VORSTER – THE MAN

John D'Oliveira

ernest stanton publishers

ERNEST STANTON (PUBLISHERS) (PTY.) LTD.
Nicholson Street, Denver,
Johannesburg

FIRST PUBLISHED DECEMBER 1977
REPRINTED JANUARY 1978

Photoset in 12 on 13 Baskerville by Pointset (Pty) Ltd.
Printed and bound by Keartland Press, (Pty) Ltd, Denver Johannesburg.

ISBN 0 949997 34 X

*For my Mother
and for Sandra, Michael
and Robyn.*

The Vorster family, photographed at Groote Schuur in Cape Town in April, 1977, when the youngest grand-child – named Martinie Steyn Vorster, after her grandmother – was christened. The photograph shows from left to right: back row: Pieter Vorster, Willem Vorster, Mr Vorster, André Kolwer (Elsa's husband). In front of them are: Retha (Pieter's wife), Marie (Willem's

wife), Mrs Vorster, and Elsa Kolwer. On their laps are: Kolbe Kolwer, Sumari Vorster, Martinie Steyn Vorster (both Willem and Marie's children), Martèlize Kolwer and John Kolwer.

Photo: Die Burger, Cape Town.

Preface

By his nature, Vorster is a formidable man to anybody other than his family, his closer friends and his associates. To his enemies and his critics he can be cold and formal – sometimes to the point of rudeness. To those South Africans who oppose his political views and to many foreigners, he is unsmiling, cold, tough, formidable and intolerant. Even to those who support him politically and admire his political acumen, he is little more than the tough, competent politician they read about, or hear on the radio, or see on their television screens. This is the Vorster that the masses know. His public face is there for all to see. It is apparent to both his political opponents and his supporters.

Obviously there is a great deal more to the man – and, just as obviously, this information is not to be gleaned from his political adversaries, casual acquaintances or those who have felt the lash of his tongue or the weight of his security laws. To find out what forces, events and influences moulded him, to find out what motivates him, to find the man behind the dour public mask, I had to go to those who know Vorster well – and the only people who really penetrated the formidable aura which Vorster's nature wraps around him are his family, his close friends and his close associates. So this book is based largely on the collective memories and views of these people. If this makes for a degree of bias, then I declare that bias here and now.

For myself, I have come to know Vorster well over the past ten years. He has come to trust me and I have come to respect him, despite our diametrically opposed political viewpoints. The political frameworks within which we think are vastly different. According to my beliefs, almost everything that he does is wrong. Equally, according to his nature and his beliefs, almost everything that I believe in is wrong. In a sense, these attitudes are understandable in a country such as South Africa where the forces of history and different cultural backgrounds have produced men and women of greatly differing political views.

So, in order to try to show what kind of a man Vorster is, I cannot do otherwise than try to examine him within his own cultural and historic framework. Because of my own strong political views, it would be a mistake to make value judgements on his beliefs, his policies and his actions.

In 1971 I arranged an interview with Vorster to mark the fifth anniversary of his election as Leader of the National Party and his subsequent appointment as Prime Minister. As the Star's Political Correspondent, I had had considerable contact with him and I realised that there was a great deal more to the man than the public mask which the people of South Africa and the world knew so well. I concentrated on his personal attitudes rather than on the major political issues which had been adequately canvassed in the weeks and months preceding the interview. The Star ran the interview straight – verbatim answer followed verbatim question – without much introduction, without conclusions, without any predigesting of information. In the days that followed, I received dozens of telephone calls from people who wanted to tell me how much they had enjoyed reading the interview and how much the plain, unvarnished question-and-answer format had told them about Vorster, the Prime Minister. I got the same response when I met people. They had learned more from Vorster's own, unprocessed words in that interview than from anything else they had read about him.

This confirms my belief that the plain facts often come closer to the truth about people than the most skilfully written book or article. Thus it is that this book is based largely on Vorster's own views and explanations, on the views and observations of the people who knew him and who still know him. And I have tried to use their own words as much as possible throughout.

I am not a political scientist. I am not a historian. I am not a politician. I am a reporter . . . and it is as a reporter that I have written this book in an effort to fill out the picture which South Africans and millions of others have of Balthazar Johannes Vorster. Deliberately, I have kept my own views and observations to a minimum.

Just as deliberately, I ended the narrative at 1970 after Vorster had almost annihilated the ultra-conservative Herstigte Nasionale Party. I did this because it would have been impossible to do justice in a single book to both Vorster the man and Vorster the Prime Minister. In any event, the years that followed revealed little more about the nature of the man – and it is Vorster's nature that this book is all about.

Because a large proportion is based on tape-recorded interviews with people who were trying to cast their minds back ten, twenty, thirty, forty years or more, there may be some inaccuracies. I have done as much checking as I can and those inaccuracies which might remain are irrelevant because they do not interfere in any way with the picture of Vorster that has been painted by the people I spoke to and the sources I consulted.

Throughout the period of writing, people asked me whether Vorster required that I should give him the manuscript before publication. The answer is: NO, Vorster required nothing of me. However, because I was trying to pull together facts on his life, I asked him to examine each chapter to help eliminate factual inaccuracies. He did this very carefully, but making a minimal number of changes (in Chapter One, for instance, he changed coffee to tea, twice). He asked me to leave out one or two anecdotes which he said dealt with incidents which he could not remember and which he doubted he was involved in. He made no request for any changes whatsoever in the format of the book, its style or the light it threw on him. While he carefully tempered his own criticism of some people, he did not quibble when others recalled some of the things he had said. He would examine this sort of thing, sigh almost imperceptibly, and say: "Well, it did happen . . .".

This book would have been almost impossible had it not been for my access to Mrs. Vorster's "files". From the time Vorster re-entered politics as a Nationalist, she kept scrapbooks of Press cuttings culled from most South African newspapers: everything which directly mentioned her husband and much which reflected the events of the day. Added to this was a generous sprinkling of personal letters, programmes of events and other mementoes. By now the scrapbooks fill perhaps ten metres of shelf space and the job of keeping them up to date now largely involves the Vorsters' personal staff. To a writer such as myself, those books were invaluable.

Nor would this book have been possible without the mass of accurate and objective information provided in the annual Survey of Race Relations, published by the South African Institute of Race Relations, Johannesburg. I drew heavily on these surveys because of their known accuracy and the ease with which information could be located, not to mention the value of the conciseness of that information. Perhaps I am biased towards the surveys because of their editors' penchant for unprocessed, unbiased information.

At the time of writing, the situation in the opposition political parties was fluid and changes in political allegiance possible. For instance, the Progressive Reform Party absorbed the Japie Basson group and became the Progressive Federal Party.

Finally, it is no coincidence that the book consists of 13 chapters because the number 13 figures so prominently in Vorster's life. He was born on December 13, 1915, the family's 13th child. When he became Prime Minister on September 13, 1966 he was in his 13th year in Parliament and he was 13th in cabinet seniority – which meant that he was 13th in the Verwoerd funeral procession. And, at the time, his golf handicap was 13.

John D'Oliveira.
Johannesburg.
October 1977

1 *Childhood*

Balthazar Johannes Vorster was born on December 13, 1915, in his parents' modest tuishuis[1] in the small but busy Eastern Cape village of Jamestown. But his story does not start there. It reaches back in time to the first stirrings of Afrikaner nationalism in the Cape, back to that day in 1706 when one Hendrik Bibault rode through the streets of usually sleepy Stellenbosch declaring loudly to those who wanted to listen: "Ik ben een Afrikaner ..."

Bibault became a nationalist. But Vorster was born one – and born nationalists, whether they be Irish, Afrikaner, Jew, Palestinian or Basque, cannot be separated from the history which was creating moulds for them generations before they were even conceived. Their beliefs are not the result of rational, intellectual reaction to a factual situation. Their beliefs stem naturally from the history, the forces, the attitudes and the objectives to which they become heir. For instance, during my long discussions with Vorster, he told me that his nationalist convictions (basically, his belief in the maintenance of his separate identity and the separate identities of others) came "absolutely naturally" to him: "It is like breathing fresh air ... it was something I simply accepted, something I have never questioned. Naturally I have often thought about it – especially now that I am Prime Minister – but it remains my sincere conviction that for any people in South Africa to lose its identity would lead to absolute chaos".

Thus, before one can understand a nationalist like Vorster, one must understand the historic forces which moulded his basic approach to life. All of which takes us back to the beginnings of what we have been wont to call White Civilisation at this southernmost tip of Africa.

The first White settlement was set up by Jan van Riebeeck who was sent to perhaps the most beautiful cape in the world to set up a way station to serve the mighty Dutch East India Company's ships

1. Town house.

as they sailed between their home ports and the riches of the East Indies. Five years afterwards, the Company agreed to allow the settlement in the Cape of a few non-official colonists, thus creating the first of the so-called "Free Burghers". Their numbers increased steadily though slowly. Under van Riebeeck's successor, Simon van der Stel, immigration was encouraged, the village of Stellenbosch was founded. Between 1688 and 1700, something like 200 French Huguenots arrived to complete the amalgam from which Afrikaner nationalism ultimately grew. Steadily a unique way of life developed amongst these Free Burghers. Steadily they grew to resent the ineptness of many of the Company's officials and their own lack of real political rights.

Leo Marquard[2] says of the Cape's White population at the end of the seventeenth century: "Small as the population was ... it was sufficiently numerous and influential to challenge successfully a clique of high officials who were attempting to corner the Cape market for their own private benefit. And it was showing signs of developing characteristics of its own – characteristics which stemmed from the motherland of Europe, but which were to be moulded by circumstances until, in later centuries, the name Afrikaner became the description of someone who was European by origin, but was neither Dutch nor German nor French. One of these characteristics was a strong sense of individual freedom and a hearty dislike of control by Government. This might have been expected from seventeenth-century Calvinists".

The intensity of the clash between the Free Burghers and Governor Willem Adriaan van der Stel (Simon's son) reached a peak in 1705 when they sent a petition to the Company indicting Van der Stel's administration. Feelings at the Cape ran so high that in 1706 a group of armed Free Burghers rode into Stellenbosch to confront the Magistrate. It was during this confrontation that Bibault rode through the streets of the village declaring himself an Afrikaner. Van der Stel was relieved of his position in 1707 and those first "Afrikaners" celebrated a notable political victory.

Friction between the Company's rulers and the colonists continued, leading to the formation towards the end of the eighteenth century of the Kaapse Patriotte[3]. In 1779 they petitioned the Com-

2. Leo Marquard: The Peoples and Policies of South Africa, published by Oxford University Press. Page 4.
3. Literally: The Cape Patriots.

pany on conditions at the Cape, but most of their complaints were rejected. So their leaders decided to send a two-man deputation direct to the States-General (the body which ruled a republican Netherlands), but the States-General was too busy with its own problems and the deputation achieved nothing. However, the mighty Company was tottering, the Cape colonists were expanding their frontiers, bringing them into conflict with the Blacks for the first time, and their political grievances and problems now expanded to include their disgust with the way in which the Company was protecting their interests on the Eastern frontier. By 1795 the Burghers of Swellendam and Graaff-Reinet had rebelled against the Company's rule, expelled their magistrates and, in effect, created their own mini republics.

While the good Burghers in Swellendam and Graaff-Reinet were wondering what to do next, a British fleet under Admiral Elphinstone arrived at the Cape with a request from the Prince of Orange to occupy the territory on behalf of the Netherlands – in order to protect it from the French. The Burghers resisted briefly, but soon capitulated to the overwhelmingly superior British forces. In terms of the Treaty of Amiens in 1802, the Cape was handed back to the Dutch Republican Government and it was ruled briefly by the enlightened and intelligent pair, Advocate J A de Mist and General J W Janssens.

But Napoleon renewed his war against Britain and the British Government decided that it would not allow its trade with the East to be endangered by leaving the Cape in the hands of a Government which was now an ally of France. So it occupied the Cape for the second time in 1806. Taking its duties much more seriously than the Company had ever done, the new British administration extended effective government to the limits of the new settlement. This upset the frontiersmen, who had generally lived free of any form of government control. But what upset the Burghers even more was the declaration that English would be the only official language – despite the fact that the vast majority of the Cape population could not speak a word of the language. This brought a new dimension to the dispute between the Burghers and the authority which ruled them. Now their resentment against the administration (any administration that wanted to control them) was coupled to the question of language and the embers of nationalism began to flame. And, as successive British governors deliberately set about anglicising the Burghers, the flames burned higher and higher. All of which led to two important movements which had a far-reaching effect on South African history.

The one was the Great Trek. Between 1836 and 1846 something like 10 000 men, women and children left their homes in the Cape Colony in order to live far removed from British authority. They gave as the reasons for their decision the suppression of their language and their institutions, the fact that they had no real say in the government which taxed them, the lack of protection on the frontier, the way in which the slaves had been liberated and the conciliatory attitude to the Blacks. After an incredible trek into the unknown interior, the farmers settled in what is now the Transvaal, the Orange Free State and Natal. While trying to negotiate for the transfer of land from the Zulus to the trekkers, Piet Retief and about 70 of his followers were murdered by the Zulu chief, Dingaan. The trekkers hit back about a year later after making a solemn covenant with God. They promised to keep sacred for ever afterwards the day He gave them victory over the Zulus. On December 16, 1838 the Zulus were decisively defeated at the Battle of Blood River and the Voortrekkers annexed Natal. However, to the disgust of the trekkers, the British Government decided to annex Natal in 1843 and many of them trekked back across the Drakensberg mountains to the OFS and the Transvaal.

But British authority followed them once more and in 1848 the OFS (or Transoranje as it was then known) was annexed by the "Paramount power" in Southern Africa. As a result, many trekkers moved to the Transvaal. Four years later Britain recognised the independence of the Transvaal and, in 1854, the independence of the OFS.

And so were born the Zuid-Afrikaanse Republiek and the Republiek van die Oranje-Vrystaat. At last the trekkers had achieved their ambition. Now they had their own countries where the laws would be made and the administration conducted according to their own customs and beliefs. It mattered little to them that their countries were poor, that they had little experience of administration, that they suffered from the effects of considerable internal division, that the highly individualistic trekkers were less than eager to submit themselves to the authority of even their own government. What mattered was that they had relieved themselves of the authority of England.

But not for long. In 1870 diamonds were discovered at Kimberley and suddenly a dispute arose over the ownership of the area. The Transvaal, the OFS and the Griqua chief Waterboer agreed to arbitration and the territory was awarded to Waterboer who was then persuaded to come under British authority. Both in the Transvaal and the OFS the whole thing was seen as a British trick to take over the diamond riches. Meanwhile, the Transvaal was rent by internal divisions, almost bankrupt and having great difficulty with its Black neighbours. Sir Theophilus Shepstone travelled to Pretoria with 25 mounted policemen in January 1877 and persuaded the majority of the Volksraad[4] to accept British rule. He promised them responsible government as soon as possible, but this never materialised and in 1881 the Transvalers rebelled, won a notable victory at Majuba Hill and regained their independence by way of the Pretoria Convention which gave Britain the right to veto the Transvaal's foreign policy.

In 1886 gold was discovered in the Transvaal. Down in the Cape Cecil John Rhodes, who ambitiously dreamed of a British territory stretching from the Cape to Cairo, plotted the Jameson Raid in terms of which a small force of adventurers under Dr Leander Starr Jameson would invade the Transvaal from neighbouring Bechuanaland. This would be the signal for the thousands of Uitlanders[5] on the Witwatersrand to revolt against the autocratic Transvaal regime which had denied them full political rights. The revolt never materialised and Jameson and his cohorts were easily captured by the Transvaal Burghers. Thus ended Rhodes' dream of annexing the Transvaal and then using this as a lever to bring the OFS into a wider Southern African confederation within the British colonial empire. Backed by a British public in an imperialist and jingoistic mood, Britain pressed the Transvaal hard over rights for the Uitlanders. Britain sent troops to South Africa, the Transvaal demanded their withdrawal in an ultimatum. When Britain refused, the Transvaal and the OFS (bound by treaty to its northern neighbour) went to war. For three bitter years the two

4. Literally: The People's Council. In fact, the old Transvaal parliament.
5. Literally: Outlanders. These were the foreigners who flocked into the Transvaal after the discovery of gold. The Transvaal could not mine its gold without them but the Transvalers were desperately afraid that they would be swamped politically and that their state would lose its special character. So they tried to prevent the "Uitlanders" from obtaining the vote. This was one of the major causes of the unrest on the Witwatersrand.

small republics held the might of imperial Britain at bay, the last two years of the war being a copy-book guerilla operation, with the Burghers living off the country, moving fast from one place to another and, in many cases, fighting with ammunition and equipment captured from the enemy.

Of the guerilla phase of the war, Leo Marquard[6] says: "It was a war of attrition and when Kitchener (the British commander) tried to make contact with his elusive opponents he found that practically every farmhouse in the Transvaal and the OFS was a Boer base. Strategically, he was bound to destroy these bases and he decided to burn farms. Once this decision was taken, women and children could not be left on the bare veld to starve. So they were brought into hastily improvised canvas concentration camps. The concentration camps were, for the most part, badly run and with rudimentary notions of hygiene. The result was that 26 000 women and children died of fever. There were not enough doctors and hospitals and supplies and the British Tommies themselves were dying by the thousand of fever. All the camps were not equally bad. As so often happens, a great deal depended on the common sense and the humanity of the camp commander. After the wave of indignation that swept the Cape Colony and liberal circles in Britain, improvements were made ..."

The concentration camps stamped bitterness deep into Afrikaner hearts. Despite the considerable evidence which shows that the fact that the women and children were being accommodated in the camps (instead of wandering about in the veld) meant that the Burghers could continue the war, most Afrikaners to this day believe that the British decided to "make war on women and children" in order to capture the Transvaal and the OFS for the Empire.

The terms of the Peace of Vereeniging were generous and by 1906 and 1907 the Transvaal and the OFS had been granted responsible government and both territories recovered fast from the effects of the war. Finally, the Transvaal, the Cape, Natal and the Orange Free State were brought together by an act of Union in 1910. The first Prime Minister was the leading Boer general of 1899/1902, Louis Botha. Despite the fact that the Union of South Africa was, to all intents and purposes, an independent country,

6. Leo Marquard: The Peoples and Policies of South Africa, published by Oxford University Press. Page 19.

polarisation had already started between those Afrikaners who supported Botha and his policy of conciliation with Britain and growth within the ambit of the British Empire, and those who saw Union as the beginning of yet another battle to cast off the British yoke.

So, when South Africa decided to go to war at Britain's side in 1914 and to invade South West Africa (then a German colony), there were immediate protests against participation in "England's war" – protests which grew into a spontaneous rebellion aimed at regaining the independence the Boers lost in 1902. However, the rebellion was badly organised, the forces lacked cohesion and the government forces under Botha soon defeated the rebels and captured their leader, General de Wet. For the first time on any scale, Afrikaners fought Afrikaners and Afrikaners killed Afrikaners. In a sense, this was the real parting of the ways in South Africa's White political history. Those who supported Botha, conciliation and freedom within the British Empire went one way. Those who supported the republican ideal (and thus the National Party which General J B M Hertzog and his followers had already established in Bloemfontein in January 1914 under the banner of his own declared belief in "South Africa first") went the other.

The other effect of the British occupation in 1806 and the deliberate attempts to anglicise the Dutch-speaking Burghers of the Cape was the rise of the Afrikaans language, a vital element in the whole mix of Afrikaner nationalism. On August 14, 1875 a group of men gathered in the home of Mr Gideon Malherbe in Paarl. They were unanimous on the need to fight for the recognition of Afrikaans as the language of the "Afrikaners" and they formed the Genootskap van Regte Afrikaners[7] to achieve this recognition. Shortly afterwards the GRA issued a manifesto claiming that attempts were being made to "eliminate with violence" their mother tongue and to replace it with English, concluding: "There are three types of Afrikaners. This we must keep in mind. There are Afrikaners with *English* hearts. And there are Afrikaners with *Dutch* hearts. And then there are true Afrikaners with *Afrikaans* hearts. The last group we call true Afrikaners and these, particularly, we call on to stand by us". With its monthly journal, Die Afrikaanse Patriot, as its spearhead, the GRA launched the first

7. Literally: The League of True Afrikaners.

phase of the fight for full recognition of Afrikaans. The impetus of the campaign somewhat dissipated, to be revived under the aegis, ultimately, of the National Party until Afrikaans was officially recognised as one of South Africa's two official languages in 1925.

To a large extent, thus, these twin dynamics of Afrikaner nationalism were well defined when Willem Carel Vorster moved from his home at Aliwal North to buy the 1 400 morgen farm Spitskop in the Jamestown district a few years before the turn of the century. Willem was a quiet, even taciturn man, short of stature and with the Vorster family's characteristically small feet.

He was a fiery Afrikaner, a man who was totally committed to the Afrikaner cause and to the Afrikaans language and it was only natural that when he had the opportunity of joining the National Party soon after its formation he did not hesitate. His children can remember him taking the keenest interest in politics and he spent days analysing election results and election prospects. Before any general election he would do his myriad calculations in school exercise books and then tell those who were interested how he thought "our people" would fare. And the only occasion he ever went to a cinema was when he knew the election results would be flashed on the screen. However, he was a man of deep affection (even though he was not demonstrative) and he had a dry sense of humour which reflected a keen mind. He was also a progressive farmer and a man who strongly believed in giving his children the best education he could possibly afford.

Vorster's elder brother, Dr J D "Koot" Vorster, one of the leaders of the Dutch Reformed Church in South Africa, recalls: "Father was a very quiet man, but he was a staunch Afrikaner because I remember right from the beginning when I was a little boy, he was one of the first people in Jamestown to get Die Burger[8] and he was one of the first people to join the National Party. But he never was a man to say very much. I can remember so well, for instance, when we were living in Sterkstroom they asked him to stand for election as a town councillor. He agreed but when the election came nearer and they wanted him to speak and canvass votes, he simply refused, telling them bluntly that the people knew who he was and what he stood for. So he simply sat on his stoep and

8. Literally: The Citizen. Die Burger was founded to serve the cause of Afrikaner nationalism. It remains one of the most important Afrikaans-language newspapers in South Africa, although its political influence has waned.

those who wanted to talk to him could. But he would not canvass for votes – not for love or money. However, despite his somewhat unusual approach to electioneering, he won the election, joined the council and served for a number of years as Deputy Mayor of Sterkstroom".

While in Jamestown, Willem Vorster met, courted and married Elizabeth Wagenaar, who was probably his opposite in almost every possible respect. While he was short and reserved, she was tall, handsome and outgoing. While he came from a vigorously Nationalist background, she came from a Botha background. While he was not greatly concerned with clothing and appearance, she loved clothes, adored dressing up and was always both fashionable and neat. Although her home language was Afrikaans, she spoke English fluently. While Willem was hardly ever demonstrative, she was. Both were very strong characters, but quiet Willem was clearly the boss. For instance, after their youngest daughter was born, Elizabeth and a teacher at the high school decided on the name Leone, both having become tired of the endless string of family names. When one of the Wagenaars asked her what the child would be christened, she replied Leone. He asked whether Willem had agreed to this departure from established norms and she replied that she had asked him and that he had said: "Umm". So the visitor laughed and left. On the day of the christening, the Vorster family filed into their usual pew in the front of the church, the Wagenaars into theirs on the other side of the aisle. Willem handed the Dominee[9] the christening papers and he faithfully read out the names Willem had written down: Margaretha Johanna. And that was that.

Willem felt deeply about the disabilities of the Afrikaner nation and the "betrayal" by Botha. This was vividly brought home to young Koot one day when they went into Jamestown for business: "That was the first day that I came across this thing called politics. I remember going into town with my father because I had to open and close all the gates on the way. It was his custom to go straight to the post office where the postmaster, Mr Tom le Roux, was a very good friend. He would hear the latest news from Mr le Roux while I sat on the cart holding the reins. On that day I can remember people standing about in the street in little groups, discussing

9. The title of a minister of the Dutch Reformed Church.

17

something very seriously. Amongst them was John Wagenaar. The people seemed very depressed. Then father came out of the post office looking very satisfied with himself, so much so that I could notice it. Remember now, he was not a very demonstrative man, so he must obviously have been very pleased with himself. After I had closed the gate on the outskirts of the town, I asked him: 'Father, why are you so happy and why are cousin John and all those other people so unhappy'. So he said to me: 'My son, Botha has died and now our nation will come into its own'. That was how deeply he felt about these matters."

Willem believed in education for his children and constantly told them that the best inheritance he could offer was a good education. And he believed in making them work on the farm, especially during the Christmas school holidays when the wheat had to be reaped. He told them quite clearly that no man who did not know how to work hard himself could ever order anybody else to work. And no man who did not know how to do a particular job could ever order anybody else to do that job.

Elizabeth was a character in her own right. While she confessed to the sin of excessive pride, she was warm and generous. Nobody was ever turned away from the Vorster home, nobody left without suitable refreshment and very few visitors walked out of the front door without a bottle of jam, canned fruit or something similar. She used to give away food to the poorer people of the town, so much so that in later years when she had returned to Jamestown and was living alone in the family home with her youngest daughter Margaretha (who became known as Mona from her earliest years), the two sons who ran the farm decided to bring her meat and vegetables three times a week instead of once a week – because within a day or two of the week's provisions arriving, she had handed out most of the victuals to other people.

Before any of her children were born, she went into mourning for a relative who had died. Once during the lengthy mourning period Willem remarked to her that she looked so good in black. And from that day onwards she never dressed in anything else. Despite the limitations of black set off by white and grey, she remained the most fashionable and the best-dressed woman in the area. She took mourning very seriously and Mona can remember that, when her father died, Elizabeth ordered her into mourning for three years, this being the proper period to mourn a parent.

And so both mother and youngest daughter appeared in black, grey and white.

Though she was generous, she did not easily forget people whom she believed had let her down. For instance, after Koot had been convicted in the Supreme Court in 1941 on a charge of trying to obtain information for the enemy, Elizabeth was confident that the judge, Mr Justice N J de Wet, would uphold her son's appeal because the judge was her cousin. She was bitterly disappointed when he lost the appeal and she vowed never to talk to Judge de Wet again. Later in that year, while Judge de Wet was acting Governor-General, he visited relatives in the district. One of them telephoned the Vorster home. Mona answered the telephone: "I remember this aunt of mine saying that the Judge wanted to come to look my mother up. I said that it was fine, that my mother would be at home. But when I told my mother that Oom Nick would be visiting her later that day, she was very cross because she had said that she would never speak to him again. However, she would not let me phone back and she got dressed in her very best clothes, because, after all, he was the acting Governor-General and my mother believed in doing things properly. When he knocked at the front door, my mother sent the maid to tell him that she was not available. The funny thing is that the house was built in such a way that he could clearly see her sitting in the background. But that was that and soon the whole village was talking about my mother who had sent away the acting Governor-General. I remember relatives phoning her and asking why she had done this and her reply to all of them was simply: 'I said I would never speak to him again and when I say something I stick by it'. She was like that."

Opposites though they were, Willem and Elizabeth were devoted to each other. Both loved children and they had 14 over the 20-year span between 1898 and 1918. They proved almost ideal parents, strict but affectionate. None of their children can ever remember seeing or hearing them quarrelling – or, for that matter, ever differing on anything in front of the children. The house was always full of people, apart from the many Vorster children. All of which Elizabeth took in her stride. She never appeared flustered and she was never apparently caught off balance. If the whole big Vorster family had just completed a meal and a string of visitors arrived, somehow or other she would immediately reset the big dining room table and within half an hour the visitors would be treated to a full meal – just as if she had been preparing for their arrival for days. On the farm, and to a greater extent when the family moved to Sterkstroom, the children were encouraged to bring their friends home. And the young people of the area were only too happy to oblige because of the warm, friendly atmosphere in the Vorster home, because of the hospitality and the bustle of people. There was always something to do, there were always people. It was a secure, happy home in which the children all developed tremendous affection and respect for their parents. A home in which the circumstances did not encourage the children to question their parents' values, their parents' norms. After all, when you are happy, contented and fulfilled you do not question the values that give you all this.

Both Willem and Elizabeth were deeply religious. No meal was ever taken without a lengthy grace before and grateful thanks to God afterwards. After supper The Bible was brought in and the house servants trooped into the dining room while Willem read a passage from The Book. Prayers were said and the servants and the family then went about their business. Every morning there was a special "quiet time" while each member of the family said his or her prayers. And every Sunday on the farm Elizabeth would conduct Sunday school for the children. So religion came naturally to the Vorster children – and it stayed with them for the rest of their lives.

The farm itself was on the northern slopes of the Stormberg mountains. The winters were bitterly cold and very long. Snow was regular throughout the area. The summers were relatively short and mild. Spitskop's ground was good and fertile, adequately watered by many springs. Willem farmed with cattle, sheep, wheat and, for a time, horses. The family lived in a big, rambling, comfortable house and, while there was hardly money to waste, the family wanted for nothing.

Balthazar Johannes (named after one of the Wagenaars, but soon to be called John, like his Wagenaar namesake) was born in the Vorsters' tuishuis in Jamestown, but spent his first years at Spitskop. Casting his mind back to those years, he remembers: "Every child thinks that he has the best father in the world, and we certainly thought so of our father. Although he was quiet, he took a keen interest in everything we did and he loved us very deeply. My mother was a wonderful woman with a wonderful mind – and she was the best story teller I have ever heard. She could tell a story like nobody else could. She was a tremendous cook, coping with all the diverse tastes of her family. But she took everything in her stride and when she died at the age of 77 there was hardly a grey hair on her pitch-black head. All of us developed a love of nature and the outdoors. Our house was at the foot of a mountain and the mountain was our playground. We had no toys in the conventional sense, but we made clay oxen and we made clay men, we played with dolosse[10] and kleilatte[11]. We amused ourselves and we were never bored, so much so that to this day I simply cannot take a child who says he is bored ..."

Like the rest of the children, John played with the little Xhosa children on the farm, learning Xhosa almost before he learned Afrikaans. He still speaks some of the language and explains: "I won't starve if I land in the Transkei, for instance."

The farm school which served the area was situated on Spitskop and, while the Vorster children could go there by foot, the rest of the pupils went by donkey cart. In accordance with the rules of the day, lessons were given exclusively in English and most of the pupils bitterly resented this. Koot Vorster can remember that anybody speaking Afrikaans on the playground was given a board to hang around his or her neck declaring "I must not speak Dutch". When the bell went for school to start again, the child who carried the "mark" had to write out 1 000 lines, "I must not speak Dutch". Koot complained about this to his father, believing that the fiery old Afrikaner would not tolerate such cultural blasphemy. However, Willem replied bluntly: "If you want to fight the English, if you want to live with them, then you must know their language". And that was that – despite the fact that Koot and some of the other children vigorously objected to being forced to sing "God Save The King" and "Rule Britannia". But Koot minimised his punishments by developing the technique of binding four pencils together and writing "I must not Speak Dutch" in quadruplicate.

10. The knuckle bones of a sheep. In the rural areas, the children used to play with these incessantly. For a dolos could be anything. A wagon, a ship, an animal, a soldier, a cowboy or a crook.
11. Again, in the rural areas, children used to take a long, flexible stick and mould a ball of clay on the end. This was swung back slowly and then smartly whipped forward. The ball of clay would leave the end of the stick at high velocity and would strike the "enemy" with great effect.

The Vorster children all inherited their father's nationalism and one of their favourite books was about the Boers who were executed by the British during the 1899/1902 war. Koot recalls: "We would read a portion of that book each night, us children. After we had bathed and said our prayers, we would sit on a big double bed, with the eldest reading until his voice broke with emotion. Then the next one would take over until he could read no further. And then the third and so on until, in the end, we all sat weeping on the bed. We, all of us, felt very bitter about the injustices of the war, about what the war had done to us Afrikaners. The English were the enemy and the Boers were our heroes".

In 1924 the educational needs of their big family induced Willem and Elizabeth to move to nearby Sterkstroom. Young John moved into the Sterkstroom High School which was parallel medium in its primary section (each child received his or her instruction in the mother tongue) and dual medium in the higher standards. In terms of the dual medium concept, half the classes were supposed to be given in English and the other half in Afrikaans. However, Vorster recalls that at least two-thirds of the subjects were taught in English. He entered the school as a Standard One[12] pupil, with elder brothers and sisters in school ahead of him.

The Vorsters simply transplanted their way of life from the farm to this small but bustling village. Once again, the home was big and comfortable, always filled almost to overflowing with the Vorster family and friends. Meat and vegetables came in abundant quantity from the farm which had been left in the care of two older brothers. While money was scarce, food was plentiful and the family was unaware of wanting for anything reasonable. For the smaller children (and their many friends) there was a mountain behind the house where once attempts had been made to mine coal. So there were rocks and slopes and tunnels – and the children played cowboys and crooks to their hearts' content. And, during the holidays, the children spent much time on the family farm only 64 km away.

Thinking of those days in Sterkstroom, Vorster recalls the tremendous impression made on him by the children being encouraged to bring their friends home with them at all times: "The mere fact that you knew you could bring your friends home, that

12. After a year in sub-standard "A" and sub-standard "B" the children of those years would enter Standard One and move yearly to Standard Ten.

your parents in fact expected you to bring them home, made a great difference to us children. Naturally, we made full use of this and there always seemed to be friends around. I have never forgotten this and I tried to do it with my own children, no matter whether I was a lawyer, a Member of Parliament, a Cabinet Minister or Prime Minister. Every day when they were at school and many weekends when they were at university, there would be five or six kids visiting. I felt it was right . . . and I enjoyed it myself".

At school young John immediately impressed his teachers and, from the first examination in Standard One to the final internal examination in Standard Ten, he remained at the top of his class. Like his father, he was quiet and reserved, never speaking for the mere sake of speaking. But he was popular with the other children – and his sense of humour was always evident. The school day was a long one. In the summer, for instance, the children went to school at 6,30 am, broke for breakfast at eight, returned at 8,45 and then continued until 12,45. In winter, school started at eight, broke for lunch between one and two and continued until 3,30 pm. One of John's tasks was the milking of the two family cows which grazed on the village commonage every day and which were stabled behind the house at night. Sometimes his brothers would help with the milking, but more often than not it was his task, which meant that he had to get up at 5 am in summer and a little later in winter. However, every day he had to chase them back to the commonage and, as he grew older and started noticing the village's girls, this proved an embarrassing operation. Whenever he saw girls approaching he tried to keep control of the cows while at the same time trying to create the impression that they had nothing to do with him.

Always there was his dry sense of humour. His mother would worry about fire or other disaster and would invariably send one of the children to see that everything was all right in the stable – much to their annoyance because, just as invariably, everything was just fine. One evening she sent John out. When he returned she asked whether everything was all right and he replied: "Yes mother . . . and I've said goodnight to the cows as well". On another occasion he was asked to make tea for an old lady who had become a nuisance because of her frequent, lengthy visits. He went into the kitchen, stirred up the stale tea, made sure that it contained a

23

generous proportion of tea leaves, and served it cold to the guest. And his mother often wondered afterwards why the old lady had stopped visiting them.

He was also learning a degree of tact. His sister Mona can remember that the children were allowed to eat exactly what they pleased, with her mother equally catering for their varied tastes. However, one day an old aunt came to visit. Because Mrs Vorster knew that the old woman liked turnips, she prepared them. Mona and John did not like turnips and when the old woman insisted they should eat them there was a confrontation between her and Mona. Once she had settled the young girl, the aunt turned to John and commended him for having cleared his plate. Mona remembers: "I was absolutely furious with him for giving in and I tackled him afterwards. Then he took an old envelope out of his pocket, turned out the turnips and explained that he had scratched them off his plate while our aunt was arguing with me. And he explained simply: 'That's diplomacy . . .' And I think he was only 11 or 12 years old at the time".

About the same time John desperately wanted a pair of rugby boots. He prayed for new rugby boots and he begged his father for a new pair. Father Willem asked whether there were any boots which he could wear and John replied: "I have too many boots. There are Izak's boots and there are Koot's boots and there are Piet's boots. There are so many boots". Willem asked: "Are they still all right?". John replied: "Yes, they are all still all right, there is nothing wrong with them, but they're not new and they're not mine!". Willem argued quite reasonably that if there were no rugby boots for John, then he would buy a pair, but as there were a number of pairs that fitted him, this would be a waste. After all, they were a big family.

John Vorster takes up the story: "I was very disappointed and, quite candidly, that night I prayed to the Lord as only a little boy can pray. I told Him that my father would not give me a new pair of rugby boots and that, in view of this, He should please do something about it. And as sure as we are sitting talking here now, a few days after I prayed so mightily to the Lord I arrived back from school and my mother handed me one of those little red parcel slips. It was the first I had ever received and she explained that there was a parcel for me at the post office. I ran my little legs off, signed the slip, handed it in and received a package from the postmaster. I opened it right there in the post office and I pulled out a brand new pair of rugby boots. They had been sent to me by an uncle whose son like me, had been born on the 13th of December, who was my godfather and who was very fond of me. In the box was a letter from him explaining that it was a long time since he had given me a present; that he had just bought his son a new pair of rugby boots and that he thought he would send me a pair as well. They were too big for me so I ran to Pearson's shop for all that I was worth and they gave me a pair that fitted. That was how I got my first pair of rugby boots. To this day I remain convinced that my prayers had been answered because there was no earthly reason why my uncle should send me a pair of rugby boots".

While John may have inherited many of his father's characteristics, he was exceptionally close to his mother. She doted on him to the point where it became a family joke. Elizabeth would answer that she loved all her children equally, but that John's tears were shinier than the others. And she frequently predicted that he would one day play a major role in the service of the Afrikaner nation.

John Vorster says that he first made up his mind about his future while he was in Standard Seven. The teacher asked the class to write a composition setting out what they intended doing for their careers. For the first time John Vorster registered that he would have to do "something" after leaving school and he gave the matter deep thought – to such an extent that when the time came to hand in the composition, he had not even written it. So he went to the teacher and explained that the composition had given him a great deal of trouble because he had not yet even decided what he wanted to be. Knowing him as a studious and impeccable pupil, the teacher granted him the extension. He gave the issue all the serious thought that a little boy could give such matters and he decided that he wanted to become a lawyer and enter politics to serve the Afrikaner nation. And that was that.

But already he was interested in politics. He read his father's Burger avidly and he would cut out interesting articles on world politics, much to his father's annoyance because it mutilated the paper. His older sister, Mrs Anna Arnold, told Dagbreek en Sondagnuus[13] on December 18, 1966: "John showed decided leader-

13. An Afrikaans-language Sunday newspaper which is no longer published.

ship traits even as a child. He did not use his pocket money to buy sweets like his brothers and sisters and like other children, no, he bought newspapers." Already John Vorster had attended his first political meeting. He can remember begging his father to allow him to go and his father agreed, provided he came right home "when the fighting starts". Vorster remembers: "My father instructed me to stand against the wall at the back of the hall. It's true, fighting did start because all the political meetings of those days seemed to end in a fight. But it so fascinated me that I stayed there right to the bitter end, mouth agape at what was happening. I remember it was a Nat meeting, and I can remember that the Nationalists gave the Sappe[14] a good hiding".

At school, apart from excelling at sport as well as his studies, Vorster quickly became the star of the school debating society. He was head and shoulders above everybody else and was soon made chairman of the society. He devastated his opponents with his lucidity, his logic and his ability to make words serve him. One of his old school-teachers, Mr Johann Schoeman, explained to me: "He had the typical attitude of an advocate. He was tremendously logical and he was always excellently prepared. For instance, it was always clear that he had studied his subject well, that he had read extensively and that he had the whole affair under complete control". And he summed up John Vorster, the schoolboy: "He was a quiet one, but always friendly. He knew what he wanted. If you gave him an instruction, you knew that it would be carried out to the letter. You knew that you could depend absolutely on his word. He never let anybody mess him around and there was not a single frightened hair on his head. There was steel in that young man and I can remember telling my colleagues that John would one day play a big role in society and for our volk as well. He never ever pushed himself, but you simply felt that the young man had tremendous inherent power. And I, for one, am glad to see that my feelings were accurate, that John Vorster has reached the very top of his chosen profession".

Of the debating society, Vorster recalls these hours as some of the most pleasant of his childhood: "Even today, when I think back on my childhood, my happiest memories centre on the debating

14. The abbreviation for members of the South African Party. It has stuck and to this day, members of the United Party – formed in 1934 with the amalgamation of the South African Party and the National Party – are still called "sappe".

society. I represented my school in inter-school debates from the time I was in Standard Seven and the debates were a great joy to me ..."

While at school John Vorster was a member of the Boy Scouts movement. But he never liked it and he never felt at home because everything was "English" and after two or three years, he dropped out and waited for the parallel Afrikaner movement, the Voortrekkers, to start in Sterkstroom. And when the movement started, the local Commandant was none other than Mr Japie Malan (nicknamed "Uil"[15] by the pupils because he was a small man whose face was dominated by his large spectacles) who had been his Standard Six teacher and who was undoubtedly one of the characters of the town. "Uil" Malan was one of the earliest radio hams and possessed the only radio set in Sterkstroom in those early years. He was tremendously interested in world affairs and would gather information from around the world by spinning his receiver's dial and absorbing the crackling messages. Having done this, he would arrive at school the next morning and start the day by telling his class: "Now boys and girls, this is what happened in the world yesterday ..." And thus he helped arouse an interest in current affairs in all the pupils who passed through his hands. On Friday and Saturday afternoons the older pupils could frequently be found at his house listening to the radio and/or deeply involved in a discussion on some current controversy sparked off by old Uil. Apart from anything else, Uil was a very enthusiastic Afrikaner and he helped hone to a fine edge John Vorster's determination to serve his people.

One of John Vorster's fellow pupils, from Standard One to Standard Ten, was a fair-haired young man called Gert Prinsloo, who today serves as Commissioner of the South African Police. His father died when he was a small boy and he went to Sterkstroom for his education, staying at a Dutch Reformed Church hostel for needy children. Early on he made friends with John Vorster who was already a "clever little fellow" who managed to do exceptionally well at school without having to do much learning. It was always a pleasure for Gert Prinsloo to visit the Vorster home, to absorb and enjoy the warmth and the hospitality, and he and John Vorster became good friends. Although Gert Prinsloo can

15. Owl.

remember John Vorster as a serious-minded young man, he was not above the tricks and the pranks of the day. "You know, on Guy Fawkes day, we all used to wander around Sterkstroom, we used to gather together all the donkey carts we could find, mix them up and then park them in different parts of the town. And the next day there was real trouble as people tried to find their carts ..."

And so it was that on their final day at school the future Commissioner of Police almost killed his future Prime Minister. Gert Prinsloo recalls: "We had already written matric and so there was very little to do. I can remember that it was the last day of school and some of us matrics were cleaning out the science laboratory. I came across a gas jar, remember one of those which was closed with a piece of glass smeared with vaseline. I realised the jar was full of gas, so I smelled it and it was awful. I thought I would play a joke on John so I took the jar to him, pushed it under his nose and told him to smell. He was somewhat taken aback and, as a result, must have breathed in deeply. I cannot remember what was in that jar, but John collapsed almost immediately and started foaming at the mouth. I thought he was dying and I, in turn, almost collapsed with fright. I ran to call the teacher, who gave John some milk to drink while the doctor was summoned. We took him home where the doctor attended to him. It was four days before he could get out of his bed ... I tell you, he almost kicked the bucket. I never went home for the holidays until John was well again. I tell you, that was a terrible thing ..."

However, John Vorster fast recovered both his health and his good spirits, knowing that he was about to go to the University of Stellenbosch; that he was about to implement his determination to become a lawyer, to go into politics and to serve his people.

Already, as a youth of 18, he showed all the characteristics of the man. From his father he inherited his vigorous commitment to Afrikaner nationalism, toughness of purpose and determination.

Mona explains: "To my father, black was black and white was white. There was very little grey in between and once he had taken a decision, that was that. Even as a child, John was very much like that. I don't want to say that he is intolerant or that he could not be swayed by good argument. It was just that once he had made up his mind on what was right and wrong, that was the end of it – just like my father. And, like my father, John does not do anything without the most careful consideration. For instance, right at the beginning of the Hertzog subversion in the National Party, I asked him why he was not acting against these people. He reply was simply: 'It is not yet the right time ... a person must not be overhasty'. This is characteristic of John. He has a tremendous sense of timing and, even after he has made up his mind that he wants to do something, he will patiently wait for the right time to do it. So I have just accepted that, with his knowledge, he knows what to do in this country of ours. And if it appears that he is marking time, doing nothing, then it is just that he is waiting for the right moment".

From his mother, John Vorster inherited personal generosity and a fine sense of hospitality. Like her, he loves giving presents and nobody is sent away from his home without refreshment. Very few of his guests leave without a jar of jam, some fruit, some dried boerewors[16], or some meat.

And, from both his parents he inherited a commitment to religion. To this day, he never goes to sleep without reading a chapter from The Bible, no matter what the time is, no matter whether he is in a jet flying off to Paraguay or Geneva, or whether he is out in the bush hunting. He explains: "I just grew up like that. I simply cannot close my eyes at night without reading a chapter from The Bible. I have never played sport on a Sunday and I never will play sport on a Sunday because that is the way I was brought up. Religion came so naturally to me and I am very pleased about this because it gives you strength, security and a purpose in life. You know you have a calling to perform. It is the whole base on which you stand ... I do not know of any other base and I would not give up my religion for anything in the world".

That last holiday from school was carefree. Although the boys who were still at home worked hard on the farm, helping with the harvest, John Vorster's head was already turned to Stellenbosch and he could think of little other than his happiness at being able to go.

---

16. A highly-spiced, succulent beef sausage greatly valued by the old farmers (hence the name boerewors, literally translated as farmers' sausage) because it could either be cooked, fried or grilled or dried. In its dried form it would last indefinitely.

2 *Stellenbosch University*

If the heart of Afrikanerdom beat on the platteland[1] in the thirties, then its soul was certainly to be found in the lecture rooms and the corridors of the University of Stellenbosch. Although still a relatively small university situated in a beautiful but quiet town, it was the first choice for most Afrikaners in those years. It had an aura which the younger University of Pretoria lacked and it drew the cream of Afrikanerdom – including the five men who were to become National Party Prime Ministers of South Africa: Hertzog, Malan, Strijdom, Verwoerd and Vorster.

So it was natural that John Vorster aimed for Stellenbosch. Apart from the university's reputation, his brother Koot was already a senior student, having started his theological studies at Stellenbosch in 1928. Because South Africa was still in the grip of a great depression, he knew that he would have to walk a financial tight-rope while he studied, but he nevertheless applied to the university for admission in his matric year. The university replied and sent a brochure on the institution, its history, its buildings and the courses it offered.

Still a wide-eyed platteland boy, John Vorster eagerly opened the envelope containing the brochure. "Heavens, I simply swallowed that information. I must have read the brochure ten or even 20 times. Within days I made that university my own ... through the brochure I knew every building in the place, every street in the town".

As a first-class matriculant, he obtained a bursary of £25 a year from the university. He applied for and received a loan of £30 a year from the university's Jan Marais Fund. An older brother, who was running the family farm, gave him £40 and thus John Vorster started off with £95 in his pocket knowing well that a reasonable sum for university in those days was something like £120: "You knew that you would have to turn every penny over twice ... but

1. The rural area. Literally: the flat land.

then it did not worry you because it was at the height of the depression and everyone was poor. Almost all the students at the university were in the same boat so you were no better and no worse off than almost all your friends. You had only one suit, only one jacket and only one pair of trousers, but then everybody had that and you did not feel deprived."

On the train to Stellenbosch, Vorster met a number of young men on their way to university, including young Willem Dempsey, who came from nearby Dordrecht and whom he knew slightly because they had played rugby against each other twice during the previous year. Dempsey was more or less in the same boat – on his way to university having scraped together money in bursaries, loans and a relatively small contribution from his family. They spoke about rugby, their school days and both shared their excitement over their good fortune at being able to go to university. They discovered that they were both going to be accommodated in the university's Dagbreek[2] hostel and this was the beginning of a friendship which lasts to this day.

Having digested the Stellenbosch University brochure so thoroughly, Vorster's arrival in the town was like a home-coming. The town was almost familiar and it fulfilled all his expectations. Its lovely, oak-lined streets impressed him greatly and he hardly noticed the long, two-mile walk to Dagbreek. He remembers being overawed by the fact that the Dagbreek Primarius (Head Student) was Andre McDonald, the Springbok rugby player, little realising that he would become Dagbreek Primarius himself and that his younger son, Pieter, would follow in his footsteps.

Vorster had enrolled for a B A Law degree. Sociology was not included in the subjects he needed for his degree but he had heard so much about the university's brilliant Professor of Sociology, Dr Hendrik Frensch Verwoerd, that he made it his business to attend his classes. The students were tremendously impressed by the fact that Verwoerd never used notes for his lectures and that he could take up a lecture after a break of a few days, recapping the precise words with which he had ended his talk to them earlier. This made a big impact on Vorster and, although he never spoke to Verwoerd and only attended his classes for one year, he felt the full impact of Verwoerd's personality and never forgot him.

2. Literally: Daybreak.

31

In a sense, Vorster was fortunate because Koot was already a senior student and could show him the ropes and could introduce him to many students. But his own quiet friendliness meant that he soon settled down and immediately he started taking his studies seriously.

Willem Dempsey became Vorster's room-mate, staying with him throughout his university career. Apart from already establishing a degree of rapport with Vorster, Dempsey was happy to have a room-mate who took his studies seriously. Dempsey explains: "It was not that we did not have a great deal of fun. It was just that we did things with a degree of intensity. When we worked, we worked hard, when we played, we played hard ..."

Dempsey never moved from Stellenbosch. He became a part-time lecturer in Economics and remained at the university, playing a major role in Stellenbosch's civic affairs and becoming a National Party Senator in 1970. He remembers Vorster as a first-year student in 1934: "You know, you could not help noticing Vorster. He is the sort of man who would not be lost in a crowd. Amongst a lot of students there is not much chance to rise above the crowd in your first year, but, when I think back, I am amazed that I did not see then that he would one day become something like Prime Minister. He had all the qualities. Firstly, he was very definitely intelligent. I remember working much harder than he did at university, but he still did better than I did. He had the personality, he had the gift of oratory and he was a serious young man with very definite ideas. He was purposeful and he was a Nationalist. Above all, he was a Christian person. Religion came naturally to him. He did not preach to the others; he just lived according to his own religious views. For instance, he would never study on a Sunday. Or, if somebody told a dirty joke, Vorster would simply move out of the company ... one could see that this shocked him, that this was not something that he went along with. But he was a student just like any other student. He was quiet but not withdrawn. If there was good clean fun to be had, then Vorster was there. He was a devil with practical jokes and we all had a great deal of fun because of this. Like us, he laughed a great deal and he had a lot of fun. But, like most of the students during those depression years, he knew that he would not have another chance at university, so he studied hard and he did well".

In 1934 Vorster met Flip la Grange for the first time and they

32

immediately became friends. La Grange had been at Stellenbosch for two years already, studying to become a teacher. He later worked for five years as a reporter on Die Burger[3], went farming, became involved in business in Paarl and became a Senator in 1970. Recalling his first meeting with Vorster, La Grange says: "It is a bit far in the past to remember precisely. It was just that we clicked naturally. I could sense that Vorster was worthwhile, that he was a young man of great strength, great character."

The next year, the Vorster/Dempsey/La Grange trio added another friend in Du Plessis, who soon acquired the nickname, Flooi[4]. Born and educated in Petrusville in the Northern Cape, Flooi arrived in 1936. Now head of the University's Carnegie Library, Du Plessis remembers his first impression of Vorster: "He stood out. He was not a tall man but he had a calm sort of air about him. And when the occasion demanded he would automatically take command and the others – even those who were senior to him – would defer. He was not pushing himself. He never pushed himself. It just seemed the natural thing to do."

Amongst the men who made a considerable impression on Vorster at the university were his Professor of Law, Morty Malherbe, a law lecturer, Andrew Beyers, who was later to become Judge President of The Cape, and Eben Dönges, a lecturer in civil law who captivated Vorster with his silver tongue and who later went into politics. Dönges was well ahead of Vorster in his political career, becoming a Minister in 1948. He was Minister of Finance when Vorster became Minister of Justice in 1961 and he remained Minister of Finance when Vorster became Prime Minister in 1966. Dönges retired in 1967 to clear the way for his election as State President. Although he was elected, he never took office because of his serious illness and death later that year.

Professor Morty Malherbe was one of the university characters. He had little time for fools, but he spent much time with the students he identified as exceptionally bright. And Professor Morty's mark of approval was an invitation to go for a walk on a Saturday afternoon. He would invite a bright student to his home, they would get into his car, his wife would drive them high into the mountains overlooking Stellenbosch and Professor Morty and his

3. Official organ of the Cape National Party, published in Cape Town by Nasionale Pers Beperk. Literally: The Citizen.
4. Literally: Flea.

protege would walk back, with the Professor putting searching legal, political and general knowledge questions to the young man walking with him. While the selected student might rather have watched rugby, he was deeply conscious of the fact that an invitation from the Professor indicated a great deal to the other students. And Vorster frequently walked with Professor Morty, sometimes arguing to such effect that the discussion had to be continued on the following Saturday.

Naturally, Vorster joined the Junior National Party at the university. Despite his conscious decision in Standard Seven that he wanted to become a lawyer and then go into politics, he was not yet sure whether politics would be his career. "I never thought then that I would go into parliament. Members of Parliament in those years were gods to me. I often went to Cape Town and sat in the visitors' galleries. But I never once visualised myself walking on that green carpet. Going into politics was a sort of silent ambition. You never spoke of it to anybody else and you hardly even admitted it to yourself, although the ambition was there, the attainment was just something out of your reach altogether. However, I was greatly interested in politics and so I took part in them at the university. I must say that I enjoyed every minute of them but I never saw university politics as a step towards my own political career. I just did what was needed to be done and I thoroughly enjoyed it ..."

Equally naturally, he joined one of the university's two debating societies. And, as he made his mark as an orator at school, so he made his mark at the university because of his ability to get his message across to his listeners and because he always knew what he was speaking about. As Flip la Grange remembers: "When it came to a debate, if you had Vorster on your side then you knew that you would win. He would simply pull the thing through for you".

An indication both of Vorster's tactical and his speaking talents came in 1938 when he was secretary of the Students Representative Council and Flip la Grange its chairman. In that year a group at the university wanted membership of the Afrikaanse Nasionale Studentebond[5] to be made compulsory, so that students would automatically become members on their enrolment and their membership fees would be collected when they enrolled. Pushing

5. Afrikaans National Union of Students.

the cause of the ANS were Jan Haak, later to become a Cabinet Minister, serving in the Verwoerd and Vorster administrations, Andries Stulting, a lecturer in psychology at the university, and Jaap de Vos, who was later to become a judge[6].

La Grange remembers: "Vorster and I said to each other: No, under no circumstances can we allow this. After all, you cannot build up a strong organisation if you automatically include as members both those who are for the organisation and those who are against it. We decided that we would put this to the students at a mass meeting but Vorster thought about the whole thing and pointed out that, by the nature of things, most of the people at the meeting would be those in favour of the proposal, because the three chaps had been working very hard to get support for their proposition. He suggested that we should put something sensational on the agenda so that it would attract a large number of students. So we decided that we would include a proposal that students not be allowed to wear their university blazers with ordinary grey flannels. At that time, it was customary to wear our blazers with white flannels and, though it seems a bit silly today, the question of flannels so excited the students that we had a very big crowd. We decided that I would keep the chairman's seat for the meeting, to arrange things so that our side did not suffer a disadvantage. Andries, Jan Haak and De Vos spoke in favour of the proposition of automatic ANS membership. Vorster spoke against it and he did his job so well that the students rejected the proposition. In fact it became clear before he had finished that the majority of the students had been won over to our side. There were many women at the meeting and I think that Vorster must have won them all over to our side. He was so fluent, so smooth and he would crucify the other side on their own arguments – just as he would do later in the House of Assembly".

Feelings ran so high over the ANS issue that nine of the 20 members of the SRC (including Jan Haak and Jaap de Vos) resigned in protest.

6. This is reminiscent of an element in the Nationalist Government's confrontation with the left-wing, English-language National Union of South African Students in the sixties and the seventies. One of the Government's major objections to NUSAS was the fact that it involved automatic membership. All students who enrolled at English-language universities automatically became members of NUSAS and the Government held that this exaggerated the degree to which NUSAS ideas and ideals were shared on the English-language campuses.

Thinking back to those days, Vorster remembers how thrilled he was when he was elected secretary of the SRC in 1938. "You see, the SRC owned a bicycle and the secretary of the SRC used this bicycle. Now you must remember that hardly any students had cars – not like today – and almost all of us were so poor that we had to walk everywhere. But now I had a bicycle and this not only made things a bit easier for me, but it gave me considerable status!"

Life at Stellenbosch was pleasant, even though Vorster and his friends were always short of money. During weekdays there were classes and in the afternoons and the evenings most of the students studied. Some went drinking in a nearby pub, but most did not have the money for this and generally gathered in the Uitspan[7] Cafe for coffee or tea. On Friday evenings the students usually went to the only local cinema or to the university dance club, which was an exceptionally formal affair, with the women wearing long dresses and the men tails. The formality notwithstanding, almost inevitably one or two students would be pushed into a fishpond – tails and all – after an evening's dancing. On Saturday mornings students went into town, in the afternoons they watched sport and on Saturday evenings the attraction was one of the two university debating societies. On Sundays they went to church and on Sunday evenings they tended to gravitate to the Plaza Cafe (somewhat higher class than the Uitspan) in order to see and be seen. It was the Plaza to which the students took their current girl-friends and once the students were back in their hostels, they would discuss at great length who had been seen with whom and who was obviously becoming serious about whom.

Vorster remembers the Uitspan Cafe with some affection: "It was run by the ACVV[8] and it served a very useful purpose indeed. You could get a cup of coffee for a tickey[9] and a cup of tea for four pence – so you normally went for a girl who drank coffee instead of tea. It was not a very big place but it catered for our needs."

Because of their lack of money, many of the students – including Vorster and his three friends – used to stay at the university during the two short vacations. Because they had to fend for themselves, they would pool the money they could afford and work out their

7. Literally: Outspan.
8. Afrikaanse Christelike Vroue Vereniging. Literally: The Afrikaans Christian Women's Union.
9. With decimilisation the tickey, or three-penny bit, became 2½ cents.

victuals for the week. Willem Dempsey recalls: "The standard thing was Post Toasties and milk, but, if we really wanted to treat ourselves, there would be bacon and eggs. Occasionally we would go into town for a meal. We all had water heating elements and there were some hot plates, so we managed quite well . . ."

It was during one of these holidays that the group developed their "Houdini" trick. In each room there was a big double wardrobe and Dempsey and Vorster worked out a trick based on this massive piece of furniture. One of their friends would be given a screwdriver and put into one side of the wardrobe. Then the spectators would be invited into the room and Dempsey would be dramatically locked into the other side. Everybody would be asked to leave the room and Vorster would stand guard at the door. The man with the screw-driver would then screw himself out of his side of the wardrobe, let Dempsey out and would then be screwed back into his compartment. All this was done in a few seconds. Then the room door would be opened and the amazed students would see Dempsey standing outside the locked wardrobe. The "Houdini" trick became something of a sensation, drawing more and more students every evening. Even Die Burger was attracted and sent a reporter and a photographer to witness the dramatic escape. Today, none of the participants can remember quite how the whole thing ended. But they still enjoy the fact that they fooled so many people for so long.

At about the same time, Vorster, Dempsey, Du Plessis and La Grange risked considerable trouble with another prank. On a day on which all the students were out of the hostel, they gathered every pair of shoes in Dagbreek and piled them in the middle of the quadrangle. Vorster remembers: "There were hundreds of shoes and we threw them all together. When everybody returned to the hostel and found their shoes piled in the quadrangle, there was real trouble – man, it took them weeks to sort the whole thing out! Naturally they searched everywhere for the culprits and naturally we threw all our own shoes into the pile because otherwise they would have known immediately who was responsible for the trick".

Not everything went Vorster's way. He remembers having drunk coffee with Flooi du Plessis and Flip la Grange at the Uitspan: "On the way back to the university we were all walking together. I was wearing a new pair of white flannels and you must understand just how important white flannels were to students at the University of Stellenbosch. You had to wear them with your blazer and while you might go to university without almost anything, you did not go without your white flannels. Look, a girl simply would not go out with you if you were not wearing your white flannels. I had on a brand new pair of flannels and I was very proud of them as we walked back to the university. A municipal refuse lorry stood opposite the Conservatoire of Music in Van Riebeeck Street and I hardly noticed that Flooi and Flip dropped slightly behind me as we passed the lorry. Suddenly they grabbed me and tossed me right into it. I fell deep into the rubbish and you could hardly recognise my new pair of flannels. I was very cross. But then, what could one do but laugh it all off?"

On many evenings the students would talk deep into the night, discussing politics and allied subjects. Vorster was usually at the centre of one of these discussion groups. Flip La Grange says: "Vorster was a serious young man. Rather than go to the pub or the cafe, we would sit down and discuss matters of importance. You must understand that these were the years of smelting[10] and feelings were running very high indeed and we discussed the whole affair over and over again. Apart from all this, there were student politics – things which today seem irrelevant but which were of vital importance to us then. Vorster's room was certainly one of the places in Dagbreek where students gathered for regular discussions on politics, world affairs and student politics, and always he seemed to be at the centre of the discussion".

In his last years at the university, Vorster moved into a three-bedroomed flatlet in Dagbreek. In one of the other bedrooms was J J H "Joggie" Victor, who is now Secretary to Parliament. As the

10. Literally: fusion. The depression of the early thirties prodded the National and South African Parties towards coalition. Following the crisis created by the British decision to go off the Gold Standard, Hertzog and Smuts formed a coalition government with Hertzog as Prime Minister and leader of the new United National South African Party, later to be called simply the United Party. Dr D F Malan, the Cape Nationalist leader, was vigorously opposed to the idea and he broke away from Hertzog in 1934 to form what was sometimes referred to at the time as the "purified" National Party. It meant Malan and his followers were moved into the political wilderness and, in the 1938 General Election, the National Party gained only 27 seats compared with the UP's 111. Within Afrikaner circles, the debate over fusion was a heated and divisive one and, to this day, some older Nationalists still look with disdain on the "smelters" or fusionists, despite the fact that many of them returned to the National Party after Hertzog broke with Smuts over the war issue in 1939.

junior, it was Victor's task to make coffee. He used to make pot after pot as the students talked until the early hours of the morning. "I can remember listening to them talking about law and politics, but I kept out of the discussions because I was a junior. They talked until deep into the morning. I listened and made coffee. What impressed me about Vorster in these discussions was the fact that he was always the practical one. While many of the others approached matters from a technical or an academic point of view, Vorster was always practical. When you listened to him speaking, you knew exactly what he meant."

As Vorster remembers: "Students talk and talk. We discussed all the world's problems and we solved them too because you know that students are very clever and have all the answers. When you are that age there is nothing that you cannot do, no problem that you cannot solve. We were all Malan men and we were opposed to smelting. We talked whole nights through and we were very fiery about our politics. We knew all the answers".

Vorster became chairman of the Junior National Party at the University in 1937 and held the office until he left after 1938. And it was after a party meeting in the same building which housed the Uitspan Cafe that Vorster met Tini Malan. They were leaving the building after the meeting. Tini broke from a party of friends and turned towards the boarding house where she was living. Vorster was walking in the same direction and he fell into step with her, thus starting the romance which led to their wedding in 1941.

In many ways Tini Malan was made for Vorster. She was the daughter of P A Malan, a leading lawyer in Worcester, a good, active Nationalist and for many years chairman of the Board of Nasionale Pers, the organisation which printed Die Burger. He was one of the founder members of the National Party in Worcester and thus Tini grew up in a politically aware home. Tini can remember her mother making the children read both Die Burger and the English-language Cape Times. "My mother was a very ardent reader of newspapers and she insisted that we should read them too. She was particularly determined that we should read the leading articles so that we would know what was happening. She impressed on our minds the fact that you cannot read a newspaper without reading the leading articles".

She had three sisters and one brother and was born in 1917, the youngest of the Malan girls. Mrs Malan did social work on a voluntary basis and kindled an interest in her youngest daughter. The family was an exceptionally happy one. "It was just the times we were living in. The gardens were big, we had lots of places to play. My mother was a very good housewife and she taught us how to make ends meet. Things were very different in those days. You did not go into a shop and order clothes, you made them yourself. All the members of the family would do their bit and we managed despite the difficulties of the depression".

Although she claims that she had to study very hard in order to make the grade at school, Tini was bright, alert, practical and positive. Her mother taught her how to keep house and, to this day, there is very little that Tini Vorster cannot do – whether it is slaughtering an ox and making hundreds of kilograms of boere-wors or whether it is coping with a sudden and unexpected inflow of guests.

She enrolled at the University of Stellenbosch for a degree in social work and looked forward to her first meeting with the already legendary (at Stellenbosch) Dr Verwoerd. "He was a wonderful man. He would walk into the class without papers and he would lecture us for 40 minutes. He absolutely inspired us and I always look back and regard it as a great privilege that I could sit in his class. He had tremendous charisma and he made an impact the moment he walked into a room".

Recalling her meeting with John Vorster, she says: "It was to-wards the end of my third year and he was in his fourth year. I think it was in September 1937. I was very interested in politics and I attended a meeting of the Junior National Party. He was one of the speakers and I can remember being very impressed because he certainly knew what he was talking about. As I left the meeting, my friends turned to the right and I turned to the left on the way to my boarding house. Then this man walked with me and that was the beginning of the story. It started as a casual thing, but then we went out again and again. But not too often because there were exams to prepare for. In any case, things were different in those days and us young people did not see each other every single night like they do today".

Vorster was chairman of the Junior National Party at the university in 1937 and 1938, and in 1938 he was student organiser for Bruckner de Villiers when he fought Henry Allen Fagan (who later became Chief Justice of South Africa) in a by-election in

1938. Fagan, a one-time Nationalist, had gone with the majority of his colleagues into the United Party. De Villiers was a Malan man and he fought under the colours of the "purified" National Party. Like the rest of the young Nationalists at Stellenbosch, Vorster was vigorously opposed to the union between the National and the South African Parties and he did everything he could to help his candidate. This help notwithstanding, De Villiers lost by 34 votes and Fagan went on to become a Cabinet Minister in the United Party Government.

Flip La Grange remembers one of the incidents of the election campaign: "Bruckner called Vorster and told him that Fagan was going to hold a meeting at Pniel, a Coloured settlement near Stellenbosch. Bruckner wanted Vorster to attend the meeting to hear what promises Fagan was making to the Coloured people. Once he knew this, Bruckner could decide on his own strategy and, if necessary, outbid Fagan. Bruckner told Vorster to take a friend along and he said that he would pay for us to take a taxi to Pniel. I was then in my final year and Vorster asked me to go along. I said to him: 'Look John, do you know what you are doing? Do you understand that you are secretary of the SRC at this university and I am the chairman? And can you imagine what will happen if they catch us at a Sap meeting in the dark of the night?' He replied that this was the risk that we ran and that I should come with him nevertheless. In those days we used to wear hats with wide brims and we each put one of these hats on, tying them on our heads with string because the wind was blowing hard that night. We did not disguise ourselves further and took a taxi to Pniel where we easily found the hall. We did our best but the windows and the doors were closed tight against the wind. We listened at the windows and we listened at the doors but the wind was blowing so strongly that we could not hear anything at all. We did not want to go inside because that would have been taking too much of a risk. So we went back to the university, our mission ending in absolute failure".

It was during this campaign that Vorster addressed his first "adult" political meeting: "Old man Bruckner de Villiers phoned me at the hostel and told me that one of the speakers for a meeting he was holding at Durbanville had fallen out. He did not know why but he was sending a taxi to take me there and would I please hold the fort. I like to think that that first meeting of mine was a great success".

At university, Vorster first met Japie Basson[11]. While Vorster headed the Nationalists, Basson was the leader of the comparatively small band of Fusionists at the university. They were in the same hostel but Vorster had very little to do with his young political opponent. "Quite frankly, I never liked the man. I do not want to beat around the bush. I did not like him and that was that – although during an election when he was in the National Party, I addressed a meeting for him in his constituency and he addressed a meeting for me in mine. But at Stellenbosch we were political enemies and feelings were running very high in those times".

Tini Malan left university at the close of the 1937 academic year, only a few months after meeting Vorster. By this time they were "going steady" and it seemed certain that the romance would develop further. Partly because of the reputation Dr Verwoerd's course at the university had developed, Tini Malan had no problem in finding a job. For a few months she worked with the Board of Aid in Cape Town before she joined a massive survey of the conditions under which the lower-paid railway workers lived and worked. While she was in Cape Town she maintained her contacts with Vorster. Then she moved to Port Elizabeth and literally started riding the rails.

She was responsible for the survey in the Cape Midlands System. With a nurse, she criss-crossed the region, stopping off at every little station, siding and ganger's cottage. They travelled by passenger train, by goods train and often on a ganger's trolley. She did this for two years, regularly reporting on her work to her superiors in Port Elizabeth. She saw Vorster only very rarely during this period, but the relationship deepened.

Vorster wrote his final examinations at the end of 1938. He obtained distinctions in two subjects. "It was just an ordinary pass, no *cum laude* business. I was so busy in my final year, what with being chairman of the SRC, the Junior National Party, the Intervarsity Committee, the Students' Legal Association and the

11., Jacob Daniel du Plessis Basson, became a Nationalist eventually and entered Parliament in August 1950 as the National Party Member for Namib in South West Africa. On May 31, 1961 he left the NP to help form the National Union. With the 1961 general election the NU entered an election pact with the UP and Basson became the NU Member of Parliament for Bezuidenhout. In 1966 the NU was dissolved and he joined the UP. And when the UP killed itself off to form the New Republic Party in July 1977, Basson and his supporters merged with the Progressive-Reform Party to form the Progressive Federal Party.

Debating Society. In addition, I was Bruckner de Villiers' election agent at the university. I was also Primarius of Dagbreek and, because we did not have a professor living in the hostel, the Primarius had virtually to run the hostel and sort out all the problems himself".

Looking back on his university days, Vorster remembers: "The difference between us in those days and the young people of today is that we were kids and we enjoyed life to the full. We did not have many opportunities, but all the opportunities which came our way we enjoyed to the full. It was not a right but a privilege to be at university and we knew that if we failed a single year that we would not come back again. There was no second chance – and you knew it. We were serious as students. When we played, we played to the full and when we worked, we worked hard. We were serious but we had a great deal of fun. There was never a dull moment and we were never bored. In fact, there simply was not enough time to do all the things we wanted to do".

Before he left the university, Vorster had already arranged a job as registrar to Mr Justice H S van Zyl and accommodation with his older brother Koot who was now a minister of the Dutch Reformed Church, living in Cape Town with his family.

Vorster regarded 1939 as an interim year, the year before he started private practice as a lawyer. However, what he did not know as he left the university was that 1939 would be a crucial year for him, a year in which he would come to the political cross-roads and take a decision that would affect the rest of his life.

3 *The Ossewa Brandwag*

While Vorster was in his final year at the University of Stellenbosch, preparations were being made in different parts of the country for the celebrations to mark the centenary of the historic Battle of Blood River during which the Voortrekkers finally broke the might of the Zulu nation. Following the murder of Piet Retief and his party of 70 Boers and 30 Hottentot servants by the Zulu King's impis in the Royal Kraal of Umgungundhlovu, the Boers in Natal suffered severely. By the time they were able to collect their scattered forces, some 500 men, women and children had been killed and the Zulus had captured 20 000 head of cattle. An attempt to punish the Zulu King, Dingaan, failed. Retief was killed on February 6, 1838 and by November Andries Pretorius, a farmer from Graaff Reinet, arrived in Natal with a large trek – and cannon. A commando was quickly organised and the Boers set off to attack the Zulus.[1]

The commando was called the "Winkommando" (The Victorius Commando). On the way Sarel Cilliers made his covenant with God and the Voortrekkers advanced believing that victory was assured. On Saturday, December 15, 1838, the Winkommando established its laager[2] on the banks of the Ncome River (translated from Zulu, this means the "pleasant" river). The Standard Encyclopaedia of Southern Africa describes the battle: "The Winkommando consisted of about 470 men while the strength of the Zulu force is estimated at 12 500 warriors ... The Voortrekkers were equipped with much superior weapons. From behind the wagons they fired their muzzle-loaders and flint-lock muskets loaded with ball, shot and slugs. The main shortcoming of these weapons was the lengthy

1. Standard Encyclopaedia of Southern Africa, published by Nasau Limited. Volume Two, Pages 367 to 376.
2. When encamped or when threatened, the Voortrekkers would draw their wagons into a defensive circle, often with thorn-bushes and branches of trees closing the gaps between the wagons. While the women would load the rifles from within, the men would lie under the wagons and fire at the enemy. This was known as a laager.

reloading and the gunpowder in the pan easily got wet in rainy weather. The Zulu warriors entered the battle with shields and assegais. To be able to use their assegais effectively, they had to come as close as possible to the defenders ... Two hours before dawn everybody was ready. A dense fog covered the ground, but at daybreak it cleared completely. When the first Zulu attack started, the firing was so heavy that the enemy could not be seen through the smoke. The attack had scarcely been repulsed when a second was launched which could not be beaten back until it had almost reached the wagons. Meanwhile, hundreds of Zulus had hidden in a donga, where Sarel Cilliers with about 80 men went to attack them during a short lull in the fighting. When the Zulus, who had again withdrawn to about 500 yards, hesitated to launch a third attack, Pretorius sent some men to draw them out in order to consolidate the victory. The cannon were also fired against the last of the Zulu reserves who, in conjunction with the main force, made a final fierce attack lasting almost an hour. When the force of the attack began to weaken, Pretorius sent out a few hundred horsemen who met with determined resistance. Only after a third sortie were the Zulus finally put to flight and the Winkommando finally pursued them for several hours. Towards midday, when the pursuit was called off, more than 3 000 corpses were counted around the laager. Only three Voortrekkers, including Pretorius himself, were wounded and none were killed. A solemn thanksgiving service was held ..."

A church was built at Pietermaritzburg and the Day of the Covenant is still marked throughout South Africa by ceremonies with a religious and nationalist overtone. If Nationalist Afrikanerdom has a holy day, then that holy day is December 16.

The 1938 centenary celebrations came at a low point in Afrikaner nationalist morale. Fusion in 1934 had almost wiped out the National Party with which Hertzog had ruled the country for so long. In the 1938 General Election the United Party won 111 seats to the National Party's 27. Many Nationalist stalwarts remained in the UP and Dr D F Malan and his followers were desperately trying to rebuild their party's national infrastructure. Afrikanerdom felt politically divided and economically depressed – having suffered more heavily than the English-speaking section as a result of the depression and the droughts of the thirties.

Centenary festivals were planned for Pretoria and Blood River, the Pretoria festival to co-incide with the laying of the foundation stone for the Voortrekker Monument on a hill overlooking the South African capital city. Against this background Mr Henning Klopper, chairman of the South African Railways and Harbour's Afrikaanse Taal- en Kultuurvereniging[3], conceived the idea of two ox-wagons trekking through South Africa to each of the festival sites. The idea was accepted, but little did those involved understand just how the symbolic trek would touch Afrikaner hearts.

The Standard Encyclopaedia of Southern Africa[4] describes the trek: "The trek was intended to be only an unpretentious and symbolic reconstruction of Voortrekker life; but it gradually developed into a great national demonstration ... Instead of two trek routes, there were eventually 14, which brought almost every town in the country into the route of at least one of the 12 wagons ... In every town along the routes of the wagons, a local festival committee was responsible for the organisation of the festivities. From the very moment when the wagons were acclaimed by a crowd of 10 000 at the foot of the Van Riebeeck statue in Cape Town on August 8, 1938, the trek became a triumphal procession. Not only in the towns but everywhere along the route crowds gathered and were deeply stirred by the sight of the wagons, which had by now become the centre of celebrations unprecedented in South African history. These simple wagons symbolised to the Afrikaner his entire history and nationhood ... Enthusiasm found various modes of expression along the route. From Worcester onwards almost every town had its commemorative beacon or some little monument or other (often imprinted with wagon wheels) in memory of the trek. Women came out in Voortrekker dress at all these festivities and many of their menfolk grew luxuriant beards".

More than 40 000 people attended the celebrations at the site of the Battle of Blood River and more than 100 000 the laying of the foundation stone for the Voortrekker Monument.

With some of his student friends, Vorster went from Stellenbosch to Cape Town by train to watch the wagons set off from the foot of the Van Riebeeck Monument on August 8. He was 23 years old and, if anything, the flame of Afrikaner nationalism burned

3. Mr Klopper came to Parliament in 1943 as MP for Vredefort. He became Speaker of the House of Assembly in 1961 and continued in that capacity until his retirement in 1974.
4. Pages 280 and 281.

more brightly within him as a result of his political activities at the University of Stellenbosch. He looked on the wagons and the crowds and felt immediately that this could lead to a revival of Afrikaner nationalism: "The date remains inscribed in my memory. I can remember a feeling of well-being, of satisfaction, of elation. You know, it is very difficult to describe an experience such as this to somebody who has not gone through it himself. But it was a spiritual revival, it was something holy and sacred".

After his final examinations at the university and in preparation for the job that he would start in Cape Town on January 2, 1939, Vorster moved in with his brother Koot and his family. Koot was heavily involved in the organisation of the symbolic trek and the festival that would be held in Cape Town on December 16, 1938 to mark the centenary of the Battle of Blood River. He was president of the festival organising committee, although he was still a comparatively young man at 29. As the time for the festival approached Koot pitched a tent on Cape Town's Rosebank showgrounds and did the final work from there. Younger brother John went with them and they shared the tent with Hervormde Church minister The Reverend Van Rhysen. Koot remembers that week: "The whole thing was very real for both of us. John helped me in every possible way and I recall that his help was considerable. We did not discuss the trek or the significance of the centenary. You must understand that we thought alike on these issues. Our involvement was completely natural and we just threw ourselves into the organisational work with all our hearts — we were part of it, a natural part of the whole thing".

John Vorster came away from the Cape Town festival, which was attended by a crowd of between 30 000 and 40 000 people, feeling that a new era for the Afrikaner had begun. For himself, he felt that his spiritual batteries had been recharged.

After the wagons had passed through Bloemfontein in late October, 1938, a number of leading Afrikaners met in the home of Dr J C Pretorius in Bloemfontein. Chairman of the meeting was Dominee C R Kotzé who later wrote in a privately-published booklet: "People wanted some organisation or another which would perpetuate the wonderful spirit of the Ossewatrek ... it was decided to form such an organisation and call it the Ossewa-Brandwag[5]. The organisation would be based on the Voortrekker's

5. Literally: The ox-wagon sentinels.

commando system and it was decided that Colonel J C C Laas, who as an officer in the Defence Force had to travel throughout the country, would provisionally become the head of the organisation"[6].

The OB was conceived as a cultural organisation which would operate in parallel with the National Party and the newly formed Reddingsdaadbond[7] to help bring about Afrikaner unity and an Afrikaner republican revival. Ultimately, because of events, it would do almost the opposite, dividing Afrikaners as never before.

Working in Cape Town as a £250-a-year registrar to the Judge President, Vorster was naturally drawn to the OB. It took some time before the OB took root in Cape Town, but in September 1939 Vorster was invited to a meeting in the vestry of Cape Town's Groote Kerk[8] where it was decided to form a branch of the OB in the city. Those present included Koot Vorster, Dr Eben Dönges and Frans Erasmus, a prominent nationalist who would later become Minister of Defence in the first National Party cabinet in 1948 and John Vorster's predecessor as Minister of Justice. Although John Vorster did not have any first-hand knowledge of the organisation, he had read about it. "Quite frankly, I liked what I had read and I went to that meeting fully prepared to join. It did not require any persuasion on anybody's part. I saw the OB as an organisation like the Reddingsdaadbond, an organisation that would help put the Afrikaner on his feet again. The OB was a cultural organisation and I saw no conflict in interests between my membership of the National Party and membership of the OB. In fact almost all National Party politicians of that day joined the OB".

While in Cape Town, Vorster maintained close contacts with his friends at Stellenbosch. Often he would catch a train and spend the weekend there. Flooi du Plessis can remember an evening when they sat talking politics until the early hours of the morning: "In politics we more or less agreed to differ. For instance, I would never join the OB and I think John thought that I did not have a

6. Kotzé later resigned from the OB, largely because of his dissatisfaction with the direction in which the Kommandant-General, Dr Hans van Rensburg, was taking it.
7. Reddingsdaadbond: Literally: The League of the Rescue Deed. It was an organisation formed in 1939, also as a result of the sentiments generated by the Symbolic Trek, to rescue the Afrikaner from economic distress and to help him achieve his rightful place in commerce, industry and finance. It was dissolved in 1957 because its functions had been taken over largely by other organisations.
8. Literally: great church.

political idea in my mind. However, our political differences have not affected our friendship at all. He is that kind of man. Once he is your friend, he is always your friend".

Soon after joining the OB, Vorster left for Port Elizabeth to join a firm of attorneys. He had already decided to practise as an attorney rather than as an advocate because in those post-depression years it was not easy for a young and untried advocate to make a living. He did not want to take the risk of going to the bar because he believed that he would need enough money to keep himself for at least two years until he could build up an acceptable practice. As he had no money and as he was deep in debt because of the money he borrowed for his university education, he decided on joining a firm of attorneys. And he chose Port Elizabeth because he saw an advertisement in Die Burger from a firm there looking for a young man to join their staff. To Vorster, his salary of £25 a month was an extremely good one. The post had the added benefit that he would be in the same city as Tini Malan.

At first he found a room in a boarding house in Havelock Street in which Tini Malan also boarded. Later he moved to a boarding house in Port Elizabeth's North End just opposite the newly constructed law courts. He paid about £7 a month for his room and board and he considered himself a rather fortunate young man.

His first day at the office was potentially traumatic: "I remember that day well. I arrived at the office and the senior partner gave me a file dealing with a court case. He told me that the State had closed the case; that the State in fact did not have a case and that all I would have to do was to apply for the discharge of the accused and that I would get it. I had only a few minutes at my disposal and I paged through the file. Well, without any experience it was difficult to tell whether the State had a case or not, but the senior partner assured me that the prosecution would not oppose the application. However, I said to myself 'Heavens alive, what will the magistrate think of this young, fresh lawyer coming into the court for his first case and then having the audacity to ask for the discharge of the accused?'. Anyway, orders were orders and I walked over to the magistrate's court, found the prosecutor (Mr E O K Harwood, now Attorney-General for the Cape), introduced myself to him and spoke about the case. I admitted that I was as raw as raw could be but that I had been told to ask for the discharge of the accused. He conceded that he did not have a case and said that if I applied for the discharge of the accused, he would not oppose me. So I promptly got up when the court resumed and asked for the discharge of the accused. The application was granted by the magistrate and so you could say that I won my first case on the first day that I practised law. I never saw the accused except as he stood there in the dock and to this day I cannot even remember what he was charged with".

Vorster never did anything else but court work. He never allowed himself to be drawn into mundane matters such as estates and property transfers. He liked the courts. He liked the battle of wits, the legal arguments and the cross-examination of witnesses. Even today he still holds that the things he enjoys most include addressing a court, cross-examining a witness and speaking on the floor of the House of Assembly.

One of his colleagues in the law firm, Mr Joseph Kitching, told a newspaper soon after Vorster was elected Prime Minister: "He was a hard-working attorney with a passion for politics. He read every newspaper he could lay his hands on, chiefly looking for reports of political speeches. It did not matter what the speech was about or from what point of view it was made, provided it was a good speech. He would study the reports and analyse the text if he could get hold of it. Despite his extreme political views, his colleagues had a high regard for him. He spoke with authority and it was impossible to argue with him – he had all his facts at his finger-tips ... he was devoted to his law studies and to politics and he had already proved a good fighter in the courts"[9]. One of the firm's clerks, Mrs M Tuck recalled: "I could not have worked for a nicer man. He was a popular man. He was one of us and he treated all of us alike"[10].

Soon after his arrival in Port Elizabeth, he joined a branch of the National Party in what was then the Port Elizabeth North constituency. Shortly after joining the branch, he was elected chairman of the National Party's divisional committee in the constituency. Secretary of the divisional committee was a fiery young lady of 19, Annie de Swardt, who had been born in Calvinia, who had been educated at the very English Collegiate High School for Girls and who had become secretary of the divisional committee when she was 16 years old. Dr Otto du Plessis, then editor of Die Oosterlig[11], was in command of the OB in the Eastern Cape. After Vorster had

9. Eastern Province Herald, 14/9/1966.
10. Eastern Province Herald, 14/9/1966.

50

been in Port Elizabeth for a few months, Dr du Plessis told him that he could not carry on as a General in the OB because of the pressure of work. Would John Vorster be prepared to take command in his place? Vorster agreed and the OB's Groot Raad[12] made the appointment early in 1940. Vorster's duties were to expand the OB in the Eastern Cape, to form commandos, to appoint officers and generally to advance the interests of an organisation which, under pressure of events was becoming increasingly more militant and increasingly more political.

Annie de Swardt recalls that Vorster quickly became the king-pin of the Afrikaner community in Port Elizabeth. "Each of us loved him and respected his qualities. Most of the Afrikaners were in the OB and so he became the natural leader of the community". Of her own political views and her membership of the OB, she said: "We never believed that we would get our republic by democratic means and then there was the whole war issue. The thought of South African, and especially Afrikaner, soldiers helping England in a war against Germany was totally abhorrent to me. At that time the dominant forces in my own life were my hatred of England, my love of South Africa and my desire for a republic. My hatred for everything English was a product of the kind of treatment I received in an English-medium school and an English church. For a long time at school I was virtually boycotted because I was an Afrikaner. So I accepted the direction things were taking in the early forties ..."

Like the National Party, the OB was bitterly opposed to the Government's decision to enter the war on Great Britain's side. Feelings throughout South Africa ran high and there were frequent violent confrontations between the pro-war and the anti-war factions. The one side beat up anybody in uniform and the other side beat up anybody wearing a beard, anybody who remotely looked like a Nationalist. Each side claimed in retrospect that their moves were a reaction to the provocation of the other side. Against this background, Dr J F J (Hans) van Rensburg took command of the OB in December 1940.

Hans van Rensburg was a man of considerable talents and considerable stature. He was one of the University of Stellenbosch's

11. Literally: The Eastern Light. The Afrikaans-language newspaper published in Port Elizabeth.
12. Literally: The Great Council. The OB's controlling body.

most outstanding students of German. Later he went to the University of Pretoria where he obtained his LL.B. degree. In 1924, at the age of 26 he was appointed private secretary to the then Minister of Justice, Tielman Roos. In 1930 he obtained his Doctor of Laws degree from the University of Pretoria. In the same year he was appointed Deputy Secretary of Justice and three years later he became Secretary of Justice – at the age of 35! Later Prime Minister Hertzog appointed him Administrator of the Orange Free State. He resigned in 1940 in order to become Commandant-General of the OB. As an enthusiastic part-time soldier, Van Rensburg attained the rank of colonel and at different times commanded the Sixth Brigade and the Fourth Brigade.

Van Rensburg was an unashamed admirer of German culture, of the Nazi Party's national socialism and of the man, Adolf Hitler. Although he said often that he did not intend transplanting national socialism from Germany to South Africa, the OB campaigned vigorously against the war and in favour of a republic which would be based on the concept of an authoritarian state which would have both national and social characteristics. The movement spread rapidly and at its peak in 1942 it had between 250 000 and 400 000 members in different parts of the country. A parallel organisation of even more militant Afrikaners, the Stormjaers[13] developed, with its headquarters in the Transvaal. Its relationship with the OB is still not quite clear, but the fact is that Hans van Rensburg was in command of both organisations. And, while the OB proper operated within the law, the Stormjaers very often operated outside the law and indulged in frequent acts of sabotage. And many members of the OB became accessories to their sabotage, both before and after the act.

Much has been written in defence and in condemnation of the OB. Much of what has been written is contradictory. However, this much is clear: Under Hans van Rensburg, the OB helped the German war effort, hindered the South African and Allied war effort and created an organisation that was prepared for a power-grabbing coup when the right moment arrived. And that moment would come when Germany was well on its way to winning the war, when the Allied forces (and the South African Government) faced imminent defeat.

13. Literally: The Stormhunters.

As it happened the moment never came and it must be said in Hans van Rensburg's favour that his control of both organisations was so effective and the discipline he had thrust upon them so tight that no futile attempt at a coup took place as a measure of desperation when it was clear that Germany would lose the war. It has been widely suggested that Van Rensburg was never interned because Prime Minister Smuts feared that, with his control gone, the OB and its Stormjaer wing would burst out of the tight cage of Van Rensburg's discipline. The Standard Encyclopaedia of Southern Africa[14] says: "Dr van Rensburg was never interned nor was the movement as such prohibited, probably because General Smuts regarded it as an instrument for the reasonably peaceful chanelling of anti-war feeling".

In his book, Their Paths Crossed Mine[15], Van Rensburg writes of the four years of OB/Stormjaer struggle and says of the effect these years had had: "In the first place, there is no doubt that they seriously hampered the Government's war effort. Hampered it because the Government was forced to draw off considerable manpower to guard many strategic points and essential services. A not inconsiderable military element had to be retained in South Africa as a strategic reserve for possible emergencies ... Secondly, their resolute attitude definitely stiffened the spirit of those who were opposed to the war: stiffened it to such an extent that the Government could certainly not seriously consider the introduction of conscription in South Africa despite the clamour of certain pro-war factions ... Thirdly, it achieved these results – whether they are approved of or not – with a minimum sacrifice of lives and destruction of property. The rebellion in 1914 cost the country some ten hundred lives. The anti-war struggle of the OB, which may be regarded as its counterpart in the succeeding generation, demanded a bare half a dozen, the majority of whom were shot by the police while trying to escape. Fourthly – and to my mind this is the cardinal contribution – it taught the Government (and any future government in the same predicament) that it is quite out of the question to take so fateful a decision as the declaration of war, if the majority of one of the two dominant European races in the country is bitterly opposed to that step ..."

And Van Rensburg explains in the same chapter: "The men

14. Page 396.
15. Published by The Central News Agency. Page 264.

(who did this) did what they did, not to 'help the Nazis' as their opponents so bitterly alleged. Rather, through their deeds – for which they often paid heavily – they voiced the protest of the Nationalist Afrikaner element, which felt it was being discriminated against and that it was being trod under in its own fatherland. Whether this feeling is right or not, is a question of opinion, and, for the moment, beside the point. The point is that it did exist from the highest to the lowest and that it was bitter and vehement".

In another part of his book[16] Van Rensburg refers to a speech by Prime Minister Malan and says this speech admits to the OB's "good faith towards our people's republican objective". He adds: "Admittedly it would seem that our faith was not sufficiently tempered with discretion. With that assessment we have no quarrel. On the contrary, it was within our own hearts a source of strength that we never counted the personal cost in furthering the republican cause in the midst of a war to which, from the start, our people had been opposed so bitterly. In doing so, we often broke the law – and broke it shatteringly. In a monarchial system, a National Republican struggle and what the law calls high treason must, inevitably, often be distinctions without very clearly defined differences. The history of Ireland, the Netherlands and many other countries should be sufficient evidence of this unfortunate truism. In so breaking the law, we took no pleasure. In the process we obviously endangered not only our own safety but also the security and the happiness of our homes and our families. That, also, we accepted as necessary without relishing it particularly. Nobody in his sober senses does relish that sort of thing".

The Government view of the OB was spelled out very clearly in Johannesburg when Mr Harry Lawrence, the Smuts Government Minister of the Interior, told the quarterly meeting of the Witwatersrand General Council of the United Party: "The Ossewa-Brandwag is an importation from Nazi Germany, and we should not allow that sort of thing to continue in the Union for one moment more than we can help ... I say the time has at last arrived, in the interests of democracy and of the people as a whole, when the Ossewa-Brandwag should not be allowed to continue ... The Ossewa-Brandwag is steeped to the hilt in politics and its hot-heads use its military formations for subversive purposes ...

16. Pages 207 and 208.

Let me assure you that the Government is in possession of abundant evidence that a section of the Ossewa-Brandwag has realised the possibilities of the organisation which is based on semi-military or military lines and they are using this organisation in the same way as the Nazis used their own pet organisations in Germany at the time of the Weimar Republic". The Government was standing no more of this nonsense and it was drafting certain amendments to the emergency regulations which would have the force of law. Persons who said that the only salvation for South Africa was a German victory should beware. The security code would deal with persons who indulged in this kind of threat. He added: "We still live under a democratic system of government, and, despite these pocket fuehrers who talk about new orders and the decadence of democracy, we still continue to live under democratic rule, under a system in which the individual has the right of free expression of opinion, freedom of speech and of thought and of religion."

There were cheers from the audience when Mr Lawrence said that the internment policy was being stiffened. There would be no more beer, no more newspapers and no more radios in the internment camps. Internees who tried to escape and who were recaptured would be placed in solitary confinement. Recently hundreds more people had been interned on the Witwatersrand and other parts of the Union and there were about 4 000 people in the internment camps. A number of pro-British Italians had been released but, in the case of the Germans, the policy had been stiffened. Some hundreds of Germans had been rounded up recently – not because they were guilty of subversive actions, but because no risks could be taken. There was loud applause when he said that the benefit of the doubt should be given to the State. Mr Leslie Blackwell[17] moved a vote of thanks for Mr Lawrence's "magnificent speech". He was pleased that a member of the Cabinet had at last come forward and outlined the methods which ought to be adopted to deal with subversive elements. The sooner the unhappy state of affairs was altered, the better it would be for all concerned. The public had been long-suffering and tolerant[18].

17. M P for Bezuidenhout from 1915 to 1933 and for Kensington from 1933 to 1943. He became a judge in 1949 but retired in 1954 to take up an appointment in the Rhodesian High Court. He returned to South Africa to become Professor of Law at the University of Fort Hare for two years. Until his death in 1976 he was a vocal critic of the National Government's security policies and actions.
18. The Star.

Under Van Rensburg the OB started to move into the political arena which both it and the National Party had agreed would remain the Party's sole domain. Naturally, there was a reaction from a party which was a) jealous of its position in the Afrikaner power structure; b) opposed to the OB's national-socialistic sentiments; and c) vigorously opposed to the OB concept of a non-party "authoritarian state". And Nationalists were beginning to resent bitterly the OB's claims (both covert and overt) that the cherished republic would never come to South Africa by democratic means, by the route which the National Party had consciously chosen.

In a speech to the National Party's nation-wide congress on June 3, 1941, the leader, Dr D F Malan, said that he did not want to attack national socialism as such or suggest that it had not done wonders for Germany. However "we cannot ignore the fact that the kernel of national socialism is a dictatorship or, at least, the dominance of an enforced one-party system. And this is where we must ask ourselves very seriously whether our people can adapt to this without losing their own national characteristics, or their national traditions or even their fundamental religious beliefs. We must never forget that our whole history has always been in a direction away from dictatorship over body and spirit and away from an enforced system of unity which had no place for our freedom of conscience, for our inborn human rights or our nationhood. That is why our forefathers were Protestants, Huguenots and Voortrekkers. That is why we could become an Afrikaner nation. It is in our blood"[19].

The break between Party and OB had to come. The relationship between the two gradually deteriorated and, according to the Standard Encyclopaedia of Southern Africa[20] "The OB leaders became increasingly critical of parliamentarianism and accused the political party of being a divisive factor, powerless to lead the nation to republican freedom. The Party, in its turn, mistrusted the growing political tendencies of the OB, seeing in the movement a potentially dangerous competitor with national-socialistic

19. Eenheid, Vryheid en Reg, a National Party publication which reproduced, inter alia, a speech by Dr Malan to the national congress of the Herenigde Nasionale Party on June 3, 1941.
20. Page 396.

and dictatorial leanings. In 1941, this mutual distrust culminated in an open and final confrontation ..."

Malan demanded of all Nationalists who were also members of the OB that they should choose between the two organisations. Most withdrew from the OB, but many remained – including John Vorster and his older brother Koot.

Annie de Swardt, by now Commandant of the women's section of the OB in the Eastern Cape, remembers very clearly the effects of the estrangement in Port Elizabeth, where Vorster was now a Chief General in the OB and a vigorous campaigner in the organisation's interests. "The branch in Port Elizabeth North had to choose a new management. The Malan ultimatum had not yet been given, but the strains within the Party were very apparent. John Vorster's and my own connections with the OB were well-known and we were asked by the branch to choose between the Party and the OB. I can remember Vorster's words as if I heard them yesterday. He told the branch: 'Both organisations are for the Afrikaner, the one in the party-political field, the other not. I am loyal to both. If the one does not want me then it will have to kick me out. I will not resign'. I told the branch that I endorsed everything that John Vorster had said. The meeting asked us to leave and the two of us walked out together. I can remember that we were both very moved and distressed – and later we were kicked out of the Party".

In discussing his OB years, Vorster vehemently rejects any suggestion that he was involved in violence. "There was no violence in the Cape throughout the war. Mr J A Smith, the leader of the OB in the Cape would have nothing to do with violence". He also rejects the accusation that he was pro-Nazi, explaining: "I was not pro-Nazi, I was anti-British imperialism, in fact the official reason for my internment was not that I was pro-Nazi but that I was anti-British. Our attitude was that we should remain neutral, that we had no quarrel with Germany and that we were not part and parcel of the war. We believed that it was a British war and that consequently we were not involved ... in my area the OB was a cultural-political organisation".

However, Vorster certainly believed in those years in the OB concept of an authoritarian state and he certainly believed that the Afrikaner would not get his republic by way of normal democratic means. Flip la Grange remembers an occasion when Vorster visited him in his flat in Vredehoek some time after his appointment as a Chief General in the OB. La Grange had himself become a member of the OB but resigned when Malan told Nationalists to make their choice: "John and I argued for a whole night. The argument centred on this: John did not see how the Smuts government could be toppled by democratic means. I said there was only one way and that was through the ballot box. I remember writing to him afterwards, once again pleading that there should be no violence – because I took it they meant to use violence. John went away unshaken in his belief that there was no other way to serve the Afrikaner cause, to give Afrikaners control of South Africa. We simply could not find each other that night. I argued like Dr Malan argued that you could only get the Smuts government out by voting them out. Vorster argued at the time that he had no faith in democratic methods, that democratic methods would not get rid of the Smuts government and that 'other methods' should be used. We agreed to differ, but this did not affect our friendship".

About the same time, Vorster visited Cape Town with two of his OB adjutants. He invited Flip la Grange and Flooi du Plessis to lunch. Flooi recalls that the two OB adjutants were both much older than the 25- or 26-year-old Vorster: "Flip and I both said to him: 'Get rid of these two old boys first and then we can eat'. He replied that they were supposed to be with him. But we said: 'Not a damn, we will not have lunch with these two old men'. He agreed and we had a quiet and very enjoyable lunch together, with John just the same as he was when we were students together".

Meanwhile, Vorster was campaigning hard in the Eastern Cape. One of his friends and a fellow-member of the OB, David Johannes Malan, who waş working in Port Elizabeth as a public prosecutor and who later married fiery Annie de Swardt, recalls that Vorster was a "fantastic" speaker: "The audience hung on every word ... remember these were difficult times and feelings ran high. The meetings were always big, very well attended and very heated". Annie recalls that Vorster frequently attacked and ridiculed Dr Verwoerd, who was then editor of Die Transvaler[21] and bitterly opposed to the OB: "I remember him frequently quoting Dr van Rensburg's degrees of comparison: 'Verward, verwarder, Verwoerd"[22].

21. Official organ of the National Party of the Transvaal.
22. Literally: Confused, more confused ...

Vorster married his university sweetheart, Martini Steyn Malan, at Worcester on December 20, 1941. Bestman and groomsman functions were performed by his two university friends, Flooi du Plessis and Flip la Grange. Du Plessis and La Grange went to Cape Town shortly before the wedding to hire the top hat and tails outfits that the occasion required and La Grange can recall being troubled about wearing spats: "I can remember well how I laughed at the spats. I mean it was something very strange for me as an Afrikaner to be wearing spats ..."

Neither of them can recall much about the wedding, except that it was very pleasant and attended by a number of people. Of course, Vorster made an excellent speech. However, on the Vorsters' silver wedding anniversary, Flooi du Plessis wrote them a letter: "... we are now on holiday at Gordon's Bay and a few minutes ago I took a turn through the bathers and the sun-bathers. Not a single female there was even nearly as lovely and as desirable as you were 25 years ago, Tini. It is probably unnecessary to say: John do you remember how beautiful your bride was? The most indelible image of your wedding remains the peach-blossoms on the cheeks and the radiant beauty of the bride. And you John, apparently bold and completely relaxed, as if you had done this thing countless times before! Just us who were near to you and who could read deep into your eyes could get an indication of the wonder and the joy you were experiencing. Yes, it was impressively moving. But it was also joyful for us. In the bridegroom's camp there was very little of the rather silly talk that I have heard tell of; naturally thanks to the innocence of the bestman and the groomsman. I remember a little philosophical speculation about sin and duty in which even the bridegroom participated. Did you have a premonition then already, John, of how familiar you would become with striped pants, top hat and tails? Oh how Flip and I fitted and found fault with the clothes when we had to hire our outfits from Payne and Bonnier in Darling Street ...".

The wedding was a warm and carefree affair. Old friends met again and spoke of their days at the university. Political differences were forgotten despite the fact that so many of the guests came from different sides of the gulf that now separated the National Party from the OB. A notable absentee was Vorster's older brother Koot who was serving a three-year sentence in the Pretoria Central Prison after being found guilty by Mr Justice Jackie de Villiers of contravening the Official Secrets Act. It was alleged that Koot tried to get information about naval installations at Simonstown. Because of a serious liver complaint, Koot spent the first eight months of his sentence in hospital in Cape Town and was then moved to Pretoria.

He recalls his imprisonment: "I was never interned and I always used to say that I was one better than the ordinary plebs who went into the internment camps. I was very well treated and I had no trouble at all. I had no bitterness about what happened. I knew what I was doing in the OB and I knew that the Government would act against me sooner or later – even if the charge was a trumped-up one. One of the things jail did for me was to restore my health. I was told in 1936 that, because of my liver complaint, I would never be able to work again. However, in God's providence, I had to go to jail in order to get well again because there I never had to do a thing and I was freed from the tremendous pressures under which I operated in Cape Town. That is why I hold no grudge against anybody because I realise that in God's providence I had to go to jail in order to recuperate completely. Those were not wasted years because I regained my health and I largely completed the work for my doctoral thesis".

Whenever John Vorster visited Cape Town in the years before his brother's imprisonment, he stayed with Koot and his family. Of these times, Koot Vorster says: "We never discussed political philosophy, the whys and the wherefores of the OB. We were always in full political agreement. We believed the same things and we did what we could, not counting the consequences. In those days we were absolutely convinced that, as Afrikaners, the only way that we could serve our people was through the OB. I can vividly recall my feelings at that time – and this is not an after-thought because I spelled it all out to an official at the time who refused me petrol coupons because he said that I was pro-German. I told him that if the Germans should come to South Africa and try to do to us what the English had done and were doing, I would be the first to fight them tooth and nail. My idea, and I think it was John's idea as well, was that we were Afrikaners. We never had an axe to grind with the Germans. Our traditional enemy was the English and we felt that very strongly indeed. We were not so much pro-German but anti-English and pro-Afrikaner. We wanted to be free of the English and we wanted our republic. I can swear to you on The Bible that if the Germans would have come here and tried to act as a superpower over us, I would have been the very first to go into the front line against them. We in the OB wanted to create an organisation that would be able to take over the country at the right time and then enter into negotiations with the Germans, thus obtaining our Afrikaner republic".

In discussion with me, Dr Vorster conceded that if he was in Government today and if an organisation like the OB came into confrontation with his Government's authority, he would act against it just as effectively as the Smuts Government acted against the OB: "That was why we took our medicine at the time without complaining. We realised what might happen to us. We went into this whole thing with our eyes open. In effect, we lost the war, we lost our chance and we took our medicine. That is why I have no rancour or hard feelings. We were in opposition to the Government of the day, they saw us as a threat and they locked us up. We never queried their right to do it".

Back at the Vorster family home in Jamestown (the family had moved back from Sterkstroom), the imprisonment of their minister son was a blow. In fact it hit the family harder than did John Vorster's later internment. Miss Mona Vorster explained: "Remember, Koot was a minister of religion and it is a terrible thing for a minister of religion to go to jail. Apart from this, he was the first Vorster to go to jail. I will never forget the day Koot's sentence was confirmed. It was a nagmaal (communion) Saturday and in a small place like Jamestown everybody knew everybody else's business very quickly. And now we have to go to church, walk right through the congregation to our traditional pew right in front of the minister. So I asked my mother whether she wanted to go to church that afternoon, whether the whole thing might not be too much for her. She was furious. She asked me how I could possibly think this. What was there to be ashamed of? And she said: 'All right now, I'm telling you that we are going to church and the dominee will say something in his prayer and if I see any one of you wiping a tear, there will be trouble.' So we had to move through that church, sit down in the front pew and go through the whole service without showing any kind of emotion at all. It was not easy because, after all it is not nice to think of your brother in jail, not nice to think that you will not see him for something like three years — but that was my mother's attitude. I remember that the dominee prayed for us to get the strength. And, you know, you do get strength to face these things and you come out of them stronger".

Despite Koot's imprisonment, once the Vorsters had settled down to married life in a house in Newton Park, in Port Elizabeth, it never occurred to Tini that John was heading for trouble. "I knew he was involved in things, but I never thought this would lead to internment and that sort of thing. I never thought the Government would regard his activities as serious. Remember, John was working, I was working, we were busy with this, that and the other thing and I simply never gave it a thought".

At many of the Vorster meetings in different parts of the Eastern Cape was a young policeman – the same Gert Prinsloo who had been so close to Vorster while they were at school in Sterkstroom. Despite a good school record, the depression meant that Prinsloo could not go to university. So he joined the police force in 1933, became a detective and was serving on the so-called "suspect staff" when Vorster was in Port Elizabeth. And the "suspect staff" had the job of keeping an eye on the anti-war people, the men and women the Government of the day considered real and potential subversives. So Constable Gert Prinsloo attended one Vorster meeting after another and reported to his superiors on what the young OB Chief General was saying. However, this did not prevent them from renewing their friendship. "I knew what he was doing and he knew what I was doing, but there were no hard feelings at all. After he was married, he stayed in a house in Newton Park and I often visited him and Tini. We played bridge and I remember well how warm and friendly those evenings were. You must know I was a single man then staying in the police barracks and I thoroughly enjoyed the warm, friendly, relaxed atmosphere in the Vorster household . . . not to mention Mrs Vorster's cooking".

Prinsloo can remember an occasion when both the suspect and the policeman arrived at a meeting together: "I cannot recall whose car broke down. It may have been mine or it may have been his. However, what I can remember is that one of us stopped for the other. We both knew that we were going to the same meeting and so the one gave the other a lift and we arrived at the meeting together, in one car. I remember there were people who gave us some funny looks. But I had my job to do and he had his role to play and we both accepted each other."

Vorster was much in demand as a lawyer and he defended a number of his OB colleagues. One of these was General Jan Moolman, in charge of the Cradock area and one of the first OB men to be charged under the emergency regulations of the time (Moolman later switched from the National Party to the United Party, becoming the UP Member of Parliament for East London City from 1962 to 1974). Vorster recalls that one of the charges against Moolman centred on an alleged statement in which he referred to the Khaki Ridders[23] insultingly. "He repeated at a meeting in Steynsburg something I myself had said often: A Khaki Ridder is like a skunk, you cannot see him, you can only smell him. I can remember that, under cross-examination, I managed to throw so much doubt on the credibility of the crown witnesses that I asked for his discharge at the end of the crown case and I got it too".

Vorster's last case before his internment involved a rather complex dispute between two farmers over an ox which resulted in the arrest of one of them on a charge of stock theft. Vorster spent three days in Jansenville defending his client. The whole town attended the, for Jansenville, sensational trial and the people were sharply divided into two camps over the issue. Vorster managed to get his client discharged and that evening there was a tremendous party for the now free farmer, his friends, his supporters and his lawyer. Vorster recalls: "My client was a good old UP establishment man and everybody at his party was vigorously pro-war. I remember the old man telling me that he had asked for me to be instructed to defend him and that it did not matter whether I was OB or not – as long as I got him off. At any rate, I was the guest of honour at the party and I thoroughly enjoyed myself. I thought then that I had done a very good job and I still think so today."

But time was running out for John Vorster. And he knew it.

23. Literally: The Khaki Knights. A more or less informal organisation which fiercely supported the war effort and which passed on information to the authorities regarding the activities of the anti-war faction.

4 Detention without trial

On September 23, 1942, the telephone rang in Vorster's law office. It was a policeman who asked him politely whether he would not step across to their offices in the New Law Courts, on the other side of the road. Vorster was not surprised and he had half an idea that the Government was finally taking action against him: "I knew something was up because one had one's contacts in the police force. I knew that old man Bill Coetzee, the head of the CID in South Africa, was there and, naturally, when they phoned me it was a question of putting two and two together. But I went. I said to my typist that they wanted to see me across the road and I walked across the road and I never came back".

Vorster was told that he was under arrest and he was taken to his home in Newton Park. The house was thoroughly searched but nothing was found which interested the police. Then he was taken to the police cells in the New Law Courts building. "They locked me up and they forgot about me. The cell was small, no bigger than 10 by 12 feet and I stayed there for 24 hours out of 24. It had no furniture whatsoever and a very small bench attached to the wall. There was a flush toilet in one corner and there was a mat upon which you slept and there was a blanket. Being a police cell without a kitchen, the police had to buy the food for the prisoners. In those days they were allowed a sixpence a meal for every prisoner. Consequently they bought a meat pie and a cup of tea at a café across the street and that was the only food we had three times a day until my wife and another lady could organise to get some food to us".

After three weeks he was transferred to the Baakens Street police station in Port Elizabeth's central business district. "They took this Black woman out of the cell and they put me in. Heavens alive, there it was awful. The cells were below the level of the ground and extremely murky and I stayed in that cell for ten days. I was never out of the cell even for exercise ..."[1].

more serious contraventions, there was a series of "coolers", small cells about seven foot square in a corrugated iron building. One of the internees[11] wrote later about the "cooler": "Only two blankets lay on the cement floor. In one corner was a Bible and no further reading material was allowed. In the summer the heat was almost unbearable and, in the winter, one almost died of the cold. In the winter the cooler well lived up to its name ... in the summer it had a paralysing effect. In the tiny room the convicted internee had to think day and night of his sins. Only an hour's exercise was allowed in the morning and in the evening ..."

At first the Koffiefontein camp was divided into two, with the Afrikaners on the one side and the Italians, in the original camp, on the other side. Later some Frenchmen were interned between the Afrikaners and the Italians and, by February 1943 the Afrikaners' neighbours included Italians (by now divided into fascists and Badoglioti), communists and Germans. Security was strict. The camp was surrounded by sentry posts and by towers equipped with powerful lights and machine guns.

When Vorster arrived at Koffiefontein, the internees included his old friend from Port Elizabeth, Dawid Malan, Advocate J F "Kowie" Marais, and a tall (2 m) detective Hendrik van den Bergh who would later play a key role with Vorster in the fight against subversion in South Africa.

Marais had arrived at Koffiefontein in July 1942 by way of the Ganspan camp. Born in Wellington into an intensely and actively Afrikaner nationalist family, Marais obtained a law degree at Stellenbosch two years before Vorster arrived at the university. For a while he worked on Die Burger as a court reporter and later he was offered a job as an Afrikaans announcer in Cape Town for I W Schlesinger's old African Broadcasting Corporation. While in Cape Town he reported for the radio on the 1938 symbolic Ossewatrek and eventually travelled with one of the ox wagons to the site of the monument at Blood River. He felt the same upsurge of Afrikaner nationalism that so many thousands of his compatriots felt throughout South Africa at the time. Later this upsurge of emotion led him to membership of the Stormjaers. His story is a fascinating one:

"By the time the war broke out, the South African Broadcasting

11. Herman Luitingh, writing in Agter Tralies en Doringdraad.

Corporation had taken over from the ABC and I then worked for them in Johannesburg. I think it was in August 1940 that one of the Stormjaer officers came to me and said: 'Look Kowie, we want to build transmitters in order to establish a sound and independent form of communication between the different centres. We believe that Hitler is going to win the war and, if he does and if he lands in England and if England is defeated, we are going to have an uprising in South Africa because the English will not be able to do anything about it. We will overthrow the Smuts Government and naturally, in the process of the rebellion, the system of communication will be disrupted. In order to avoid confusion and chaos, it will be necessary to have transmitters and receivers under our control in different parts of South Africa'. So I got one of the engineers at the SABC to design a small but powerful transmitter. Of course, when construction started, we had to get all the parts on the black market. We even stole some of them and I even seem to think that one of the valves was stolen from a therapy machine at the hospital in Bloemfontein. We had five depots staffed by young men who knew something about radio and electricity and we started building transmitters at these depots, two were in Pretoria and three were in Johannesburg. I realised that, if any of this activity came to the notice of the police, we would be in for the high jump. And it did happen. The depot in Sydenham came under suspicion. The chaps were putting the finishing touches on to one of the transmitters and one of them took it to his place of employment to have certain holes drilled. This alerted someone or other who reported his suspicions to the police. The police then followed our man to the place in Sydenham. It was a private garage and I had already assured the owner that if anything should go wrong, we would take all the blame and absolve him completely. We told the police that the owner had nothing to do with the illegal operations. I was arrested with three other chaps and spent a few days in police cells in Johannesburg. Then we were sent to the Ganspan camp which was an old age settlement the Government had taken over.

"I joined some other chaps in digging a tunnel. It was about 56 yards (51 m) long and it took us from the middle of April, 1941 (a few weeks after our arrest) until October 11. We effectively made our escape and immediately went on the run. Our comrades in the OB and the Stormjaer movement looked after us as we went our different ways. Later I could not stand hiding away any longer and I decided to come out in the open. I disguised myself and adopted the name Rossouw. At first I worked as a shop assistant in Heilbron and later I found a job in an attorney's office in Vrede-fort. Later it appeared that one of the chaps with me had kept a diary in which both my name and my pseudonym appeared. The police caught him and got a look at his diary. I got a warning from Johannesburg that the police were on my tracks but I did not think the danger was very great. In any case, building up an entirely new identity was going to take too much trouble. However, the report from Johannesburg was a well-founded one and I was arrested in July 1942 and sent to Koffiefontein".

Speaking of the OB and the Stormjaer movement, Marais says: "There must have been about 300 000 members of the OB and about 40 000 members of the Stormjaer movement. By the begin-ning of 1942, the Stormjaers had sufficient explosives in various caches to cause an enormous amount of damage by way of sabotage in South Africa. But the commanding officer of the Stormjaers was a very close friend of the Commandant-General, Dr Hans van Rensburg, and no order went out except from these two people. Discipline was exceptionally strict. You were not allowed to make a move of any kind without somehow or other getting the OK from the K-G or the Owerste[12] . . . I tell you, we had some very wild and irresponsible elements in the Stormjaer movement but Van Rens-burg and the Owerste controlled them very firmly indeed and carefully considered anything which might cause bloodshed. The Stormjaer top command always reminded us that if we shed blood, this would follow us through history, it would follow and stain both the movement and whatever we stood for. We were told over and over again that we were not to waste lives and, as things happened, less than a handful died. Our objective was sabotage that would not cost human life but which would keep troops in South Africa and away from the war".

After his arrest, Marais was taken to Jagersfontein and from there he was moved by car to Koffiefontein: "I arrived while all the chaps were on morning parade. I still had my moustache and glasses which I had used as a disguise and one of the people stand-ing in the front row looked at me and asked one of his friends: 'What's this little Jew they have brought here?' And then some of

12. Literally: The Chief.

my camp mates from Ganspan said: 'Ag no, its old Kowie, the barefoot advocate from Ganspan' ... and then I was taken to my bungalow".

Hendrik van den Bergh came to Koffiefontein by an entirely different route. He was born in Vredefort in November, 1914. His father was a post office official who later became a building contractor. Van der Bergh was named Hendrik Johannes after his grandfather and it so happened that, as a result of an estrangement between his mother and his father, he was largely raised by his grandfather. His family were fiery Afrikaners, with his father a veteran of both the Anglo-Boer War and the 1914 Rebellion in which he fought with General de Wet and was captured with him. Both father and grandfather fought in the Anglo-Boer War and were prisoners-of-war in Ceylon. However, as Van den Bergh remembers it, there was only a very mild political atmosphere in both his father's and his grandfather's homes. They hardly ever talked politics but the whole family were ardent admirers of General Hertzog, the Free State Nationalist leader. Van den Bergh was educated in Vredefort, but, because the depression weighed so heavily on the platteland, he had to leave school in Standard Nine. "As a result of the English War, the Rebellion and the depression, my people were not wealthy. We had enough food, but we had no money. I was very conscious of the battle my grandfather had to keep us clothed, fed and accommodated and so I decided in Standard Nine that I would leave school and help him provide for the family ... remember it was the depression and I know that at one stage my grandfather worked as a labourer in the street with a pick and shovel for 3/6d a day ..."

In 1933 he joined the Special Service Battallion, created by the Government to provide a home for young men during the unemployment of the depression and to give them a foundation for later employment, generally in one government department or another. The SSB was operated on military lines and attached to the Union Defence Force's headquarters at Voortrekkerhoogte, just outside Pretoria. "I remember arriving in Pretoria. I was one of the first 16 youths in the SSB and when we arrived at the camp there was no accommodation for us. There were no tents, no messes, nothing. But some military tables stood outside one of the buildings and we ate at them when we arrived. There was only bread, but what struck me was that there was butter, jam and cheese – and we could eat as much as we liked ... to me it was a fantastic experience".

At one stage, Van den Bergh was selected for possible training as an officer in the Defence Force. However, after being questioned by the selection panel, he told them that he did not want to become an officer but that he wanted to join the South African Police Force. "I really do not know why I said that to them because, after all, selection for officer training would have meant an immediate and impressive jump in my status and my pay. At school I had wanted to be a doctor of medicine, but, of course, that was impossible. My brother was a policeman, but I think there was a deeper reason for my statement to that selection panel. At Vredefort, one of our neighbours had a son in the Police Force. His name was Abraham 'Apie' van Zyl and I think he was about six years older than I was and at the time he was stationed in Johannesburg. Johannesburg! We children in Vredefort had never been to Johannesburg, we had only heard the adults tell of this great place. Well, one day we were sitting under a willow tree next to a stream eating watermelons and listening to Apie tell of the big city. There were about ten or 12 of us boys listening to him. He was our hero and he told us about communism. Communism? But I was the youngest and I was too young to ask questions, so I just sat there with my mouth shut. Heavens, communism? This was the first time that I heard tell of communism. And he told us what the communists were and how they intended taking over South Africa. This must have been in 1928 or 1929 and he told us how the communists were trying to get the Black Man on their side and how they infiltrated organisations. I remember this conversation very clearly indeed and I remember him telling us: 'I say that we are going to have a Black Prime Minister in South Africa within 50 years ...' The older boys asked him how he knew all this and he answered that he had learned it in the police force, that he had read about it and talked to people about it. That conversation must have made a tremendous impression on me because it has remained with me all my life. Little did I know then that it would one day be my task to help prevent a communist plot for revolution in South Africa. But it is also clear that the decision to go to the Police Force was not my own. It was a decision of the Higher Hand. It is the Higher Hand who said: Go to the Police Force, that is where I need you ..."

Van den Bergh was a big and tough young man, standing 6'4½"

(2 m) and weighing 180 lb. (81,6 kg). After writing an entrance examination in February, 1934, he went to the Police Depot in Pretoria for training and was nominated as leader of his troop during training (the troop of 34 was later to produce three generals and a brigadier). After training, the whole troop was posted to Johannesburg. His first posting after a month at Marshall Square headquarters was to Booysens police station, which in those days served what amounted to a rural area. Later in the year, after a spell in Orlando he was transferred to the detective branch as a probationer. In 1938 the Johannesburg liquor squad was "cleaned up" following a scandal and Van den Bergh was transferred to the new squad.

Later he left the liquor squad and did general detective work at Marshall Square. By now he was a sergeant and much of his time was taken up with the investigation of homicide cases. On January 20, 1942, Van den Bergh was summoned to the Divisional Criminal Investigation Officer's offices. He found a number of his detective colleagues there. "We did not know what was happening. They called in one of the chaps to the officer's office and when he came out he was almost exploding he was so cross. But he was some distance from where I was standing so that I could not hear what he was so angry about. Then they called in Max de Wit, who is now chairman of the Transvaal Provincial Council. When he came out, a number of officers followed him and he could not tell me anything. Then we were told to go into the office and we formed up in two rows in front of the DCIO, a Major Kruger. We stood facing each other and Major Kruger said with his heavy lisp that he was very sorry to tell us that he had orders to arrest us. Then one of my colleagues, who was standing opposite me, came to search me. I realised then that the one row of detectives knew what this was all about while we knew nothing. I must tell you that in that moment, as he stepped forward to search me, I became a man, I matured, suddenly I knew what I was. I became a mature person for the first time in my life ... that feeling that coursed through me while I was being searched made me what I am today. Until that point I had not taken any interest whatsoever in politics. Old papa Kruger said then that we were being arrested because we were all members of the Stormjaer movement. In my case this was absolute nonsense because I had never belonged to either the OB or the Stormjaers. But I tell you what happened. One of my police friends, Nicholas

Vorster, who is now my brother-in-law, enrolled me in the OB without my knowledge. Then we were locked up in the police cells. A few days later I was sent to Koffiefontein. I can remember that day so well. By that time I was a widower (I had married a Welsh girl who later died) and I had a three-year-old daughter who was being looked after by my mother. I can remember as if it was yesterday how I lay in my camp bed that first night. The full moon shone through the window right in my face and I thought: This same moon is shining in Johannesburg where my daughter is ...."

Vorster arrived at the outer gates of the camp on December 17, 1942. At first he was taken to the camp stores where his own clothing was taken from him and replaced with camp issue: "We got a pair of velskoens[13], two pairs of socks, one pair of short pants, one pair of long pants and two very rough black shirts such as the train drivers used to wear. We were also given a broad-brimmed felt hat like those issued to the Cape Corps[14] and a black overcoat, two pairs of pyjamas, two sheets and two blankets. And then they marched you into the camp proper with your goods and chattels. The camp was circled by a fence about 18 inches high. About ten feet further there was another fence about six feet high with rolls of barbed wire on top and beyond that was a ten-foot barbed-wire fence. Outside the last fence the armed guards patrolled constantly, never more than about 50 yards apart. The sentries had orders to shoot anybody who moved into the no-man's-land between the 18 inch fence and the six-foot fence ...."

Vorster recalls that he felt a sense of relief when he was thrust into the camp: "Firstly, you have left the terribly small police cell and, to you, the space available at Koffiefontein is fantastic. And you are now amongst friends – and lots of them. You can move around, you can talk to people, you have space, sunlight, open air ... and, in any case, you had already come to terms with yourself in jail ...."

Thus it was that Vorster slept more easily that night than he had done since the day he was first arrested in Port Elizabeth.

---

13. Literally: Skin shoes. Shoes similar to those made by the Voortrekkers and reproduced on thousands of farms and hundreds of rural settlements in South Africa. Simple, cheap and relatively comfortable.
14. The Cape Corps was recruited from Coloured people during the Second World War and intended to serve the White troops as a service battalion. However, in the later years of the war the Cape Corps soldiers fought with their White compatriots.

6 *Camp Life*

Vorster soon settled down to life in the camp. He had already promised his wife that he would not try to escape (because she feared that he might be shot in the process) so he tried to make the most of his indefinite internment and to prepare for the day when he would be released. Once he learned the camp routine he realised that he would have to try to earn some extra money in order to supplement his meagre shilling a day allowance – especially because if any of the Koffiefontein prisoners escaped, all the internees at the camp were fined £1. He remembers: "I realised that the only thing I could try for was to become a potato peeler. Then I would get an extra shilling a day. I must tell you that this was a very sought-after job because it meant that your camp pay was doubled. I badly needed the job because I wanted a portrait of myself done by Dr Kranz and I wanted Fobian to make me a white tunic jacket. Each cost £1 and so I needed the potato-peeler's job ... the material for both the painting and the jacket was provided by tearing one of our sheets into two pieces, the one went to Dr Kranz and the other went to Fobian. So, for most of my time in Koffiefontein, I slept with only one sheet..."

Vorster made an immediate impact on the camp community, not because he thrust himself forward or because he tried to get involved in the camp administration, but because his leadership qualities were so evident. Apart from anything else, he came to the camp with a reputation as the youngest of the OB's Chief Generals. The mere fact of his high rank assured him of status in the camp. But his personal qualities were quickly recognised by his fellow-internees. Kowie Marais remembers: "He impressed me immediately as a quiet, pleasant man, a man with a sense of humour, a man who never lost his cool and who did not have a frightened hair on his head. He was humorous but not flippant ... what was serious he treated seriously ... but he was a tremendous companion, a man who always had an anecdote to tell. He had presence and he became very popular because of his personality and his quiet friendliness. Later I got to know him better and came to admire his planning ability, his strategic cunningness and his qualities of leadership".

Vorster moved into hut number 48. One of those already there was David Malan who recalls that Vorster was almost immediately elected House Father: "He was so obviously a leader, that we put him in charge of the hut, despite his comparative youth. In the camp he was still the same quiet, but humorous man I had known in Port Elizabeth. He was universally liked and respected ... he was so genuinely human".

But Chief General or not, South Africa's future Prime Minister had to do the chores just as the rest of his comrades. For a week at a time he was the house orderly (even when he later became Camp Leader) and had to make all the beds, sweep the floor, do the dusting and the tidying up. In the central dining room, each hut had a separate table and the orderly had to set the table. After the meal he had to wash up for everybody. "When you were on duty, you had to make early morning coffee for the house, you had to set the table for breakfast at eight o'clock, wash the dishes, tidy the hut, make the beds, make 11 o'clock coffee, set the table for lunch, wash the lunch dishes, make four o'clock coffee, set the table for dinner, wash the dinner dishes, make nine o'clock coffee ... all this only happened once every 16 weeks, but I tell you it took some doing".

Most of the internees were Afrikaners and members of the OB. There were a few Germans and a solitary Irishman. "There was this Irishman, Dr Kirby who, I think, practised at Elgin. He was a pukka Irishman and he was violently anti-British. But he could not speak much Afrikaans and so he was the only man in the camp who spoke English. I remember that he came into my hut one day and he was particularly angry with the English over something or another. He said to me: 'Jy moet nooit weer met my Engels praat nie, ek gaan die verdomde taal nooit weer oor my lippe neem nie'[1]. But that was just for that day. The next day he spoke English again. We got on very well together and I played many a game of chess with old Dr Kirby ... he had a beard and he was as Irish as Irish could be".

---

1. "You must never speak English to me again, I am never again going to let that damned language pass my lips".

From time to time tensions mounted in the camp. Like the "mossie-war"[2] which flared up suddenly and then died down again. A number of the internees cultivated vegetables on a small piece of ground. When the first shoots appeared above the surface, the mossies could not resist them. The gardeners objected and immediately started planning their annihilation. However, the mossies had their allies. Some of the internees had tamed them and made pets out of them. The tamed mossies repaid this felicitation by chirruping away. One afternoon the pro-mossie faction noticed that a large number of mossies had been killed and maimed and they learned that the gardeners had declared war on the birds. This sparked off great conflict in the camp which divided into pro-mossie and anti-mossie factions. However, as the vegetables matured and the birds lost interest in them, the temperature of the dispute dropped and eventually it was all but forgotten[3].

Tension of a real and potentially serious kind began building up at the beginning of 1943. It reached its peak with a routine search of the camp. The authorities were looking for an alleged offender. They demanded that the camp leadership hand over the man. The leadership refused and tension within the camp mounted explosively, with many of the internees arming themselves with makeshift weapons and preparing for a final confrontation with the "khakis". They knew that the military would be back soon to get their man.

Different versions of the incident exist. However, it seems that a force of about 200 soldiers marched into the camp, armed with pick-axe handles or long truncheons. They searched the camp for the alleged offender. The version printed in Agter Tralies en Doringdraad reads: "The officer commanding the soldiers ordered the comrade to give himself up when he was finally tracked down. However the House Father of the house in which he sought refuge refused. At this critical moment, the Camp Leader and the commanding Stormjaer officer intervened and told the soldiers that they would talk to the comrade. The Stormjaer officer told the comrade: 'Today we can hammer the khakis in the camp into the ground, but they will fire on us from outside and it is not us who will suffer for the consequences of our deeds, but the innocent, our wives and children. We cannot fight machineguns with

2. The mossie is a small bird, generally known as a Cape sparrow (Passer melanurus).
3. The "mossie-war" was described in "Agter Tralies en Doringdraad".

our bare hands'. The comrade agreed to leave the hut but the House Father said: 'We will only hand him over at the gate'. The khakis then marched in close file towards the gate while the comrade was carried shoulder-high by the internees who had formed a procession ... The internees had to hold hands to allow the khakis to get through the gate. When the last few rows were almost through, one of the khakis threw a two-inch steel ball into our midst and it caught one comrade on his elbow. This set off a wave of rage within the camp and one of our comrades plucked out a bread-knife. Things suddenly became serious. 'Take your soldiers out more quickly, our chaps are becoming mad' one of our leaders called out to the soldiers and the khakis rushed through while a quick skirmish took place just before the gate. The khakis on the other side of the gate were on the point of opening fire with a machinegun, but the Camp Commandant stopped them. In the meanwhile, some of the internees formed a cordon to prevent their comrades from bursting through the gate in a wild rage ... quickly the gates were closed and the older comrades pleaded passionately with the others in an effort to calm them down. When the Camp Commandant saw this, he ordered his soldiers to leave the terrain ... after about two weeks the tension started ebbing away. This crisis led to a reform of the camp leadership and a sharpening of the duties of our Dienswag"[4].

Kowie Marais was right in middle of the fracas. "I was standing at the gate. I simply did not realise the temper of the men around me or the seriousness of the situation, despite the fact that a machinegun had been placed facing the gate, about twelve yards from us. The machinegunner was standing behind it and it was trained right on our gate ... fortunately Botterbul[5] kept his cool and so did our officers. When I think back on that incident, I still go cold because it was as close to dammit that the shooting would have started – and if shooting started that afternoon in Koffiefontein, it would have echoed throughout South Africa. I was holding my breath once I realised just what could happen because I knew that if even one of us was shot, The Commandant-General and the Owerste would have great difficulty in restraining their men ... it would have been revolution."

4. Page 33.
5. Literally: butter bull. It is an Afrikaans expression generally used to describe a large man whose bark is worse than his bite.

Vorster was there too. "I tell you that was one devil of an eruption. If it was not for Christiaan de Jager, who later became a professor at the University of Pretoria, many chaps would have been killed that day ... De Jager helped save the day by closing the gate and preventing our chaps from getting through. I hate to think of what the repercussions would have been outside the camp had the machineguns started firing that afternoon".

After the near-explosion, the OB command in the camp decided to apply stricter discipline. According to camp documents, at 4,25 on April 26, 1943, Vorster, as Secretary of the Camp Council, announced that the camp authority would consist of General C L de Jager, who would be responsible only to the Commandant-General (of the OB) and to the "nation outside". Dr J Trumpel-mann would be head of the administrative section, General M J Toerien would be Head of the Dienswag and General B J Vorster would be Secretary. (Commandant-General Hans van Rensburg later confirmed these appointments.) Shortly after the announcement, General de Jager called the internees together and told them: "A record will be kept of all the occurrences and incidents in our camp life. We are all striving for a republic, a new and a better state. Let us all show by our actions that we are responsible enough for this state. Offenders' records will later be available in a Volks-museum for everybody to read"[6].

This threat of ultimate exposure to the "nation outside" was effective and helped towards stricter discipline in the camp. How-ever, this did not interfere with the internees' sense of fun, with the practical jokes or with their interminable attempts to laugh at the expense of the camp authorities. And in this form of activity the "Kaalvoet Advokaat", Kowie Marais, was the star. Koffiefontein became very cold during the winter months and the internees shivered in their cold concrete-floored huts. And while they froze, they could see the guards outside the perimeter fence smiling smugly and warming themselves at coal fires outside the sentry posts. The camp authorities refused the internees permission to make similar fires and Marais thought that if the internees had to do without fires, then the guards would have to as well. The next day the camp censor read to his consternation in a number of letters being sent out of the camp: "Prepare yourselves for a

6. Dagbreek en Sondagnuus, January 29, 1967.

surprise. These days the camp guards sit and doze beautifully next to their coal fires ...". This was the end of the fires for the guards.[7]

Vorster can remember that representatives of the International Red Cross visited the German and the Italian camps and that the internees in these camps received food parcels and comforts from the Red Cross. "But they never came to see us and to take a look at the conditions in our camp ...". However, a relatively effective postal service operated between the Germans, the Afrikaners and the Italians. The Italians had managed to construct a radio set which they operated clandestinely for a long time. News bulletins were prepared from radio reports, written down on paper which was tied around a stone of suitable size and then pitched from one camp to another. Small packets of biscuits and packets of cigarettes travelled the same route.

In June 1943 General de Jager was released and Vorster followed him as Camp Leader, a considerable tribute to his obvious leadership qualities because he was then 28, much younger than most of the other internees. Because of his low-key approach to the administration of the camp, the tighter discipline that he slowly but steadily imposed went almost unnoticed. He remembers getting on relatively well with the Camp Commandant. "I got on very well with old man Japie van Rensburg, who was a decent fellow trying to do a difficult job as best he could. But I did not get on at all with his second-in-command who was nothing more nor less than a Boerehater[8]. Nobody could get on with this chap at all".

Vorster did not receive any kind of an allowance for the job, only "a lot of kicks in the pants". Because of the shortage of suitable accommodation he had to do his considerable administrative work while sitting on his bed. As with previous Camp Leaders, one of his major preoccupations was keeping the internees busy and maintaining morale and discipline. "I think we succeeded very well because there was never a single suicide in the Afrikaner camp and, given the circumstances of our internment, there were relatively few really serious conflicts".

As advocates, Vorster and Marais spent much of their time drafting (in sevenfold) appeals for the release of internees. A great deal of effort went into these appeals and, according to Vorster, none

7. Dagbreek en Sondagnuus, January 29, 1967.
8. Literally: Hater of farmers. Used to describe somebody bitterly opposed to and prejudiced against Afrikaners.

was ever successful. "You sent the appeal off and nine months to a year later you got a roneoed document saying that your appeal had been heard and dismissed. Nobody's appeal was ever successful ... I know because I appealed and I was turned down ... I still have both the copy of my appeal and the reply".

Marais has high praise for Vorster's abilities as Camp Leader. "Once he took over, the whole machine started running much more efficiently and smoothly and there was improved discipline because he had the loyalty and the trust and, I can almost say, the friendship of almost all the internees. I think where Vorster really scored was in his dealings with the camp authorities. The rule was that every morning – or, at any rate, almost every morning – after the early parade, they would send in two camp orderlies who would escort the Camp Leader to the Camp Commandant, Colonel van Rensburg. They would discuss any difficulties, the quality of the food, incidents involving guards or internees and that kind of thing. I can remember other Camp Leaders told us very little of these discussions and, in fact, they were supposed to keep quiet because the camp authorities regarded the discussions as confidential. However, Vorster came back every time and told us exactly what had happened, what he had said to the Camp Commandant and what the Camp Commandant had said to him. During this period, I came to realise that Vorster was a negotiator of quite unusual calibre. He knew exactly how far he could go – with both sides – without really creating a confrontation, and on what points he could stand firm and on what points he could negotiate. He was a really excellent negotiator and he won our respect and our trust because he took us into his confidence ... I suppose there were one or two people in the camp who said: 'Vorster is a fool' or something like that, but I would say that 95 per cent of the chaps were solidly behind him".

Not only did Marais come to respect Vorster's negotiating ability but also his strategic and planning abilities. "I really got to know him well when we planned an extensive escape project early in 1943. It was a really involved project and I will not go into the mass of preliminary detail that was meticulously worked out. It was organised that three men would escape one night. These men were cunningly organised into the hospital tent which stood outside the main gate into our camp. We knew that the relief guards did not carry ammunition and that they got their ammunition from the

94

people they relieved. As they walked in the outside gate would not be locked because the guard at the gate would be waiting for the relieved guards to come out. At the one o'clock in the morning change of guards, the three so-called patients rushed out of the hospital and through the outside gate before the gate guard could lock it. The guards were busy exchanging ammunition clips when this happened and our chaps had vaulted the last low gate before the first shots were fired. Everything went strictly according to plan and our chaps got clean away. Just as we planned it, the military establishment called on every possible camp guard to go out and look for them that night, the next day and the following night, leaving the camp guards sadly depleted. This set the stage for the second phase of the operation – the mass breakout. We had planned that we would put the power station out of action by shorting the power lines leading into the camp. We were going to do this by taking the chains which supported the mattresses on our beds, connecting them and by throwing them over the bare overhead wires at a given moment. All this worked according to the plan but the chains were not good enough conductors or that sort of thing and all that happened was that there were a lot of sparks and no power-station failure. So this part of the operation did not succeed ... because of the miscalculations of our technicians, rather than the mistakes of the planners. Vorster was excellent at this kind of operation. He was such a cool sort of a planner. No emotions at all, weighing up one thing against another ... he really is one of the greatest strategists that I have come across".

As Camp Leader, Vorster gave the nod of approval to another escape project: the big tunnel. One of the men involved in this operation was Piet Riekert, then a 25-year-old official in the Department of Customs and Excise. In 1938 Riekert obtained his B A (Economics) degree from the University of South Africa by extra-mural study. In 1938 he was also caught up in the wave of emotion which accompanied the symbolic trek, helped by the heritage of vigorous Afrikaner nationalism on both sides of his family. "Afrikaner nationalism was simply a part of myself, part of my make-up, part of my very being. I never consciously thought about it, I never really challenged my own beliefs until the war came ... nationalism was simply the only thing I knew". A big (2 m) man, Riekert joined the Stormjaer movement and he was arrested on May 14, 1943 for allegedly taking part in a robbery aimed at supplementing OB funds. Despite the fact that his colleagues (all English-speaking and pro-war) were prepared to swear that he could not possibly have been involved because of the time factor, he was placed in solitary confinement for two months during which time he was questioned continuously.

In July, 1943 he was sent to Koffiefontein. Like any newcomer, he was welcomed by the internees and then questioned extensively about what was happening "outside". He met Vorster shortly after his arrival. "When I look back, I think my overall impression was that here was a man who was respected greatly by the internees. I soon found out that the reason for this was his very proper dealings with the camp authorities. On the one hand, he never tolerated nonsense from the internees and, on the other hand, he stood up firmly to the camp authorities whenever this was necessary. He was always strictly correct to both sides and he had the confidence of both sides. He behaved in such a manner that at least two or three of the internees predicted that he would one day reach the cabinet, possibly even becoming Prime Minister. I must say that I did not take this very seriously at the time because we did not ourselves believe in parliamentary democracy ...".

The full story of the Koffiefontein tunnel would make an epic in itself. This is Riekert's version:

"It was decided that we would make the entrance through the floor of the hut which operated as the camp bakery. One night while a concert was being held, we cut through the concrete floor of the bakery, being very careful to keep intact the piece of concrete we took out. The entrance was in one corner. The fellows made a special paste of cement, soap and fat which was placed in the cracks between the tunnel 'door' and the rest of the concrete. This 'dried' within a few minutes and took the same colour as the rest of the floor. With a bit of dust spread over it, it was absolutely impossible to detect. The sand from the tunnel was disposed of in what I think was a very clever way. We got some of the internees of a hut on the other side of the camp to get permission to start a garden. They got picks, shovels and wheelbarrows from the authorities and there was tremendous activity, making vegetable beds, digging furrows and that sort of thing. The authorities simply did not realise that the amount of ground dug out of these interminable furrows was getting bigger and bigger. This was necessary because the ground at Koffiefontein was white chalky soil and the authorities had carted blue Kimberlite[9] into the camp and covered the parade ground with this stuff so that they would immediately notice if anybody was trying to dispose of ground from a tunnel. I suppose they thought that this clever precaution was enough and never thought that we might get past it. At any rate, we made special sand bags from old sugar pockets and the chaps used to fill these in the tunnel and then carry them under their coats to the 'garden' hut where they would hand the bag over for disposal of the soil, at the same time collecting an empty bag. The drawback was that we had to wear coats even in the summer.

"We went straight down for about twelve feet, then we pointed the tunnel towards the perimeter fence and, we hoped, ultimate freedom. Eventually the tunnel was 130 feet long and I tell you it was a great business getting chaps conditioned so that they could work in that damned tunnel. It was so claustrophobic that we would have to take a prospective tunneller into the first portion of the tunnel for a few minutes a day. Then we would increase the time he was there, until we knew that he could take the first part of it. Then we would take him in further and further until he learned to control the feeling of claustrophobia sufficiently to work in the tunnel. Nevertheless, it was terrible. I was perhaps the biggest of the tunnellers and I can remember how bad I felt as I inched my way along the tunnel which was not very much wider than my own body. Every now and again there were way stations burrowed into the walls of the tunnels so that one chap could pass another and it was terrible if, just as you reached the chap in front, he needed to go back and you had to push yourself backwards on your stomach until you could ease into a way station and he could pass you. At first ventilation was easy. As we got deeper, we made a ventilation pipe out of old jam tins connected with rags dipped in fat. Air was fed into the tunnel by a bellows but later this proved insufficient and we made quite a powerful fan out of a hand-operated grindstone. Because of the need for secrecy, we would cover the tunnel and push the ventilating fan out of sight the moment somebody approached. Sometimes the ventilation was 'off' for up to an hour at a time and, heavens alive, we sweated in the tunnel when this happened.

9. Kimberlite is the bluish shale in which diamonds were discovered in great quantities in Kimberley.

"We dug for ten months. I myself suffered from nightmares during the first few months that I was tunnelling and I am certain that, when the time came for escape, not more than a third of the camp internees would have been prepared to buy freedom by crawling through that tunnel. To our great joy, we completed the tunnel undetected. This was a Friday and we had prepared everything for an escape the following Tuesday. Friends from the Transvaal would come by car and fetch us from the vicinity of the camp on that Tuesday night. On the Sunday evening about 300 soldiers marched into the camp, went straight to the bakery and started demolishing the concrete floor. They started from the wrong end and it was only on the Monday afternoon that they came across the entrance. They sent in a Black man with a piece of string to determine how deep the tunnel was and how far it extended. After a few hundred feet of string disappeared, they sent a soldier in with a torch and he found the Black sitting close to the entrance, with a pile of string at his feet. He was simply too terrified to go any further. So the officer who was second-in-command of the camp went in himself. After about two minutes he burst out and they started looking on the surface for signs of the tunnel. Eventually, on Wednesday morning, they found the small pipe we had pushed through the surface at the tunnel entrance for air. Then they took a pick and opened the tunnel up. Naturally we were tremendously disappointed, especially in view of the fact that we had come so close to success. Quite obviously there was a spy in the camp because, how else would they have known to come straight to the bakery?

"The authorities demanded the names of the tunnellers from Vorster, warning that the whole camp would be punished if the names were not given. We were told that we would not get any more hot water, that the camp shop would be closed down and that other privileges would be withdrawn. This was in May and seeing that winter was approaching, this could have been very nasty for us. Vorster quite correctly and with the support of all of the internees – or, should I say, the vast majority of the internees – refused to give the names and the whole camp was punished for about a month. The effects of the punishment were reduced because cigarettes, tobacco and things like toothpaste could be obtained by rock post from the adjacent camps ..."

Riekert admired Vorster's handling of the tunnel affair, but also remembers Vorster's negotiating ability. "He always managed to retain the trust of both sides. For instance, he never went to the authorities with an unreasonable request or complaint. He carefully sifted the wheat from the chaff and all of us knew that we had to have a strong and well-reasoned case before we could ask him to take it up with the authorities. On the other hand, the camp authorities knew that he would never come to them with nonsense – and they knew that when he did come with something, he would stand his ground. As a person, I can remember that he was always friendly and helpful, although at some times he appeared a bit aloof. Always, he had a tremendous sense of humour".

The bakery was next to Vorster's hut and he wished the tunnellers well with their task. But he made it quite clear that he would never go into the tunnel himself, explaining it to me one day: "No matter how sweet freedom might have been, I must tell you that I would rather have received my pension in Koffiefontein than go into that tunnel"[10].

The spy who revealed details of the tunnel to the authorities must have been one of the few who escaped detection by Hendrik van den Bergh who was in charge of the camp's anti-espionage operation. It was his job to try to identify spies who were deliberately planted in the camp by the military authorities. When a spy was identified, it was usually made so obvious to him that he was withdrawn almost immediately.

Van den Bergh himself organised a meticulous and successful escape while Vorster was Camp Leader. Van den Bergh tells the story: "Danie Taljaard was one of my friends and shared a hut with me. While we were there, his mother died and he asked the camp authorities for parole so that he could attend her funeral. But he was refused and he turned to me after parade one afternoon and said: 'Hendrik, now you must help me escape'. Look, he hated that bunch. He hated the Government and the internment authorities because they did not want to let him attend his mother's funeral. We had discussed possible escape plans for many months and I said to him that the only possible escape plan was one of those that we had already worked out, but that he would need a partner. I told him that he should take with him a fellow called Willem

---

10. Piet Riekert eventually got his doctorate in economics and became economic adviser to the late Dr H F Verwoerd when he was Prime Minister. He continued in the position after Vorster took over.

Willers, who had been a detective before his internment. We got Willers appointed as deputy manager of the camp shop and Taljaard as his assistant. Every Friday the additional meat which we had ordered for the camp – and paid for ourselves out of the camp shop's profits – was delivered by a soldier by the name of Jacobs, who brought it in a light delivery vehicle. I had observed the movements of this vehicle for a long time and knew exactly how it operated. Jacobs and I were already on speaking terms. Taljaard looked very much like this man Jacobs and we decided that when next the meat was delivered, we would overpower this Jacobs and that Taljaard would put on his uniform. We would cut out the bottoms of some of the boxes in which the meat had been delivered and Willers would hide under these boxes. It all worked very well, but remember that it took us six months to plan and finally execute it. For instance, I arranged with one of the guards to smuggle money into the camp for us, some £55 or so, for Willers and Taljaard to use after they had escaped. Everything went according to plan and the two men got clean away, with Taljaard posing as a soldier . . .".

The camp authorities' respect for Vorster is illustrated by a story told by Kowie Marais. "On one Sunday afternoon there was a stone-throwing episode. We were all resting on our beds when we heard the machine-guns going. We all rushed outside and found that the Italians in the neighbouring camps – now divided into fascists and so-called communists – were throwing stones at each other and the guards were firing the machine-guns over their heads in an attempt to calm them down. Despite the machine-guns, all of us rushed to the fence which separated our camp from the two Italian camps. Many of us climbed on to the fence, which we were not allowed to do, and shouted support for the fascists. The leader of their stone-throwing faction was the well-known motor racing driver Dr Mario Mazzacurati who came from the north of Italy and who had a band of his northern Italians with him. Things started to look ugly because, in the camp atmosphere, anything like that stone-throwing affair could have developed into something really nasty. Then Botterbul (Colonel van Rensburg) came along, walking in the passage between our camp and the Italians. Things were not looking too bright and he asked us: 'Please gentlemen, go back to your bungalows'. Of course, we did not even hear him and, even if we had, which of us would have listened to what old Van Rensburg was saying? Then I heard him say: 'Will somebody please call General Vorster'. Now this was something unusual, for the Camp Commandant to recognise an OB officer's rank – and in front of so many people. So somebody called General Vorster and Botterbul said to him: 'General Vorster, look, this is a quarrel between other people. Can't you ask your people to go back to their bungalows?'. Vorster replied: 'All right'. Then he turned to us and said simply: 'Comrades, please disperse and go back to your bungalows because this has nothing to do with us'. They obeyed him without question and almost instantly. But the real significance of this incident to me is the fact that Botterbul used Vorster's OB title, thus signifying the respect he had for him".

Apart from his other qualities, Vorster was recognised as the star speaker in the camp. He was in great demand whenever the internees celebrated one of the Afrikaner festival days, especially the Day of the Covenant on December 16 which was particularly relevant to those Afrikaners who believed that they were being interned because of their commitment to their long-desired republic. One of the internees, a Dutch Reformed dominee, Ds. E G Norval, spoke in 1966 about one of these speeches. "On October 10 we asked Vorster to speak at the camp festival in honour of Kruger Day[11]. The enthusiasm, fire and conviction with which he entranced the camp audience that evening is unforgettable for me ... I will never forget his enthusiasm ... and right then I was convinced that he would one day lead our nation ... I remember that about 40 internees constituted a guard of honour for Vorster that evening. For the purpose, 40 neat bush jackets were made out of camp sheets. The buttons were carefully and artistically carved out of wood ..."[12].

Another man who was deeply impressed by Vorster the speaker was Professor Stoker who can remember arriving late on one of the occasions when Vorster was speaking. "Because I was late, I joined a few of the internees who were listening at a window. I was so impressed with John Vorster's speech that night that I turned to one of the other chaps and said to him that I was certain that this man would one day serve in the cabinet ... all the qualities for leadership were there". Of Vorster the man, Professor Stoker com-

11. October 10, Kruger's birthday, still celebrated as a public holiday in South Africa.
12. Dagbreek en Sondagnuus, September 18, 1966.

ments: "He was already in the camp when I arrived and he made a definite impression on me when I first met him. As I got to know him, it seemed that he was a man who thought very clearly indeed, a man with a determined will who could not only discipline others but who could also discipline himself. He was a sober-minded person, with fixed principles, strong ideals but always reasonable and friendly. He also impressed me as a man with very deep Christian commitments".

Johann van Zyl Alberts, the man who ran the camp shop at Koffiefontein for a while[13], recalls the Day of the Covenant celebration on December 16, 1943. "The authorities had told us that we would not be allowed to hold the meeting which had been planned and at which John Vorster would be the main speaker. But we went ahead and gathered at the appointed time next to the dam in which we swam. Soon there was a concentration of soldiers on the other side of the wire, opposite the point where we were gathered. I can remember that there were armoured cars and machineguns and that the camp second-in-command told us that the meeting had been prohibited. I cannot remember whether he said that they would shoot if we went ahead. At any rate, Vorster just simply stepped on to the little platform, told us: 'Comrades, we stay here', and went ahead with his speech – and I can remember that speech as one of the best I have ever heard him make. I am certain that there would have been real trouble had not the Camp Commandant, Colonel van Rensburg, arrived and cooled his chaps down. This van Rensburg was a very good chap and he did his best to do his job as reasonably as possible. However, that incident showed us just how cool and brave John Vorster was. It also showed us how good he was at assessing just how far he could go in a given situation ... I cannot remember what the repercussions of the incident were, but I almost think that we were put on short rations for a time. But it was really worth it over and over again ...".

All good or bad things come to an end and so did Vorster's internment. It seemed to the internees that there was no pattern to the way in which the authorities released the people in Koffiefontein, so every release tended to come as a surprise to the people

13. Van Zyl Alberts is now the publisher of the weekly news magazine, To the Point, in South Africa.

concerned – this despite the fact that the internees knew whether people were going to be released or not or whether extra people were due for internment. This was established when the rations were collected for the next day's cooking. If the number of people in the camp was 450 and rations were given for 445 only, the story soon spread that five of the comrades would be released the next day and, in most of the huts, internees teased each other, saying that the rest of the camp would "see my heels tomorrow". All would watch anxiously the next day for the corporal who came to seek out the men due for release. He would come into the camp pushing a little trolley for the released internee's belongings. After seeking out the lucky man, he would give him a few minutes to pack and then escort him out of the camp proper. In most cases, the internees were only too happy to get out as soon as possible.

Vorster was too pre-occupied with his manifold duties as Camp Leader and paid very little attention to the stories of the number of people who would be released on a given day. So it was with some surprise that he looked up from his bed on February 11, 1944, and saw the corporal at the door of his hut, asking for detainee 2229/42. "He told me that I should pack up my things and be ready to leave within half an hour. It was some time in the morning and I said: 'No fear, you've had me here for more than a year and I have got business to finish. I have got to hand over to the other guys and you can come and fetch me at three o'clock in the afternoon'. I was in a hurry to get out, but I had to hand over the affairs entrusted to me in a proper way".

And so Vorster handed over, packed his meagre belongings and walked through the gates of Koffiefontein to the Smuts Government's version of house arrest.

7 *Back into Politics*

While Vorster had been in the camp a number of people outside worked feverishly for the release of internees. One of these was Senator Ignatius "Naas" Raubenheimer, a veteran Nationalist politician who would petition the then Minister of Justice, Dr Colin Steyn, and who would find people who were prepared to take responsibility for paroled detainees. He arranged Vorster's release and found that the authorities would accept Vorster's parole to the Town Clerk of Robertson, Mr Gert Van Rooyen, an old friend of Vorster's. And Naas Raubenheimer was at the Koffiefontein camp gate to take Vorster to Bloemfontein where he would catch a train to Robertson.

Vorster remembers: "I never knew a thing about the arrange-ments. When I was taken to the camp office, they told me that a 'fellow by the name of Van Rooyen in Robertson has accepted responsibility for you, here's a rail warrant for Robertson and now shove off'. Naas Raubenheimer took me to Bloemfontein where I was supposed to catch a train for Robertson immediately. The booking clerk in Bloemfontein was one of our chaps and it was arranged that I could not get a seat on the train to Robertson for two days. So we telephoned my wife who came to Bloemfontein immediately and we stayed together in Bloemfontein illegally for two days before I went to Robertson".

The reunion was one of the highlights of the Vorster's early years. They had been married only for nine months when he was detained in Port Elizabeth and she had only once been able to fight her way through the security bureaucracy in order to visit him at Koffiefontein. While they were together in Bloemfontein, they did not know when they would next see each other. They could talk about the future and try to make plans, but they did not know for how long he would have to stay in Robertson.

Vorster left for Robertson without a penny in his pockets. "When I left the camp I had no money at all. I never asked my wife for any money because I knew that she was almost as poor as I was and I did not want to take anything of the little that she had. Because I did not have any money I spun the yarn to the other guys in my compartment that I never ate or drank on trains. I remember when the other chaps ordered early morning coffee, I was as thirsty as I could possibly be, but I never let on and persisted with the story that I never ate or drank anything while on a train".

In Robertson he was confined to Van Rooyen's house under the Smuts Government's version of house arrest. "You had to get a permit for everything. You had to get a permit if you wanted to go to the bioscope. You had to get a permit if you wanted to go shopping. You had to get a permit if you wanted to go to Cape Town and then you had to get your permit stamped by the control authorities at the Clarendon School and you had to get it stamped again when you returned to Robertson. You even had to get a permit to go to the local swimming bath ... and I still have this particular permit today".

Fortunately there were also permits for jobs and Vorster successfully petitioned the local control officer for a permit to work for a firm of attorneys in Robertson.

While in Koffiefontein, Vorster had promised his comrades that he would try to see the Minister of Justice as soon as he was released to discuss camp conditions with him. He told the story of his visit in the House of Assembly on May 16, 1960: " .... while I was in the camp I wrote several letters to the then Minister of Justice ... I begged him to come to the camp to investigate conditions for himself. When I was released, I promised my comrades there that I would go to see the Minister in Cape Town to discuss conditions with him. I came. With the kind assistance of the then Senator Raubenheimer, I requested an interview with Dr. Colin Steyn to discuss the affairs of the Afrikaner with a fellow Afrikaner. He refused to grant me an interview, despite the fact that I was in the lobby of the House of Assembly with Senator Raubenheimer, near his office. Do you know what his answer was? If I was not out of Cape Town by 6 pm, he would have me arrested again. And only because I came to the Minister of Justice to have a discussion with him about the affairs of Afrikaners ..."

In that same speech he referred to the Government's appeal board to which internees could appeal for their release: "If you were lucky, you received the reasons for your internment three months after you had been interned. Let me now read out one of my reasons as I still remember: 'The authorities are in posession of information that you harboured interned fugitives'. Then you ask who those fugitives were and when you harboured them and where and they tell you that this is not relevant. That is the only charge you received. Then you appealed to the tribunal – an old and decrepit advocate appointed for the purpose – and then you waited exactly 12 months after you appealed ... and then you received a little note to say that your appeal had been considered and dismissed. And that little note was printed for it was sent to all of us ...".[1].

After three months in Robertson, Vorster heard that a firm of attorneys in Brakpan was looking for somebody. "I got a permit to go to Cape Town to see the Chief Control Officer, Sir Theodore Truter. I put my case to him and asked him whether I could be transferred to Brakpan so that I could start work seriously and set up my home again. He refused and I went back to Robertson, packed my bags and went off to Brakpan where I was given the job and where I started practising again. Because we still had so many things to sort out, my wife remained in Pretoria for a while ... I had been practising in Brakpan for about three months when they arrested me again one day as I was coming out of court. I was not surprised because I knew every policeman there by the time and although officially nobody knew that I was John Vorster the ex-detainee and the OB Chief General, unofficially everybody knew. I was taken to the Benoni Magistrate, an old Hollander by the name of Carstens. He knew me well because I had appeared in front of him on a number of occasions. He said he was very surprised to see me, although he had my file in front of him. I can remember the interview very well. He said to me: 'I suppose you're just one of these young men who have been misled'. So I said to him: 'On the contrary, sir, I don't want to mislead you. If you read through my file you will see that I am accused of misleading other young men'. After a while he said to me: 'Ag, you go home now and I will see you right'. So I went home and a couple of weeks or months later, I cannot remember exactly, I got a telegram from Alf Trollip, who was then Member of Parliament for Brakpan and whom I had come to know well as a fellow attorney, telling me that all restrictions on me had been lifted. For the first time since

1. Hansard, 16/5/1960.

September 1942, I was free to do as I chose again ..."

But although life was free, it was not necessarily easy. "You mustn't forget I had nothing. I had lost everything. I had nothing at all when I restarted in Brakpan. Heavens alive, we were as poor as church mice and I had to borrow money from Volkskas in order to reclaim our furniture which had been in storage ever since my wife left the house in Port Elizabeth. But, once my wife had joined me, we set up house again in Brakpan and started living normal lives. I must say that we have never regretted the decision to live in Brakpan and our 14 years there were amongst the happiest of our lives ..."

Now pre-occupied with establishing himself once again, Vorster had little time for politics. In any case, it was now 1944 and it was clear that Germany would lose the war and that the OB was a spent force although its top men were still very active. But its main purpose now was helping the families of internees and helping ex-internees rehabilitate themselves. While Vorster did not take part in politics as such, he did a great deal to help OB colleagues and their families.

But the break from politics would not last for long. Hans van Rensburg realised after the war that the OB was finished and that the members of the organisation would have once again to get into the mainstream of Afrikaner politics. But feelings within the National Party were still so bruised that a reconciliation was impossible. So he urged OB members to join the Afrikaner Party, then led by Klasie Havenga[2], knowing that the Afrikaner Party and the National Party would have to come together at some time in the future. Vorster recalls: "I was very perturbed about the rift between the OB and what was now the Herenigde Nasionale Party[3]. I spoke to Hans van Rensburg about this in the OB's offices

2. Havenga served as MP for Fauresmith from 1915 to 1940, first as a member of the National Party but, after fusion in 1934, as a member of the United National South African Party. He returned to Parliament as leader of the Afrikaner Party in 1948 and MP for the constituency of Ladybrand. In 1953 the Afrikaner Party merged with the National Party. From 1948 until he followed Dr D F Malan into retirement, Havenga served as Malan's Minister of Finance.
3. When he refused to follow Hertzog into fusion with the South African Party in 1934, Malan formed the so-called "Purified" National Party – that is, "purified" of un-Afrikaner elements. When Hertzog and his followers broke with Smuts (who then became Prime Minister) over the war issue in 1939 and returned to the fold of the National Party, it became the Herenigde Nasionale Party. Literally: the Re-united National Party.

in the Sanlam building in Pretoria. Hans Van Rensburg felt as I did and he felt that there was only one way to deal with this rift and that was for the OB members to join the Afrikaner Party and for Havenga to come to an agreement with Dr Malan, the leader of the National Party. We realised that it was impossible for the OB to come to any agreement with Malan in view of everything that had happened in the past. The only way to get unity again would be for the OB to submerge itself totally within the Afrikaner Party. I know that many chaps will tell that this man and that man were indispensable for Malan and Havenga getting together. I do not want to say for a moment that other people did not play a part. There are many people in those years who tried to get people together. But this much I know: The man mainly responsible for them getting together in the end was Hans van Rensburg and I want to spell his name in capital letters. He went to see Mr Havenga and he put the position to Havenga very clearly. Havenga accepted the position."

Vorster's discussions with Van Rensburg over the future political role of the OB members took place in 1946 and both he and his wife subsequently joined the Afrikaner Party. With a handful of other people, they organised the Afrikaner Party's congress in 1947. The congress was a great success and Vorster was considerably impressed by Havenga's sincerity. "He was a sincere and likable man but he was not really a leader. I would say he was like a vine. He wasn't a tree, he was a vine. At first he grew on Hertzog and later on Malan".

Because of the success of the 1947 congress, the Vorsters were asked to head the organisation for the congress arrangements in 1948 – again in Brakpan. By now Vorster was a member of the Afrikaner Party executive, the youngest of the members as he was the youngest of the OB's Generals – this despite the fact that his own political ideals were closer to those of Malan than they were to those of Havenga. Not that there was very much which separated the two men, with the exception of their attitudes to the OB.

Between the two congresses there was the 1948 General Election and Vorster was determined to go to Parliament, even though prospects for the Afrikaner and the National Parties looked bleak. After all, when Parliament was dissolved before the election, Smuts' United Party had 89 seats and the Herenigde

Nasionale Party had only 49 seats. The Labour Party had six seats, the Dominion Party had three, there were three Natives' Representatives, two independents and one member of the Central Group. The Afrikaner and National Parties entered into an election agreement which involved, *inter alia,* that the National Party would concede certain seats to the Afrikaner Party which would have the right to nominate its own candidates.

Vorster takes up the story: "I was nominated as the Afrikaner Party candidate in Brakpan but Malan refused to accept this because I was an OB officer. Havenga called me in to Johannesburg to see him and he explained the position to me. The meeting took place in the offices of Die Vaderland[4] which was then the Afrikaner Party's newspaper. Havenga was very annoyed at Malan's attitude but I said to him: 'Don't worry about it. Forget about it. I will stand as an independent in Brakpan and it will not be necessary for you to quarrel with Dr Malan or anybody else about this, I can look after myself, I have always looked after myself and I am quite capable of fighting the election as an independent'. A really funny thing happened in Brakpan because after I was nominated as a candidate by the Afrikaner Party, the Herenigde Nasionale Party in Brakpan also nominated me as their candidate. So the HNP Executive sent Jan de Klerk[5] to Brakpan to undo this decision by the Brakpan Divisional Committee, but what Jan de Klerk did not know was that I had also been invited to this meeting. He was greatly surprised when he saw me there and he told me that he did not think it fair that I should be at the meeting. So I told him in reply: 'I'm not pushing myself in. I was invited to attend the meeting and if the meeting tells me to leave, then I will go immediately'. The meeting unanimously confirmed their invitation to me to attend and so I stayed. Jan de Klerk then explained the Party's position. He said that the Party now wanted to nominate a candidate in Brakpan and that he had been sent to

4. Die Vaderland, published in Johannesburg by Afrikaanse Pers.
5. Jan de Klerk was then an organiser for the Party. He became a Senator (representing the Transvaal) in 1955, a few months after being appointed Minister of Labour and of Public Works, by Prime Minister J G Strijdom. Verwoerd retained him in the cabinet as Minister of Mines (58 to 61) and of Interior (61-66), of Education Arts and Science (61 to 66) and Information (66). Under Vorster, he served in the Education Arts and Science and Information portfolios until 1968. He then became Minister of National Education, in which capacity he remained until he became President of the Senate in 1969. He retired in 1976.

the town in order to invite nominations from the Divisional Committee. So the Committee said it was perfectly prepared to nominate a candidate and, while Jan de Klerk sat back, they promptly nominated me again – unanimously. Well there were certain recriminations after that and I stood down for two weeks while I invited the HNP to nominate a candidate. I promised them that I would withdraw and support their candidate because I knew that Brakpan was a difficult seat. But they obviously decided to leave Brakpan to its fate. When no nomination was forthcoming from the HNP after two weeks, I said: 'OK, then I carry on'. And it was in those two weeks that I lost that election because it meant two weeks in which I did nothing, two weeks in which my election organisation did nothing . . . and two weeks is a long time when you are fighting for the Afrikaner cause in a United Party stronghold – especially when you are fighting on a shoestring".

So Vorster fought his first election. His opponent was Alf Trollip[6] who had his office in the same passage as Vorster's and who seemed set to retain Brakpan for the UP by about 2 000 votes. In effect, the election was fought from the sitting room of the Vorster's Brakpan home. The election organisation was a small one. Money was always tight and a great deal of the canvassing was done by Mrs Vorster. The small team worked hard, long hours and they tried to make up for lack of resources with enthusiasm and sheer hard work. But they never thought that their independent candidate would ever come near victory. All they wanted was to give Alf Trollip a good run for his money.

When the results were announced, Alf Trollip had won by only two votes. Vorster appealed but the only effect of his court action was another two votes for Alf Trollip.

Vorster remembers the election: "I was tremendously pleased that we had done so well because we had no idea that we would come within reach of victory. Naturally I was disappointed, but I had enjoyed every minute of the election campaign. There was no time for recriminations. I know that if I had not stood down for

6. Trollip represented Brakpan in the House of Assembly from 1938 to 1953 and Bezuidenhout from 1953 to 1958. Verwoerd brought him back into Parliament as a nominated Senator in December, 1961. Trollip served as Minister of Labour and Immigration from 1961 to 1966 and as Minister of Indian Affairs (1966) in Verwoerd's cabinet. Vorster retained him as Minister of Immigration and of Indian Affairs from 1966 until 1968 when Trollip retired from the cabinet. Two years later he retired from politics and left the Senate.

two weeks, we would have won. I know that if the HNP had not been so antagonistic, I would have won. I know that had Dr Verwoerd, who was then the editor of the Transvaler, not written a leader just before the election telling Nationalists not to vote for me, I would have won. Incidentally, Dr Verwoerd later spoke to me and told me he was sorry for that leader. At any rate hundreds of people came up to me after the election and sympathised with me because I had only lost because of what they believed was the stupidity of the National Party. But, while I might have agreed with them, my main feeling was one of elation at having come so close. I can remember that some time after that 1948 election old man Harm Oost said to me: 'John, you will find later in public life that you are going to gain far more, politically-speaking, from the fact that you lost by two votes rather than winning by two votes'. And, you know, he was perfectly right. Everybody felt sorry for you. You got letters from people you never knew. You can imagine, people felt sorry for the chap who lost by two votes – especially under those circumstances. I became known through-out the country as the man who lost the election by two votes. But nobody would have remembered me as the guy who was fortunate enough to have won by two votes. Such is life."

In between political involvement in the Afrikaner Party, the Vorsters settled down in Brakpan. Elizabeth was born in 1945, Willem in January, 1950, and Pieter in December 1951. The Vorsters liked Brakpan and found themselves fitting into the Afrikaner community without any problems. While Vorster built up his practice as an attorney, Mrs Vorster became involved in things like school committees and other organisations. For years she served on the Rent Board in Brakpan and thoroughly enjoyed the work. She remembers: "I always say that we can go back to Brakpan any time. We enjoyed it very much there ... we were part and parcel of everything that went on in the town".

In 1951 the Afrikaner and the National Parties merged and, by way of this back door, Vorster became a Nationalist again as did so many of his OB comrades. Finally, after almost a generation of strife, "Afrikaner unity" had been achieved and, having lived up to its name of the Herenigde Nasionale Party, the HNP then became simply the "National Party".

Meanwhile, Vorster was doing well as a lawyer. His courtroom abilities were being recognised and he appeared in cases in

111

different parts of the Witwatersrand. But he was also becoming increasingly involved in the affairs of the National Party in Brakpan and felt that there was a strong chance that when the 1953 General Election came that he would be able to gain the Party's nomination. However, this was not to be. "I was offered the National Party nomination in Nigel, which borders on Brakpan. But I refused because I said to them that I had lost my honour in Brakpan in 1948 and that I was going to regain it in Brakpan. Then I was called to Jan de Klerk's office in Johannesburg. The last time I had really spoken to him was when he was trying to prevent Brakpan from nominating me. Now he urged me to accept the Nigel nomination, saying that Mr J G Strijdom, leader of the National Party in the Transvaal, wanted me in Parliament and Nigel was a better proposition than Brakpan. I had not yet met Strijdom, but from what I subsequently heard, it was partly due to my fame as the chap who had lost Brakpan by two votes that I came to his attention. I won by 700 votes or so and my law partner, P W du Plessis, won Brakpan by 47 votes. We were both tremendously pleased."

The next day, a telegram arrived for John Vorster. It said simply: "Heartiest congratulations comrade. Remember my words in the camp. Now you are there, let my prophecy come true. Your good fortune and happiness is my joy". It was signed: Oom Tiny Rautenbach and it took Vorster right back to his days in Koffiefontein, to a day in December 1943 when a number of internees were sitting together, talking about the future. Amongst them were Vorster and Tiny Rautenbach. They spoke of what would happen after the war was over and when they were released. Rautenbach said that he did not know what would happen to him, but that he was certain of Vorster. "One day, John, you are going to become Prime Minister of a Republic of South Africa". Vorster still has the telegram. The only thing that grieves him is that Tiny Rautenbach died before he could see his prophecy come true.

Parliament was not a strange place for Vorster. He had been there on many occasions as a politically active Stellenbosch University student and on one occasion Dr Malan had called him to his parliamentary office to discuss Stellenbosch University affairs with the young chairman of the Stellenbosch University Branch of the Junior National Party. How did he feel when he walked in there for the first time as an MP in 1953? "You know that

14. *October, 1958. The Vorsters photographed a few hours after his appointment as a Deputy Minister.*

15. Port Elizabeth, December, 1961. The Vorster family photographed on the Windsor Castle, en route from Durban to Cape Town for the 1962 parliamentary session.

16. 1961, Minister of Justice.

17. *A Cape Times poster displayed on September 12, 1966 and accurately pointing to South Africa's next Prime Minister.*

Photo : Louw Pretorius.

it has happened but you still feel that it is all a dream. After all, in your own mind you thought that only gods came to Parliament and you did not look on yourself as a god. You had the feeling that you, as a mere mortal, were standing on the heights of Olympus. However, I must confess that the feeling did not last for many weeks because you soon established that the gods had feet of clay ... and it gradually dawned on you that you must not be afraid of these chaps because they are more afraid of you".

Although Vorster dismisses his maiden speech as "ordinary, worse than average" there are still Members of Parliament who can remember it and many of them said to themselves that young Vorster was a man to be watched.

Vorster himself decided to play his role as a new MP in a low key. "I said to myself: 'Look John, you're a backbencher and you behave yourself as a fresher at university should behave'. After all, I had given this advice so often to freshers at university and later on I gave it to many a newcomer to Parliament. I believe to this day that you must never push yourself because you run the risk of pushing yourself right out of things. It is your contemporaries who must pull you up, it is not for you to push yourself up. A pusher has never arrived anywhere in Parliament because Parliament is a great leveller. You cannot make yourself arrive in Parliament. It is your colleagues who decide when you have arrived. When your colleagues show that you are a man to take note of, then you have arrived. So I behaved like the fresher that I was and I think those first five years were the most enjoyable years that I have had in Parliament. There was no responsibility whatsoever ...".

But his colleagues fast recognised Vorster's qualities and he probably addressed more meetings in constituencies other than his own than any other backbencher in Parliament. During his period in "the kitchen", as MP's fondly think of the backbenches, he addressed meetings throughout South Africa, including those constituencies held by Ministers Dönges and Erasmus. This was a sure sign that his colleagues were busy "pulling him up". He was in considerable demand during the 1958 General Election campaign and played a role beyond that of the average backbencher. During the first session of the Eleventh Parliament, Prime Minister J G Strijdom died and Verwoerd, then serving as Minister of Native Affairs, took his place. When Parliament went into recess on October 10, 1958, there was considerable discussion amongst the

Nationalist MPs because they somehow sensed that things would never be quite the same again. Strijdom had been the last of the fiery Afrikaner Nationalists to whom the quest for an Afrikaner republic had been life itself. Verwoerd thought beyond this – although he was the man who eventually ushered the Republic in – and was already clearly on the road towards the ultimate partition of South Africa. Like his other colleagues, Vorster had tremendous admiration for Verwoerd's capabilities and his intellectual capacities. But he did not think that Verwoerd had noticed him at all.

Shortly after Parliament went into recess, Vorster visited Pretoria to fetch his daughter who was then a boarder at Afrikaanse Meisies Hoërskool. "I was a bit early and so I went to Omie van den Heever's[7] office in the central part of the city. I often visited Omie when I was in Pretoria because old Omie always seemed to be up on the latest political gossip. And I was interested at this stage because Verwoerd had just taken over and a cabinet reshuffle was in the air. Apart from this, one of Dr Verwoerd's first bits of legislation following his election as Prime Minister created the new posts of Deputy Minister. So there was going to be quite a shuffle at the top. I was interested, not because I thought there was even the most remote chance that I would be selected myself, but because I was interested in the careers of my colleagues. While I was talking to Omie, Dirk Uys[8] came in. We talked for a while and, as Omie did not seem to have anything worthwhile to tell us, I took my leave and so did Dirk. When we got to my car, he said to me: 'Heavens alive, you're a godsend to me. I must go to the Union Buildings[9] because Verwoerd has called me there in order to make me Minister of Agriculture'. I said: 'Congratulations' and he replied: 'Hasn't Verwoerd spoken to you yet?'. I replied that he had not and Dirk said to me: 'Well, I tell you that he is going to

7. Daniel Johannes Gertruide van den Heever, then MP for Pretoria Central, later to become Deputy Speaker and Chairman of Committees in the House of Assembly.
8. Dirk Cornelius Johannes Uys, MP for Bredasdorp from 1948 to 1953, for Caledon-Bredasdorp from 1953 to 1958 and for False Bay from 1958 to 1970 when he became a nominated Senator. He served Verwoerd as Minister of Agricultural Economics and Marketing from 1958 to 1966, as Minister of Lands from 1964 to 1966 and as Minister Agricultural Credit and Land Tenure in 1966. He remained in the Vorster cabinet as Minister in charge of the various agricultural portfolios until his retirement in 1972.
9. The magnificent buildings, designed by Sir Herbert Baker which have served as South Africa's main government building since 1913.

make you a Deputy Minister' I told him nonsense and he said that he was prepared to take a bet on it. I thought he was joking and I dropped him at the Union Buildings, collected my daughter and went home to Brakpan. This was a Friday. Saturday passed and I did not give Dirk's talk a second thought because I really thought he was pulling my leg. On Sunday night we went to bed early and I was deep into a very interesting book when Hannes Visagie, who later became Member of the Provincial Council in Nigel, phoned me to ask whether I knew anything about the cabinet reshuffle. He spoke to me for a long time and I had just started on my book when the telephone rang again. I think I picked up the phone and said rather brusquely 'Yes?' There was a lady on the other end who said: 'Good evening Mr Vorster, this is Mrs Verwoerd here'. I recognised her voice immediately and I realised that it was not anybody pulling my leg. I got the fright of my life and she said: 'Mr Vorster, my husband would like to speak to you. Would it be convenient for you to see him at his office tomorrow at 12,30'. I said yes and then I told my wife about the call ..."

The Vorsters were quite capable of putting two and two together. It now seemed certain that Dirk Uys had not been joking and Vorster was about to take a major step towards political power. On the Monday they travelled to Pretoria full of excitement and just a touch of apprehension. "When I got into Dr Verwoerd's office, he told me that he wanted to make me Deputy Minister of Education Arts and Science and of Social Welfare and Pensions. I said to him: 'Doctor, I hope you know what you are doing because I know nothing about education, arts or science. However, my wife is a social worker. I think you are making a mistake'. He replied a little sharply: 'It is not for you to judge. I am the one who must judge ... the swearing-in ceremony is on Wednesday, just see to it that you are there.' Then my wife and I went off to a tearoom for something to eat and we went home to Brakpan. I never saw myself as a Deputy Minister of Education Arts and Science and of Social Welfare and Pensions, but I was pleased because it was obvious that Dr Verwoerd trusted me and that he had confidence in my abilities ..."

Verwoerd appointed only four of the six Deputy Ministers the change in the constitution had provided for. Marais Viljoen was given the responsibilities of Mines and Labour, P W Botha became Deputy Minister of the Interior and F E Mentz became Deputy

Minister of Bantu Administration and Development[10]. Vorster, the young MP for Nigel, received the least interesting and politically glamorous of the deputy ministerships. However, his Minister, J J Serfontein, was neither dynamic nor really effective, partly because his wife was extremely ill for much of the time Vorster was his deputy. This meant that Vorster was thrown in the deep end of executive politics and, for much of his time as a Deputy Minister, he took the decisions which were normally the Minister's perogative. And he piloted all the two departments' legislation through Parliament something that would give him extremely valuable experience for his time as Minister of Justice.

There was not a great deal of reaction to Vorster's promotion. However, he received a letter of congratulations from the Nigel Town Council and Die Burger's astute political columnist, Dawie[11], recorded in a single paragraph on October 23, 1958: "John Vorster's promotion has gladdened me most. During and after the war he went through deep waters and, at one time, it must have seemed to him that everything had broken down ... but he persevered and, as a sober idealist, he started building a new future. The world is now open for him".

At least one English-language newspaper took notice of the new Deputy Minister when he referred to the approaching Provincial Council by-elections as "trials" for the coming of the Republic. The Cape Times commented in a leading article on November 20, 1958: "One, Mr B J Vorster, a spokesman for Transvaal reaction, has informed the country that the provincial elections will be a 'trial' for the republic ... we suppose we must regard ourselves as lucky that occasionally some minor politician takes time off to give us notice of what has been decided for us ..."

10. Marais Viljoen became Minister of Labour and of Coloured Affairs in 1966. He served Vorster as Minister of Labour (66 to 72), of Coloured Affairs (66 to 69), Coloured Relations and Rehoboth Affairs (69 to 70), Interior (1970) and Posts and Telegraphs (70 to 72). After three years as a Deputy Minister, Botha became Minister of Housing in 1961. He held this portfolio until 1964. However, he also served as Minister of Community Development and of Coloured Affairs from 1961 to 1966. He served as Minister of Public Works between 1964 and 1966 and became Minister of Defence in 1966. Vorster retained him in the Defence portfolio in which Botha still serves. Mentz resigned in 1960 and moved into political oblivion, although he later became slightly involved with the ultra-right-wing Herstigte Nasionale Party.

11. The pseudonym under which the Editor of Die Burger (Literally: The Citizen) wrote a weekly political column.

In Cape Town for his first session as a Deputy Minister in 1959, the "minor politician" from Nigel had the task of guiding the highly controversial Extension of University Education Amendment Bill through Parliament. The measure provided for the creation of separate university colleges (later to become autonomous universities) for the different South African race groups, with the barring of most Coloured, Indian and Black students from South Africa's so-called "open" universities – the Universities of Cape Town, the Witwatersrand and Natal[12]. The Opposition fought the measure vigorously, claiming serious interference in university autonomy and the application of a racist ideology to the universities. When the Opposition gave notice that it would oppose the first reading of the measure[13], it also gave Vorster notice that his baptism would be one of fire.

With his Minister ill, Vorster started the parliamentary ball rolling. His performance was such that Nationalist newspapermen applauded and even Opposition commentators showed reluctant admiration. Serfontein later entered the debate himself, but there was a sharp contrast between his performance and Vorster's. The Cape Times Gallery Correspondent, Adderley, commented on May 1: " . . . Mr Serfontein had quite obviously realised that his reply to the third reading debate on the University Apartheid Bill was probably the worst performance put up by any Minister in the whole 11 years of Nationalist rule. What made it worse was that his deputy, Mr John Vorster, had not two hours before nearly turned the whole occasion into a debating victory for the Government". Die Stem[14], an Afrikaans language newspaper which claimed it was politically independent, wrote of the debate on May 3: "Two National Party ministers (sic), J J Serfontein, Minister of Educa-

12. These universities were able to admit Black and Brown students, but this right was almost eliminated by the Nationalist Government with the passing of the Extension of University Education Act in 1959 which made provision for separate university colleges for Black, Coloured and Asian students.
13. In terms of South African parliamentary procedure, bills are read three times in both the House of Assembly and the Senate. The first reading is almost always a formality, in effect, permission to debate the bill. The second reading debate determines the principle or the principles of the bill. This is followed by a committee stage in which the detail of the bill is examined and debated. Then comes the third reading, which deals with any changes that might have been made during the committee stage and with the bill in its entirety. To oppose the first reading has come to mean, in South Africa, most vigorous disapproval of any message.
14. Published in Johannesburg by the Argus Printing and Publishing Company.

tion Arts and Science, and B J Vorster, Deputy Minister, gave an opposing example of how personality can swing a debate from one side to another ... while Mr Vorster's deft, sharp arguments all but annihilated the Opposition's arguments, Mr Serfontein allowed himself to be led around the bush, to be enticed into ambushes and to be almost torn to shreds by an Opposition that fought like terriers".

With this performance, Vorster gave the political establishment the clearest possible notice that he was cut out for bigger things. For the rest, Vorster did those seemingly dull things which fall to the lot of the Deputy Minister of Education Arts and Science and of Social Welfare and Pensions. He attended Day of the Covenant celebrations. He laid foundation stones by the score. He unveiled plaques. He smiled as Nigel named its new industrial estate 'Vorsterskroon'[15]. He made party speeches, he attended first nights and he was present at countless civic functions. In a sense, Mrs Vorster, with her deep interest in social welfare, was in her element as they visited children's homes, institutions for the aged and became involved in other aspects of social welfare. And she started keeping cuttings of newspaper reports which referred to her husband – not realising that this would one day become a major undertaking[16]. Vorster had a meeting almost every night and, Mrs Vorster went to all of them. His youngest sister, Mona, moved in with them and helped look after the children. Both saw the new job as a challenge and, in Mrs Vorster's words, it kept them "very, very busy".

On February 3, 1960, Vorster crowded into the Parliamentary dining room with the rest of South Africa's parliamentarians to hear the British Prime Minister, Mr Harold Macmillan, make his famous "winds of change" speech – a speech which echoed through Africa and the world and which, in a sense, marked the watershed in South Africa's international relations in that it heralded the parting of the ways between South Africa and the West over South Africa's race policies.

Towards the end of a first-ever tour of African countries by a serving British Prime Minister, Macmillan confronted the White rulers of South Africa, said all the polite things and added: " ... all

15. Literally: Vorster's crown.
16. It was Mrs Vorster's cuttings which provided much of the material for the later part of this book.

this proves your determination as the most advanced industrial country in Africa to play your part in the new Africa of today. As I travelled round the Union, I have found everywhere, as I expected, a deep preoccupation with what is happening in the rest of the African continent. I understand and sympathise with your interest in these events and your anxiety about them. Ever since the break-up of the Roman Empire, one of the constant facts of political life in Europe has been the emergence of independent nations. They have come into existence over the centuries in different forms with different kinds of government. But all have been inspired by a deep, keen feeling of nationalism, which has grown as the nations have grown. In the twentieth century, and especially since the end of the war, the processes which gave birth to the nation-states of Europe have been repeated all over the world. We have seen the awakening of national consciousness in people who have, for centuries, lived in dependence on some other power. Fifteen years ago, this movement spread through Asia. Many countries there, of different races and civilisations, pressed their claim to an independent national life. Today, the same thing is happening in Africa".

Referring to his African tour, he said: "The most striking of all the impressions I have formed since I left London a month ago is the strength of the African national consciousness. In different places it might take different forms. But it is happening everywhere. The wind of change is blowing through this continent. Whether we like it or not, this growth of national consciousness is a political fact. Our national policies must take account of it. Of course, you understand this better than anyone. You are sprung from Europe, the home of nationalism. And, here in Africa, you have yourselves created a free nation, a new nation. Indeed, in the history of our times, yours will be recorded as the first of the African nationalisms. And this tide of national consciousness which is now rising in Africa is a fact for which you and we and other nations of the Western World are ultimately responsible ... As I have said, the growth of national consciousness in Africa is a political fact and we must accept it as such. This means, I would judge, that we must come to terms with it. I sincerely believe that, if we cannot do so, we may imperil the precarious balance between East and West on which the peace of the world depends ..."

Macmillan went on to discuss Britain's reaction to the "winds of change" in Africa, of the way in which Britain had done and would do her Christian duty in the face of the new challenges. He emphasised Britain's non-racial approach to these challenges and he told his audience: "It may well be that in trying to do our duty as we see it, we shall sometimes make difficulties for you. If that proves to be so, we much regret it. But I know that, even so, you would not ask us to flinch from doing our duty. You too, will do your duty as you see it ... as fellow-members of the Commonwealth, we always try and, I think, we have succeeded in giving South Africa our full support and encouragement, but I hope you won't mind my saying frankly that there are some aspects of your policies which make it impossible for us to do this without being false to our own deep convictions about the political destinies of free men to which in our own territories we are trying to give effect. I think therefore that we ought to face as friends together – without seeking, I trust, to apportion praise or blame – the fact that in the kind of world of today, this difference in outlook lies between us ...."

In his reply, Prime Minister Verwoerd accepted Macmillan's straight talking and, in turn, said that South Africa looked critically on some aspects of British policy in Africa " ... we see ... that there may be great dangers inherent in those policies. The very object at which you are aiming may be defeated by them". But he pledged the South African Government to the fullest co-operation in seeking prosperity for South Africa, Great Britain and for Africa itself.

Listening intently was the Deputy Minister of Education, Arts and Science and of Social Welfare and Pensions, totally unaware of his own destiny, unthinking that he would have to follow Verwoerd and that it would fall to him to try to come to terms with an African continent much more severely affected by the "winds of change" than the one Macmillan had visited.

Vorster remembers the speech well: "I could see Verwoerd was under a very great strain as he listened to Macmillan. But we later heard that, although Macmillan had been staying with the Prime Minister, he did not show Verwoerd a copy of his speech. So Verwoerd had to both listen intently and formulate his reply while Macmillan was speaking. And I think that our man did a magnificent job. The speech itself came as a bit of a shock to me because it made me realise that Britain had taken sides and that Britain's side was not a pro-South African side. The impression the speech made on me was that we were, in fact, expendable in Britain's eyes". Did it ever enter his mind then that he might one day have to face the full blast of the "winds of change"? "Ag no. Heavens alive, it never entered your mind".

Meanwhile, events were in the making which would affect profoundly both Vorster and his future political career. While the African National Congress, South Africa's long-time voice of Black nationalism, planned its campaign against the so-called "Pass laws"[17], the more militant, break-away Pan-Africanist Congress announced its own campaign. This involved calling on all members to leave their reference books at home and to present themselves at police stations for arrest. The slogan for the campaign was: "No bail, no defence, no fine". The object was to embarrass the Government by flooding its penal machinery. The demonstrators were told that, if the police refused to arrest them, they should return again and again until arrested. They were also told to ensure that there was no violence. But violence there was – including the Sharpeville tragedy in which police fire killed 67 Blacks and wounded 186. There were disturbances in Cape Town in which more people were killed and injured. And there were demonstrations and sporadic outbreaks of violence in other parts of South Africa.

The Government reacted by banning public meetings in all relevant magisterial districts on March 24, 1960. On March 28, legislation was introduced to ban the PAC and the ANC. On March 30 a State of Emergency was declared and hundreds of people were arrested in different parts of the country in a pre-dawn police swoop. More disturbances followed on a wide front. It was a time of high tension for both White and Black. Citizen Force units were mobilised and the London Daily Mail reported on March 31: "After today, things can never be the same again in South Africa. The 12-year-old pattern of Apartheid Government is breaking up ... the feeling grows that Verwoerd's Government is tottering ...".

In South Africa itself the unhappy events sparked off a great

17. The various laws and regulations controlling the movement of Blacks to the urban areas and which have existed in South Africa in one form or another since the days of British rule. The whole system was considerably tightened up by the Nationalist Government with the Abolition of Passes and co-ordination of Documents Act in 1952.

deal of White soul-searching and political re-thinking. However, the Verwoerd government continued its course and, armed with emergency powers, the authorities largely smashed the organisation behind the protests. It is clear, in retrospect, that these events strengthened Verwoerd's determination to take really tough action against "subversive" elements in South Africa. And it is possible that he had already made up his mind that the then Minister of Justice, Mr F C Erasmus, was not up to the task.

Much of the unrest centred on Cape Town and Vorster can remember taking a great interest in what was happening: "When about 30 000 Blacks marched on the Caledon Square police station, Hendrik Luttig[18] and I walked over from the House of Assembly to watch the procession. It was led by a young Black man, Phillip Kgosana and thousands of Black people milled around the police station and its environs. We talked about the serious and troublesome times ... but it was not my reponsibility at that time and it was only later that I realised that this was the beginning of really big trouble".

1960 was to provide yet more drama. On January 20, Verwoerd announced that the Government intended holding a referendum on the question of making South Africa a republic. A simple majority would give the verdict, one way or another. The referendum campaign got under way during the second half of 1960, with Vorster playing a part beyond that of his formal status as a Deputy Minister.

An obvious indication of his growing status in the Party came on August 19, 1960 when Verwoerd wrote to him telling him that the Cabinet had decided that Vorster should introduce the motion at the national congress of the Party in Bloemfontein on August 30, calling on South Africa's White voters to declare themselves in favour of a republic. Vorster recalls: "The letter came as a very big surprise. I would mislead you if I said that I was not greatly honoured. You see, you got the idea that you had arrived. After all, it was a nation-wide congress[19] and there were only four motions

18. Luttig, then MP for Mayfair, left politics in 1965 to become the South African Ambassador in Vienna.
19. The National Party in South Africa is a federal organisation, consisting of autonomous parties in each of the four provinces and in South West Africa. Their affairs are co-ordinated by a Federal Council. Each party holds an annual congress and nation-wide congresses are only held rarely.

before the congress and this one was the most important. With my background, it was particularly gratifying to be able to propose this motion because it was the culmination of almost everything that I had strived for, lived for and worked for. Everything almost that had taken me into the National Party, into the OB and back into the National Party again".

The motion was accepted with acclamation, after Vorster told his enthusiastic audience that the main purpose of the campaign was to create real unity in South Africa[20]. Later Vorster was elected as Jan de Klerk's alternate on the National Party's Federal Council – a position of considerable importance for a young Deputy Minister. He was elected to replace Mr Hans Abraham, who had resigned to become Commissioner-General to the Xhosa National Unit[21] and who subsequently dropped into political oblivion.

The referendum was held on October 5, 1960 and the result showed 850 458 voters in favour of a republic and 775 878 against. The average poll was an almost incredible 90,75 per cent so strongly did both sides feel about their viewpoints. Apart from anything else, this meant that South Africa was about to break with the British Crown for the first time since 1806 – and John Vorster was right there amongst the cheer-leaders.

However, the break was to be with more than the British Crown. In March, 1961, Verwoerd went to London for the meeting of Commonwealth Prime Ministers. On March 31 he told them that South Africa had taken the steps necessary to change to a republic. With his permission, the meeting discussed South Africa's race policies and two days later the South African Press Association special correspondent in London sent a flash message to South Africa : "South African Prime Minister, Dr Verwoerd, has withdrawn his application for South Africa's continued membership of the Commonwealth as a republic ... this was announced in a final communique". The same day Verwoerd explained: "In the light of opinions expressed on behalf of other member governments regarding South Africa's race policies, and in the light of their future plans regarding the race policies of the Union Government, the Prime Minister of South Africa informed the

20. Pretoria News, 30/8/1960.
21. The Commissioners-General served as the Government's representatives in the different homelands in a sort of pre-ambassadorial function.

other Prime Ministers this evening that he had decided to withdraw South Africa's application for continued membership of the Commonwealth as a republic"[22].

Vorster sent Verwoerd a telegram immediately: "Thank you for rescuing the nation's pride".

While the White nation's pride may have been rescued, South Africa now stood exposed as never before to Macmillan's winds of change. However, Afrikanerdom was on the brink of achieving its greatest ambition, the republic, and Verwoerd was welcomed as a conquering hero when he returned to South Africa. In the euphoria of the weeks that followed, the celebrations, the speeches, the coming of the republic on May 31, 1961, few Afrikaners understood that their biggest battle was yet to come. Few understood that, given the National Party's steadily increasing electoral support, the arrival of a republic was only a matter of timing. The real battle was about to start and that battle would be keeping what they had now won, fighting internal subversion, fighting attempts to isolate and destroy South Africa, coming to terms with Africa, applying the official race policy in such a way that there would not be a repeat of the events of 1960.

On July 22, 1961, the Vorsters were visiting M. J. De la Rey Venter, MP for De Aar-Colesberg, on his farm in the Colesberg district. It was a Sunday night and the cold of the Karoo winter seeped into the house. The Venters and the Vorsters sat clustered around the fire after dinner talking and joking. Then they quietened to listen to the nine o'clock news over the radio. To their surprise they heard that Italian President Giovanni Gronchi had accepted Mr F C Erasmus, the South African Minister of Justice, as South Africa's new Ambassador in Rome. The announcement took South Africa by surprise because, it seemed afterwards, an Italian official had released the news prematurely. It should have waited until Verwoerd announced his cabinet changes at the beginning of August. Vorster declines to discuss his reactions to the news, but the fact is that the family left for Pretoria the next day and he was in his Deputy Minister's office in the Union Buildings about three pm.

"As soon as I got to my office, I telephoned P W Botha to hear the latest news. He told me that he had something extremely

22. Die Transvaler, 16/3/1961.

important to tell me and could I come down to his office for a cup of coffee. I went down to his office and, as I shook hands with him, the telephone rang. He picked the phone up and I had the idea that it was Fred Barnard, Dr Verwoerd's Private Secretary. He turned to me and said: 'Heavens, Dr Verwoerd wants to see me urgently'. So I went back to my office, telling him to see me as soon as he had finished with Dr Verwoerd – after all I wanted to know what the extremely important matter was that he wanted to discuss with me. A little later he came into my office and he was about to tell me what the extremely important matter was when my phone rang. It was Fred Barnard and he said that I should come to Dr Verwoerd's office urgently. So I left and, to this day, I do not know what P W Botha wanted to see me about. As I walked to his office, I had the feeling that he wanted to appoint me as Erasmus' successor. When I got there, Dr Verwoerd told me that Erasmus was leaving the cabinet, and that there were two vacancies in the cabinet, that he was offering the one to P W Botha[23] and that he was offering Justice to me. I cannot remember exactly what we said to each other. I want to meet the man who can remember everything that is said at a time like that ... you're flabbergasted, its the culmination of your political career, you want to get home to tell your wife and family about it. You feel elated. You feel that you didn't look for it, you didn't aspire to it, you did not scheme for it, but now it has come your way. There are very few other things that can bring that feeling. But I do remember saying to Dr Verwoerd that he should let me deal with the threat of subversion and revolution in my own way. I told him that you could not fight communism with the Queensberry Rules because if you fight communism with the Queensberry Rules, then you will lose. He agreed with me and said that he would leave me free to do what I had to do – within reason. I do not want to be critical of Frans Erasmus, but I knew that I would handle the situation differently. It is perfectly natural as a lawyer and as a Deputy Minister that you look at your colleagues and you think how you would deal with a particular situation if it was your responsibility. Slowly in my own mind I had, perhaps unconsciously, been accumulating thoughts and ideas on how South Africa should deal with subversion ...."

No announcement was made at this stage but there was

23. See footnote 10.

speculation about Erasmus' successor. The Sunday Times reported on July 31, 1961 that Vorster would succeed Erasmus. Speculation about a cabinet reshuffle built up until August 1, 1961 when Verwoerd announced an early general election, to be held on October 18. The Rand Daily Mail reported on August 2 that the Prime Minister was known to be planning a clean-out of Nationalist moderates and of older parliamentarians. And it tipped B J Vorster, "one of the Party's young extremists" as the next Minister of Justice.

Ten hours after announcing the coming poll, Verwoerd revealed his cabinet changes, but explained that further changes would be made after the election. As predicted, Vorster became Minister of Justice but was asked to take on the Education Arts and Science portfolio until after the election. His former boss, J J Serfontein, remained in the cabinet with reduced responsibility, retaining only Social Welfare and Pensions.

While Nationalist newspapers spoke of the cabinet being strengthened, the Rand Daily Mail commented on August 3, 1961 that Vorster was known to have strong-man qualities and that he therefore fitted readily into the strong-man posture Verwoerd expected from his Minister of Justice. On the same day, the London Daily Telegraph reported that a former pro-Nazi leader was now in the South African Cabinet and commented: "The cabinet changes suggest an obstinate determination (on Verwoerd's part) to pursue the doctrinaire policy of apartheid uncompromisingly. Mr Vorster, who now comes to the front ... is known for his prominence in the Ossewa-Brandwag, the underground organisation dedicated by its name to preserving the separatist spirit of the Great Trek. Germanophile in war and, in peace, resisting the reconciliation between Boer and Briton ..." The London Daily Herald reported that Vorster was a known extremist, that he had a reputation for political ruthlessness and that Nationalists considered him Dr Verwoerd's heir-apparent. Canada's Globe and Mail said in an editorial on August 16: "The shadow of the police state grows longer in South Africa. Prime Minister Hendrik Verwoerd has appointed a former Nazi sympathiser and tough advocate of Apartheid to a key position in his cabinet ... He (Vorster) is known as a very tough advocate of the Republic's race laws ..." Back home in South Africa, The Cape Times said on August 4, 1961: "Though less shrill than Dr

Hertzog and by far an abler speaker, Vorster belongs to the same school of bitter sectionalism and baasskap[24]. The Sunday Times said on August 6, 1961, that the "moderate" Cape had suffered a major setback and that the National Party was now ruled by an extreme triumverate: Verwoerd, Vorster and Hertzog.

Thus destiny had finally caught up with the man who had once been detained without trial by the South African Police Force, who had been interned as a subversive by a South African Government, and who had been threatened with arrest by a South African Minister of Justice. Now it would be his job to sit behind the same desk and to do unto others what was once done unto him.

24. Literally: being the boss.

8 *Justice*

The newspapers were right about one thing: Vorster was a strong man and he would not hesitate to change the rules when he felt the game was going against his perception of law and order in South Africa. One of his first public pronouncements after his appointment as Minister of Justice came when he addressed the 'Afrikanerklub in Bloemfontein: "I believe in the right of free speech; in the right of people to assemble, and protest. These are three inalienable rights which the people of South Africa should have. I want to announce here that I see it as my duty to protect these rights – but not without qualification. The right to free speech must go together with discipline and responsibility. People must assemble in legitimate places and have legitimate objectives. And, when there are protests, these must be conducted with dignity ... If it is required of me that I should curtail the rights of free speech, assembly and protest within the existing legislative framework, then I will do so reluctantly, but with determination because I will know that it is essential". He added that he believed in a free and independent judiciary that would apply and interpret the law; that he believed in the closest possible co-operation between all those involved in the process of the law; that he would do everything in his power to achieve this co-operation; and that he would go out of his way to work with both the Bar and the Side-Bar[1]. At the same meeting he said he would do everything in his power to eliminate the "big cancer" in South Africa – Whites who agitated amongst Blacks[2].

A few days later, addressing Nationalists in Vanderbijlpark, he called on the Press to support law and order in South Africa and he warned "agitators" that he would act against them with all the means at his disposal. He said he would act firmly in the interests of

1. Die Volksblad (Bloemfontein), 5/8/1961.
2. Die Transvaler, 5/8/1961.

18. *Vorster leaving Marks Building in Cape Town on September 13, 1966 on his way to the National Party caucus meeting at which he was elected Leader of the Party. Next to him is General John Keevey, Commissioner of the South African Police, and behind is Major Dirk Genis, a security police officer.*

19. *South Africa's new Prime Minister emphasising a point during his first speech on the steps of Parliament on September 13, 1966. On his right is the National Party's Chief Whip, Koos Potgieter, and on his left is Paul Sauer, Chairman of the National Party caucus. Standing behind Vorster with his hands folded in front of him is Ben Schoeman. On Schoeman's left is Eben Dönges. Both Schoeman and Dönges were at one stage candidates for election.*

Photo: Louw Pretorius.

20. *Immediately after his speech on the steps of Parliament on September 13, 1966, Vorster received a congratulatory kiss from his wife.*

21. *After perhaps one of the busiest days of his life, Vorster broadcast his first message to the Nation from the South African Broadcasting Corporation's Cape Town studios on September 13, 1966.*

Photo: Nasionale Koerante.

22. *Walking into Groote Schuur, the Prime Minister's residence in Cape Town for the first time.*
Photo: Nasionale Koerante.

law and order and that he would ask for more powers if this was necessary[3]. And he said that his first task would be to see to it that justice was done to all South Africans, irrespective of country of origin, language or colour[4].

True to his determination to apply the security legislation reluctantly but "with determination", Vorster soon signed a string of banning orders under the existing Suppression of Communism Act. Those restricted included Mr Patrick Duncan, a prominent member of the Liberal Party and the son of a former South African Governor-General, and Mr Joseph Nkatlo, Vice-Chairman of the Liberal Party of the Cape. In October, 1961, ex-chief Albert Luthuli a former President of the ANC was awarded the Nobel Peace Prize for "opposing violence in South Africa". Vorster refused to let Luthuli travel to Oslo to receive his award, explaining: "The restrictions on ex-chief Luthuli were imposed for good reasons which have not disappeared because a prize has been awarded to him overseas, for whatever reasons ... My duty as Minister of Justice is to maintain such restrictions in respect of affected people in South Africa for as long as it is deemed necessary[5]." Later Luthuli was given a ten-day temporary passport so that he could go to Oslo to collect his prize.

On November 1, 1961, Verwoerd announced that he had appointed two English-speakers to the cabinet (in fulfilment of a promise he had made during the republican referendum): Mr Frank Waring and Mr Alf Trollip. At the same time Vorster relinquished his temporary responsibility for Education Arts and Science to allow him to concentrate fully on the Justice portfolio. Vorster greeted Trollip as an old friend, recalling how he had lost to the old UP stalwart by two votes in Brakpan in 1948. "When Dr Verwoerd told us in cabinet that he was appointing Alf and Frankie, he turned to P W Botha and myself and said that, in terms of normal cabinet seniority, Alf would be our junior. However, in view of his age, would we have any objections if he put him above us in seniority. Before P W could reply, I said to Dr Verwoerd: 'No Doctor, I have no objections, after all, he once beat me by two votes'. We all laughed and that was the end of the story."

By now there was no doubt in anybody's mind that John Vorster

3. The Cape Times, 11/8/1961.
4. The Rand Daily Mail, 11/8/1961.
5. The Rand Daily Mail, 28/10/1961.

was going to be a tough, unyielding Minister of Justice, absolutely implacably opposed to anything which he identified as subversion, as a threat to established order in South Africa, as a threat to the republic which was still in its infancy. To him and his security policemen, South Africa faced revolution and, if it was necessary to resolve a conflict between the interests of the State and the interests of the individual, then it was the interests of the state which would win. And if his policemen had to err, then he would prefer them to err in the direction of excessive zeal in protecting the interests of the State. Vorster recalls his thinking at the time: "In normal circumstances you can play the game according to the rules. But these were not normal times, the communists were plotting revolution, bloodshed, violence and they were certainly not playing the game according to the rules. I realised that if the security forces had to play according to the rules it would be like fighting an implaccable and vicious enemy with one hand tied behind your back. I was not going to send my men into battle with one hand tied behind their backs. I saw my way very clearly right from the outset because my own experiences during the war had given me a very clear insight into the whole thing ... I knew the whole thing from both sides, from the inside and from the outside. I had no real hard feelings about my own internment. I had come out in opposition to the Government of the day, that Government identified me as a threat to established order and so it neutralised me, it did what it felt was necessary at the time. I adopted the same approach ..."

However, when it came to the administration and control of the judicial machine, he showed another side. He was reasonable and flexible and, although he warned the legal profession to keep out of South Africa's political turmoil, he proved accessible and amenable to argument when it came to the question of the administration of the justice machine. The legal profession appreciated the fact that he had gone through the legal mill himself and that he generally knew exactly what they were talking about. Kowie Marais, who was made a judge in 1955, recalls that Vorster was an excellent administrator and that he won the respect of the Bench "because we knew that he would never injure any person out of spite, or because of irresponsibility or political reasons. As far as his personal integrity was concerned, I could give my colleagues on the Bench an absolute assurance".

Vorster was going to become even tougher in the security field. In The Senate on February 15, 1962, he announced far-reaching measures aimed at protecting the security of the State. This was his reaction to a new threat to state security in the form of intermittent Black violence; but most of all to the emergence of the Umkonto we Sizwe (The Spear of the Nation) movement which claimed it would continue to fight for democracy and freedom in South Africa. Violence would no longer be met with non-violence and there would be attacks on government installations. By way of anonymous telephone calls to newspapers, an organisation calling itself the Committee for Liberation warned of impending violence. In December the NCL claimed responsibility for an explosion which damaged two pylons on the outskirts of Johannesburg. A wave of bombings and attempted bombings followed in different parts of South Africa. Vorster announced the rapid expansion of the Security Police, tightened control at the country's borders, the establishment of police mobile units, the creation of helicopter units to help the mobile groups and the extension of the Police Reserve to Black and Brown South Africans[6]. On May 12, he published details of the 1962 General Laws Amendment Bill (soon to be called the Sabotage Bill by the Opposition) and all hell broke loose around the new Minister of Justice. Vorster remembers: "When that first wave of sabotage came, I had just addressed a Day of the Covenant function at White River and I was on my way to spend a weekend in the Kruger National Park when they phoned me and told me to come back to Pretoria immediately. I turned round there and then and we headed for Pretoria. I thought about it all the way from White River to Pretoria and when I got to my office, I called for the Commissioner of Police and we discussed the whole affair. We went into the question of what legislation we had to deal with the situation and what legislation was necessary. I gave the instruction that the legislation should be drafted because I had already told my policemen that I would not send them into the fight against the communists with bare hands".

Publication of the details of the "Sabotage Bill" sparked off one of the longest and most savage political controversies in South Africa's history. Throughout the controversy and the long and

6. The Cape Times, 16/2/1962.

bitter parliamentary debate, Vorster stood implaccable and unyielding. Although he made a few minor changes in the legislation, he refused to budge on its basic content – despite accusations of Nazi dictatorship, fascism and totalitarianism. As far as he was concerned, the measure was necessary to deal with a very serious threat to state security and that was that. Basically the legislation (in the form in which it finally became law) made sabotage as serious an offence as treason and it laid down a minimum penalty of five years and a maximum penalty of death. It was based on an extremely wide definition of sabotage and it placed the onus on the accused to show that, if he wilfully committed one of the acts listed in the definition of sabotage, he was not guilty of it. It increased the State President's powers to ban subversive organisations and it provided the Minister of Justice with the power to order the "house arrest" of people he believed were a threat to the safety of the State. The Minister's powers to prohibit people from attending gatherings (in terms of the Suppression of Communism Act) were increased and it created the "gag" for all people who were prohibited from attending meetings – nobody could henceforth publish anything said at any time by anybody who had been prohibited from attending meetings.

Koot Vorster tells an interesting story about the coming of the house arrest provision. "I remember that John was with me during that time and we were discussing subversion and the threat of communism. With us was Professor T N Hanekom, Professor of Church History at the University of Stellenbosch. John asked us whether we knew of the first case of house arrest in recorded history. Neither of us knew and John said it was very interesting that two churchmen of our status did not know the story of how Solomon ordered the house arrest of Shimei. John told us that, while he was at the university he was reading this passage in The Bible when he underlined it. He cannot remember why he underlined it but, during the period that he was considering the whole issue of legislation to deal with sabotage, he read The Bible and he came to this underlined passage ...".

The story of Solomon and Shimei is told in Kings I Chapter 2, verses 36 to 46: "And the King sent and called for Shimei, and said unto him, Build thee a house in Jerusalem and dwell there and go thee not forth any whither. For it shall be, that on the day that thou

132

goest out, and passest over the brook Kidron, thou shalt know for certain that thou shalt surely die: thy blood shall be upon thy own head. And Shimei said unto the king, The saying is good: as my lord the King hath said, so will thy servant do. And Shimei dwelt in Jerusalem many days. And it came to pass at the end of three years, that two of the servants of Shimei ran away unto Achish, son of Maacha, King of Gath. And they told Shimei, behold thy servants be in Gath. And Shimei arose and saddled his ass and went to Gath, to Achish, to seek his servants: and Shimei went and brought his servants from Gath. And it was told Solomon that Shimei had gone from Jerusalem to Gath and was come again. And the King sent and called for Shimei and said unto him, Did I not make thee swear by the Lord, and protested unto thee saying, Know for certain that on the day thou goest out and walkest abroad any whither, that thou shalt surely die? and thou saidst unto me, The word that I have heard is good. Why then hast thou not kept the oath of the Lord, and the commandments that I have charged thee with? The King said moreover to Shimei, Thou knowest all the wickedness which thou heart is privy to, that thou didst to David, my father: therefore the Lord shall return thy wickedness upon thy own head. And the King Solomon shall be blessed, and the throne of David shall be established before the Lord forever. So the King commanded Benaiah, the son of Jehoiada; which went out, and fell upon him, that he died. And the Kingdom was established in the hand of Solomon".

Vorster remembers the incident: "I have read The Bible through many times because I read a chapter every night, no matter where I am, no matter what the time may be. And occasionally, when I have the time, I page through The Bible and read this and that. And while I was considering this legislation I came across this underlined portion in my Bible. I cannot say that this was the inspiration but I did come across the story at about the same time that I took the decision. You must remember that after Koffiefontein I was placed under a form of house arrest myself, so this thing was not really new in South Africa. It seemed the humane thing to do. If somebody was clearly a threat to the safety of the State then, if it was at all possible, you did not lock him up in jail but you neutralised him in his own home where he could be with his wife and kids and where he could go out and earn a living (in some cases). If he was particularly dangerous, you house arrested him for weekends as well ..."

At a Press conference called to explain the measure, Vorster said that it had been made necessary by threats of violence and actual violence. The measure was designed to "protect democracy" and he denied claims that he was creating a police state in South Africa. He said that the house arrest provisions of the Bill were aimed at allowing certain people to remain at home instead of being in jail[7]. The Bill was designed to close the loopholes in the existing legislation aimed at combating communism and were less stringent than were the provisions against subversion during the Second World War. "I know what I am talking about when I say that. I can speak from personal experience"[8]. He conceded that teenagers could be hanged for sabotage once the Bill became law and said that if juveniles were willing to be used as tools by the communists, it was unfortunate for them[9].

Reaction from the Government's opponents was bitter. The Sunday Express (May 13, 1962) called the Bill a "savage" one. The Natal Mercury (May 14, 1962) said: "Sabotage is a horrifying political weapon ... so also is the Government's General Law Amendment Bill". The Star (May 14, 1962): " ... the Government is saying, in effect, that the State is in mortal peril and that civilised principles of justice must therefore be abrogated. The familiar pattern of liberty being destroyed in defence of liberty is thus being repeated". The Rand Daily Mail (May 14, 1962): " ... it is legislation of a government with its back to the wall and in an ugly mood ... this shocking Bill is clearly the product of a dictator mentality ...". Two former Chief Justices of South Africa, the Hon. Mr A van der Sandt Centlivres and the Hon. Mr H A Fagan (the same man Vorster had helped fight in the 1938 General Election) both expressed shock at the provisions of the legislation and joined the mounting protest against the measure. The Christian Council of South Africa, which claimed to represent 3,54 million South Africans condemned the "harsh" measure[10]. The Progressive Party launched a nation-wide campaign against the Bill. Other organisations and individuals joined the vociferous

7. The Star, 15/5/1962.
8. The Pretoria News, 15/5/1962.
9. The Daily News (Durban), 15/5/1962.
10. The Cape Times, 17/5/1962.

134

protest. Scott Haig, the veteran parliamentary journalist wrote in the Sunday Tribune on May 20, 1962: "The OB is dead, Long live the OB ...". Patrick Duncan, who would one day be gagged by the legislation, asked: "What next? ... concentration camps"[11].

A bitter parliamentary debate followed, the highlight of which was a heated 37-hour debate in the House of Assembly. And, while controversy raged in the House, protests were organised throughout the country. Sir de Villiers Graaff, Leader of the Opposition, hammered the Government for a measure which meted out "civil death" to people who incurred either the suspicion or the displeasure of the Minister of Justice. Opposition newspaper cartoonists had a whole series of drawings portraying Vorster in Nazi jackboots. Public protests led to brawls between supporters and opponents of the measure. The day the Bill passed the final stage in The Senate, the Pretoria branch of the Liberal Party of South Africa laid a white wreath on the steps of the Palace of Justice in Pretoria, with a placard mourning the end of the rule of law in South Africa. The measure became law when it was promulgated in the Government Gazette on June 27, 1962. In a television programme screened to millions of British homes, Vorster was interviewed on the Sabotage Act and said that, considering what South Africa had to combat, he considered the Act humane. He agreed with the interviewer that certain provisions were open to abuse, but explained: "With our experience of communism, we have found it necessary to take wider powers than is absolutely necessary to close up all the loopholes that exist"[12].

On October 13, opening a new police station at Wolmaransstad, Vorster said: "I do not want to be tough, but I have to do my duty. I do not want to curb freedom of speech or the right to protest. On the contrary, I want to ensure that the right to protest is safe-guarded. I have to reconcile between the philosophy of freedom of speech and the safety of the State."[13].

Meanwhile, there were isolated acts of sabotage and attempted sabotage. On October 20, an explosion wrecked the offices of the Minister of Agricultural Economics and Marketing in Pretoria.

11. The Rand Daily Mail, 22/5/1962.
12. The Star, 13/7/1962.
13. The Cape Times, 15/10/1962.

Anonymous telephone callers to newspapers claimed this was the work of the Spear of the Nation. A few days later a "proclamation" purporting to come from the Spear of the Nation was sent to the Sunday Times stating that the organisation's policy was an eye for an eye and a tooth for a tooth and a life for a life. It would meet force with force and fight until White domination of South Africa was ended. There was more sabotage and serious rioting took place in Paarl on the night of November 21. In the days that followed, saboteurs damaged a pylon near Benoni, bringing down power lines. A kiosk linking signal boxes near Johannesburg was blown up. On December 4 telephone and telegraph wires between Port Elizabeth and other centres were cut and a telephone booth in Cape Town was wrecked by an explosion.

Vorster reacted to all this at a National Party rally in Alberton on October 20: "If saboteurs think I will be scared off by such explosions from taking even stronger action, they are mistaken". He said communism was a deadly danger which South Africans would have to fight to eliminate. However, there was possibly an even greater danger: the liberalistic tendencies which were being stoked up day by day by certain newspapers. "I want to warn the liberalistic elements that, in future, they may run into difficulties. They have challenged me. It is not my practice to challenge them. It is not my habit to make threats. I am giving them a friendly warning". He added prophetically: "Our struggle will become tougher and tougher. It will become necessary for the protection of White civilisation to take more and more steps."[14]. And he warned the Rand Daily Mail that it was playing with fire. The newspaper had to accept that people who played with fire got burned. If the RDM continued supporting the current of liberalism in South Africa, it would "come up against something"[15].

Laurence Gandar, the Daily Mail's articulate editor, replied in a leading article on October 28. It was an important editorial in that it encapsulated and articulated the views of Vorster's liberal critics. Gandar referred to the Alberton speech and said that it was not the first time Vorster had linked liberalism with communism. The newspaper felt it was not a moment too soon to give Vorster a friendly but very serious warning:

14. The Sunday Times, 21/10/1962.
15. The Rand Daily Mail, 22/10/1962.

"For it is a dangerous game that Mr Vorster is playing and we will now tell him – and the public – why:

● "By equating liberalism with communism, Mr Vorster, you are endowing communism in the eyes of an unsophisticated non-White population with the acknowledged virtues and values of western liberalism;

● "By identifying communism with the various non-White political movements, Mr Vorster, you are helping communism in its traditional strategy of allying itself with local nationalisms:

● "By branding leading liberals, whose bona fides are firmly established amongst non-Whites, as crypto-communists, Mr Vorster, you are making it easier for communism to pose as the true friend of the non-Whites;

● "By issuing warnings to liberal newspapers like the Rand Daily Mail, Mr Vorster, you are virtually telling the non-Whites that those who have respect for their human dignity and have a proper concern for their grievances, behave as communists do;

● "By holding up communism as the militant champion of those political aspirations amongst the non-Whites which are considered legitimate and normal elsewhere in the world, Mr Vorster, you are encouraging our non-Whites to regard communism as their principal hope for the future;

● "By denouncing liberalism and communism in the same breath, Mr Vorster, you are using the classic language of the extreme right in international politics. This kind of talk can only confirm in the mind of the outside world the belief that we have a fascist-style government in South Africa today.

"All this adds up to a massive and quite gratuitous boost for communist prestige and influence in South Africa which we are sure is the very opposite of your intentions. Through this misguided propaganda of yours, it is suddenly the communists who are depicted as the principal opponent of White baasskap, as the political force which is throwing the White establishment into confusion and causing it to react with panic measures. Surely the communists could wish for nothing better than this; it is something that they have signally failed to achieve by their own efforts up till now.

"Communism has never had wide support among non-Whites in South Africa. You are giving it the stature of a mass movement.

"To combat communism in South Africa, Mr Vorster, three things are surely essential:

● "First the conditions of life in which communism is known to thrive must be eliminated as rapidly as possible ...

● Secondly, a wedge must be driven between the communists; and thirdly the non-White political movements must be persuaded that their reasonable aspirations must and can be pursued peacefully under our democratic system.

"What, Mr Vorster, is your Government doing to meet these three essential requirements? A little in the case of the first and nothing at all in the case of the other two. This is both the tragedy and the danger of our system ... do not persuade the non-Whites that their struggle is the same thing as the communist struggle. Do not hand to the communists a monopoly of fighting for the rights of the non-White peoples. If you do these things, Mr Vorster, you will have sealed South Africa's fate and history will rightly condemn you and your colleagues for having delivered a great country into the hands of the communists".

Vorster reacted by saying that the Rand Daily Mail was very definitely on a dangerous road for itself and for South Africa. He said that his warning to the newspaper stood and that he stood by every word he had said about communism and liberalism. "No matter what can be said of liberalism in other parts of the world, it is my conviction that liberalism, as manifested in South Africa, is, according to my lights, nothing other than the precursor of communism. Evidence of this is the fact that if you tackle communism here, then every liberalist in the country cries for 14 days long. It is also typical of the communists that they use liberalism as a screen behind which they can hide and as a means to destroy democracy. Thus communism's infiltrations of all liberalist and all pseudo-liberalist organisations and institutions. In South Africa it is a fact that the communists believe in everything that the liberalists believe in, although all liberalists are not necessarily knowing and willing communists. As it is, the difference between the communists and the liberalists is getting

138

smaller and smaller, so that a person will eventually need to use a magnifying glass to see those differences[16]".

Reviewing 1962, the Sunday Times named Vorster the "strong man of the year" on December 30 and recorded that he had put 18 people under house arrest, silenced 103, listed 437 as communists, outlawed the Congress of Democrats, banned the left-wing weekly newspaper, New Age and prohibited meetings on the steps of the Johannesburg City Hall.

On December 28, the Rand Daily Mail published a picture of the Vorsters boarding the Windsor Castle in Durban en route to Cape Town for the parliamentary session. Vorster was casually dressed in an open-necked shirt. The next day an anonymous writer posted a letter in Johannesburg, addressed to: Minister Vorster, SS Windsor Castle, Cape Town docks. It read: "Vorster I enclose a picture of you and your wife. You are a very wicked man and your wife looks like a cook. Fancy in your position in this country daring to travel, you without a tie and your old girl with no hat etc. You Afrikaans people have no dignity or respect for yourselves or for us. You are all a VERY DISHONEST lot of people". The letter was duly pasted into Mrs Vorster's Press cutting scrapbooks.

The next security shock for South Africa came in the form of the Snyman Commission of Inquiry into the Paarl Riots of 1962. His urgent, interim report was tabled in the House of Assembly on March 21, 1963. He found the root cause of the riots had been the activities of a new Black political movement, Poqo (literally translated from Xhosa, this means "only" or "pure" suggesting an exclusivist Black movement). He found that Poqo was the banned Pan Africanist Congress gone underground; that it planned to overthrow the Government by revolutionary means during 1963 and to create an African socialist democratic state in which Whites would have no political rights. He urged the Government to take swift action to regain the trust of Blacks generally in the State's ability to give them protection. The same day Vorster announced that the Government would give effect to the judge's recommendations. Thus was conceived the General Law Amendment Bill of 1963 which went far beyond the suggestions made by the judge.

Meanwhile, Hendrik van den Bergh had become head of the Security Police. After his release from Koffiefontein, Van den

16. Die Vaderland, 23/10/1962.

Bergh was placed under house arrest in Vredefort. Then he obtained permission to go to Johannesburg to look for work. He was employed as a clerk by the South African Institute for Architects and he worked happily for five years until some of his old Koffiefontein police colleagues asked him to help them regain their positions in the police force – something that had only become possible because a Nationalist government was now in power. So, in 1949, they petitioned the Government. The then Minister of Justice, Mr C R Swart (later to become the first President of the Republic of South Africa), appointed a committee to investigate their claims, the period of their absence from the force was "condoned" and they were re-instated as if nothing had happened. However, they felt that they were entitled to back pay for the period of their quite clearly illegal dismissal from the force. This was rejected but they decided to leave the matter there because, after all, this was "our own" government. Ten of the most senior of the newly re-instated policemen were allowed to sit for the examination that would enable them to qualify for commissioned rank. Van den Bergh was one of those who passed and he was promoted to lieutenant. "At that time there was tremendous enmity towards us ex-internees in the police force and I was posted to what was one of the most difficult stations in South Africa: Woodstock in Cape Town ..."

He served as a detective officer in Woodstock, Bellville, Pretoria and Bloemfontein. In 1960, he was transferred to Welkom in the Orange Free State as a major and Divisional Criminal Investigation Officer. While he was there the Minister of Justice, Mr F C Erasmus, visited Welkom. After he left an Afrikaans newspaperman told Van den Bergh that the Minister had told him that he saw Van den Bergh as the future head of the Security Police in South Africa. Soon after this he was informed that he was being transferred to the Security Police in Pretoria but, before he could leave Welkom, he was sent to Pondoland in the Transkei to investigate the serious disturbances which had already led to 30 murders. After four months there, he went to Pretoria and the Security Police: "I tell you I was the most unhappy man in South Africa. I did not want to join the Security Police. Their reputation was bad in the sense that they were a force apart. They were untouchable. They did their own thing and they were answerable only to Pretoria. This created a great deal of resentment amongst

140

us regular policemen. Apart from anything else, I did not agree with the way in which the security police force was being run and so I took four months leave in order to build myself a house in Pretoria. I had just started working again when I had a serious accident in my home, receiving severe burns which kept me out of work for another three months. So it was almost a year before I really started working as the number two man in the security police force.

"Meanwhile, Erasmus had gone to Rome and John Vorster had taken over as Minister of Justice. I think that between the time when we were in camp and the time I rejoined the police force I had seen him once and I had possibly seen him no more than two or three times up to the point when I was transferred to the Security Police. Sampie Prinsloo was made head of the Security Police but I was still extremely unhappy about everything and one day I was summoned to the Commissioner of Police's office. There I found the Commissioner, General Du Plooy and Brigadier Van Den Bergh who was head of the Criminal Investigation Department. The general told me that he had discussed my position with Brigadier Prinsloo and that it would obviously be better if I was moved. He said I would be transferred to the CID as Brigadier Van den Bergh's staff officer. I was so glad that I almost went through the roof and I did not even go back to my office with the Security Police that day. I moved straight to the CID's offices and I only went to the Security Police offices the next day to collect my belongings. I was tremendously pleased because I was now back on detective work. This was the work I loved and understood and 1962 was a good year for me ..."

During 1962 Van den Bergh was offered a "fantastic job" by a top South African financier. He signed a contract but, shortly after this, Vorster asked him to take over the Security Police. After much soul-searching, Van den Bergh agreed to remain a policeman and the financier released him from his contract. "When I was asked to take over security, I had my conditions. And one of those conditions was that the security police force as it then existed should be disbanded and that I would be able to draw to the new Security Police force the men that I either knew personally or knew of as top policemen. I kept many of the old security policemen because I knew them ... and I brought in many more. I took office on January 14, 1963. I had a Minister of Police who

141

understood just how serious the threat to South Africa was and he was prepared to give us the weapons with which we could fight revolution ... I can remember saying to John Vorster once that if he gave us the weapons then we would guarantee that not a shot would be fired, that there would not be a revolution in South Africa.

"Many people have attacked me bitterly and accused me of being instrumental in the abrogation of the rule of law in South Africa. But we were fighting a revolution in those days. It was not kid glove stuff, it was war, I tell you. It was war and I saw the choice as being between revolution, violence and bloodshed and the rule of law. I looked at my own children and the children of my friends and said, as far as I was concerned, there was no time for peace-time legal niceties ... because if there was revolution, what would have happened to the rule of law then? It would have been gone, not in parts or temporarily, it would have been gone forever and completely".

Thus was born the Vorster-Van den Bergh partnership – a partnership which still exists now, with General van Den Bergh as head of the Bureau for State Security.

On April 20 Vorster told Nationalists at a meeting in Worcester that his new security bill was being framed in the full knowledge that South Africa's enemies did not play according to the rules. He added that he would ask Parliament for additional powers with which to fight subversion as often as he deemed this necessary – no matter how drastic these measures might be[17].

Three days later, perhaps the toughest security legislation in South Africa's history stood revealed – the so-called "Ninety-days Act." Apart from closing certain legal loopholes and further excluding the courts from testing the validity of certain administrative actions, the General Laws Amendment Bill of 1963 gave the Minister of Justice the right to order the continued imprisonment without trial of certain people who had completed jail sentences for special crimes. This provision was urgently needed because Robert Sobukwe, president of the banned PAC, would shortly complete his prison sentence and the Government believed that his continued detention was in the public interest. It also gave all police commissioned officers the power to order the arrest and

17. The Rand Daily Mail, 22/4/1963.

detention for up to 90 days on any single occasion of anybody suspected of committing an act of sabotage or any offence under the Suppression of Communism Act or the Unlawful Organisations Act, or anybody suspected of having information relating to the commission or intended commission of any such offence. The detainees were to be held incommunicado (except with permission of the Minister of Justice or a commissioned police officer) until such time as the Commissioner of Police was satisfied that they had answered all questions satisfactorily. No court of law would have the power to order the release of any 90-day detainee.

Again the storm of protest. The United Nations Special Committee on Apartheid called an urgent meeting to discuss this "new development". The Times, London, spoke of this "cruel and mind-breaking piece of administrative despotism" in a leading article on April 24, 1963. The Star headlined its editorial on April 24: "Guilt-edged security" and said that the legislation placed South Africans, as never before, at the mercy of the informer and the sneak. The Bill received top priority in Parliament. The United Party supported it in principle but opposed vigorously the 90-day clause. Helen Suzman, the lone representative of the Progressive Party, fought against its every step and every clause. The Johannesburg Bar protested that some of the provisions of the Bill would have as their consequence the virtual abrogation of the rule of law in South Africa. Mr J Hamilton-Russell, a UP front-bencher, resigned from the UP because of its support for the principle of the measure, saying that Vorster had become the "epitome of a Nazi gauleiter". However, in the Senate, Vorster received praise from an unexpected quarter when United Party Senator R D Pilkington-Jordon, said that, throughout the debate, Vorster had remained courteous, patient and objective. The Minister already wielded enormous powers, but had said that he had abused none of these powers – "This is a proud claim which I do not only concede unhesitatingly, but gladly ..."[18].

Thanking Mrs Vorster on May 21 for remembering her birthday, Mrs Verwoerd added to the typed letter her own handwriting: "I would like to add how proud we are of our Minister of Justice! Look after him well, everywhere I hear nothing but praise for his actions ..."

18. The Cape Argus, 30/4/1963.

On June 12, Vorster told the House of Assembly during the Committee of Supply debate on the Justice vote that Poqo had been knocked out. If it attempted to make a come-back, it would get an even bigger and better knock-out. However, it was the ANC which posed the biggest threat to South Africa. But the police were dealing with the ANC in the same effective way that they had dealt with Poqo and the PAC[19]. Giving statistics, he told the House that, since the passing of the Sabotage Act, 126 people had been convicted and none had received sentences of less than eight years. The courts were still dealing with a number of cases and there were 511 persons awaiting trial on charges of sabotage. To date, 124 Poqo members had been convicted of murder and 77 were still in the process of being tried. Action had been taken against 670 persons in connection with continued membership of banned organisations. The number of active Poqo members arrested up to June 5, 1963 totalled 3 246. There was only one inference that could be drawn from this and that was that the police had done their duty in "eradicating this cancer in our national life" ... Had it not been for the prompt action of the South African Police "these people who were foolish enough to believe it possible and who made preparation for the taking over of South Africa in 1963, would have caused a bloodbath in South Africa. There were certain incidents and certain murders were committed ... but we can be grateful that there were only a few incidents and it remained at those few incidents because measures were timeously passed by this House to deal with the position, because the police had the necessary powers to take action when they were required to do so, and because the police, in the circumstances, were exceptionally efficient"[20].

As the parliamentary session drew to a close, Mrs Suzman said it was the most disastrous in South Africa's history and she warned that attempts to enforce apartheid would mean the complete abandonment of the rule of law in South Africa. Speaking in one of the final debates of the session, she said; "Any criticism is unpatriotic, recourse to the courts of the land is in defiance of the Government ... the Government bullies, threatens and tries to intimidate anybody who offers it real opposition. And when this

19. The Cape Argus, 13/6/1963.
20. Hansard, 1963 Volume Eight, June 12, columns 7771 and 7772.

23. *An ecstatic Prime Minister sinks a long putt at the Stellenbosch golf course on the Saturday after his election.*

Photo: Harry Tyler.

24. *The Vorster family photographed at Groote Schuur, Cape Town, the week before Elsa's wedding. Pieter is on the left and Willem on the right.*

25. *A proud father escorts his daughter to the wedding ceremony in Stellenbosch in 1967.*

Photo: The Argus, Cape Town.

does not work, they resort to smear tactics. These tactics will not work with me[21].

Scott Haig commented: "It is without enthusiasm that I comment on the parliamentary observers' automatic selection of Mr B J Vorster as the dominant ministerial figure of the session. For the first three years of his premiership, Dr Verwoerd lorded it loquaciously over the House of Assembly. Last session, and again this session, he lost his jaunty superiority and lost his ascendency. More and more he has retired into the shadows ... and, as the political stature of Mr B J Vorster has become enlarged – perhaps grossly magnified out of his real importance – so that the portly Dr Dönges becomes more and more obviously one of Nationalism's back numbers ..."[22].

During 1962 and 1963, Vorster was probably subjected to more vigorous and bitter criticism than any of his ministerial predecessors. How did this affect him? "It had very little effect on me because I knew that I was doing the right thing. But it did have some effect on my children and on my wife. Even the cartoons depicting me as a jack-booted Nazi did not really worry me because I knew that they were untrue and unjust. The English Press had by that time already made up its mind that I was insensitive to any criticism, but I can tell you that the only effect of all this unjustified (to me) criticism was that it did make me insensitive to the criticisms of the English Press. I do not know how the average person feels about criticism, I only know that I am very sensitive to it in the general sense. I thought their criticism was malicious and this resulted in me becoming totally insensitive to what they were saying. To this day I feel that the English Press criticism of me is based on severe prejudice and I pay very little attention to it".

And so the 1963 Parliamentary session ended. Vorster was in full control of the police force. He had the Prime Minister's full confidence. Van den Bergh had re-organised the Security Police and the policemen were armed with greater powers than they had ever before had in peacetime. Poqo and the PAC had been smashed and the security policemen had already begun effectively to infiltrate the Communist Party and the ANC.

The stage was set for sensational events.

21. The Sunday Times, 27/6/1963.
22. The Sunday Tribune (Durban), 7/7/1963.

9 *High Drama*

Vorster and Van den Bergh formed a formidable team, backed by the toughest peacetime security legislation in South Africa's history. While communists and others planned the overthrow of the existing order in South Africa, they planned the penetration and annihilation of the Communist Party and its activist groups. Young policemen were specially selected and trained and then instructed to penetrate communist cells. This they did to great effect until Vorster and Van den Bergh could actually listen to tape-recordings of vital meetings. In addition to this, routine operations by the Security Police were slowly amassing the detailed evidence that is so fundamental to police operations. By the middle of 1963 they were in a position to sink their teeth into the Spear of the Nation, the organisation that would spearhead revolution in the country.

On July 11, 1963 the police raided the home of Arthur Goldreich at Rivonia, outside Johannesburg and arrested 17 people in terms of the 90-day clause. One of them was the ANC leader Walter Sisulu, another was A M Kathrada, a listed communist and leader of the Indian Congress. Also arrested was L G Bernstein, of the Congress of Democrats, Govan Mbeki of the ANC, Arthur Goldreich and his wife, Dr H Festenstein, Dennis Goldberg and Bob Hepple. Other arrests followed in different parts of the country and Vorster commented grimly a few days later: "There is no doubt that the police are now tearing the Spear of the Nation apart ... I am highly pleased with what the police have done[1]."

On July 17, Vorster said South Africa was now picking the fruits of the 90-day detention clause. If it had not been for the 1962 and 1963 security legislation, the police would not have had the startling success that they had with the swoop on the Goldreich home. "I sincerely hope that those who strongly objected to that

1. Die Vaderland, 15/7/1963.

legislation now realise the wisdom of the Government's move"[2]. Two days later he told the Sunday Tribune: "They wanted to crucify me when we introduced the 90-day detention clause earlier this year. The happenings of the past few days have completely vindicated the law passed at that time. And, as a result of those happenings, I am now pretty confident that we will not have any troubles in this country this year – or next year ... people must realise that the communists are playing for very high stakes indeed. These are not men who play according to the rules. To try to combat them with conventional methods is just a waste of time"[3].

It took almost four months to bring the Rivonia group to trial. By the time they appeared in court, Goldreich had escaped, but other names had been added to the list of accused. Eleven men appeared on charges of sabotage and it was alleged that seven of them constituted the high command of the Spear of the Nation. It was alleged that the 11 men had conspired with others to commit a number of acts of sabotage which were committed in South Africa in preparation for guerilla warfare and outside invasion. Counsel for nine of the accused men was Abraham (Braam) Fischer, Q.C., brilliant Johannesburg advocate, son of a former Orange Free State Judge President, respected pillar of Johannesburg society – and a totally dedicated communist.

While Vorster practised at the Bar in Johannesburg he met Fischer often: "Look, we all knew that Braam was the head of the Communist Party in South Africa. At least, everybody who knew his way around Johannesburg at the time knew it. Time almost without number I argued communism with Braam over a cup of tea in the advocates' common room in the Supreme Court in Johannesburg. He was one of the most dedicated communists that you could find anywhere in the world. But we did not argue about his role in the communist organisation or what that organisation was doing, we argued the theory of communism and that sort of thing. He argued very vigorously. You know, Braam was a very nice chap if you talked rugby to him, or gardening, or anything that was not connected with politics. But the moment you turned to politics, his whole personality, the look in his eyes, everything, changed. He was a completely different man, there was a light in

2. The Pretoria News, 17/7/1963.
3. The Sunday Tribune, 20/7/1963.

his eyes and you knew that you could never convince him that he might be wrong. Once I became Minister of Justice, I discussed Braam thousands of times with Hendrik van den Bergh and the police. We knew what he was up to but we wanted to give him enough rope to hang himself well and truly . . ."

Three days after the Rivonia men appeared in court for the first time, Vorster attended the annual dinner of the Bond van Oud Ge-interneerdes en Politieke Gevangenes[4] at the Berea Club in Pretoria where he was the main speaker. They talked, they ate, they drank, they reminisced and they sang songs, did these old "subversives" from the days of the Smuts Government. For the most part they were unaware of the irony of their gathering at a time when Vorster was deeply locked in battle with the subversives of the sixties. They sang songs like "Los van Engeland"[5], "Die sinkende vloot van Britanje"[6] and "Wat maak die OB daar"[7]. It was a time for memories, cameraderie and good cheer – not for soul-searching.

While Fischer pitted his considerable wits against the State in the Rivonia case, Vorster reacted bluntly to the International Commission of Jurists' request to send an observer to the trial: " . . . your request is tantamount to a suggestion that the trial will not be a fair one and appears to be motivated by the recent resolution of the United Nations. Our courts are at all times open to everyone and our system of justice and our independent judiciary comparable with the best in the world. I consider your request as an affront to our system of justice and our Bench and Bar. I am not interested in the name of your observer, nor will I afford him special recognition or special facilities should you decide to send one"[8].

While the Rivonia trial dragged on, Vorster announced in Cape Town that the 90-day clause would stay in force for another year. He said that the Government never knew what might crop up. However, he did not regard the clause as part of South Africa's "permanent law"[9].

4. Literally: the League of ex-internees and Political Prisoners.
5. Literally; Free of England.
6. Literally: Britain's sinking fleet.
7. Literally: What is the OB doing there.
8. The Star, 19/10/1963.
9. The Cape Times, 14/1/1964.

On April 28, Vorster received a letter from Dr Albert Schweitzer, writing from his hospital at Lambarene in Gabon. It was enclosed in a letter from Dr Schweitzer's secretary, Lotte Gerhold, who wrote: "Referring to the treason trial and the judgement that will soon be pronounced on Nelson Mandela and the accused, Dr Schweitzer sends you the enclosed line which he hopes to bring to your attention". Dr Schweitzer's brief letter read: "Dear Sir, I beg you, please not to let be hanged those in prison who await judgment of hanging". Vorster immediately hand-wrote his reply on the back of Lotte Gerhold's letter and then handed it to his secretary for typing: "Dear Dr Schweitzer, I have received your letter dated 2nd ultimo regarding the case of Mandela and others. The position is that Mandela and his co-accused are at present appearing before the Supreme Court on serious charges of sabotage, such as the blowing up of buildings and railway installations. They are being tried by an independent court which will decide at the conclusion of the case whether they are guilty as alleged and, if found guilty, the sentence is entirely in the discretion of the court".

As it happened, Nelson Mandela[10] and the other seven accused who were found guilty of sabotage were not hanged. They were sentenced to life imprisonment on June 11, with the judge commenting that the crime for which they had been found guilty was essentially high treason. But, since the State had not seen fit to charge them with this, he had decided not to impose the death sentence. Before he was sentenced, Nelson Mandela spoke in a style reminiscent of Hans van Rensburg: "I do not deny that I planned sabotage. I did not do this in a spirit of recklessness . . . I planned it as a result of a calm and sober assessment of the political situation that had arisen after many years of tyranny, exploitation and oppression of my people by the Whites . . . Africans either had to accept inferiority or fight against it by violence. We chose the latter".

Following the Rivonia verdict, there was a fresh wave of sabotage in different parts of the country. At dawn on Friday, July 3, the police throughout South Africa swooped. Hundreds of

10. Nelson Mandela was charged after the "Rivonia Raid". At the time of the raid he was already serving a five-year prison sentence for incitement and having left the country illegally.

arrests were made and the police discovered a powerful radio transmitter, time bomb mechanisms and certain "related elements" that could have been used for sabotage. Vorster told the Press that discoveries by the police during the course of these raids could possibly lead to the destruction of the communist-inspired subversive element in South Africa.[11] A few days later he announced that another radio transmitter, 100 lb (45,36 kg.) of dynamite and 50 lb. (22,68 kg.) of electrical detonators and time-bomb mechanisms had been discovered by the police in Cape Town.

Many of the people arrested in the two police swoops were members of the African Resistance Movement. And their arrest was the product of a casual remark Braam Fischer made during an unguarded moment at the Rivonia Trial. Hendrik van den Bergh recalls: "We thought we had caught all the saboteurs. On a day I said to one of my senior officers, Colonel Fred van Niekerk, that I wanted him to go to court and just sit there, keeping his eyes and ears open. One day he came back to me and said that Fischer had whispered to one of the accused: 'We are not the only people who have committed sabotage'. I said: 'OK, let's accept Braam at his word, let's take it from there ...'. I told all my offices in South Africa that, on the following Saturday morning, every member of the Security Branch should come together and discuss this statement by Fischer. I said that anybody who had the slightest idea of what he might have meant should tell me. But they came together, they discussed the thing for the whole morning and nobody could think of anything. On the Monday I telephoned Colonel George Klindt, the head of the Security Police in Johannesburg. We had a long discussion and, as a result of this discussion, we decided to arrest a Black man who had already been twice detained under the 90-day clause. We told him what Fischer had said in court and, after a while, he gave us the name of a certain person in Johannesburg on condition that we released him (the Black man) immediately. I talked to him over the telephone from my office in Pretoria. I told him we would release him the moment the man he had named had been arrested. That man was a White Johannesburg accountant. Johannesburg almost fell apart as a result of his arrest. But, by the end of the week, we had

11. The Star., 6/7/1964.

arrested almost the whole of the African Resistance Movement a communist organisation financed by Braam Fischer ..."

But their security net had not included an intense young man by the name of John Harris.

On July 24, the Vorsters were in a mildly festive mood as they made their way from their home in Pretoria to the Colosseum Theatre in Johannesburg for a celebration to mark the South African Rugby Union's 75th anniversary. Part of the celebration was a special rugby film. While they watched the screen, Vorster saw somebody with a torch, obviously looking for one of the guests: "The moment I saw this, I got the feeling that they were looking for me. I told my wife: 'I am sure that person is looking for me' and I went to him and asked him whether he was, in fact, looking for me'. He said: 'Yes, There's a detective outside who wants to see you, I went to the detective who told me that a bomb had been exploded on the Johannesburg station ..."

When Vorster got to the station, the scene was chaotic. A time bomb left in a suitcase had exploded in the main concourse of South Africa's biggest railway station at 4.35 pm. A number of people, including children, suffered severe injuries as a result of burning petrol from the bomb and flying glass from shattered windows. Fifteen were admitted to hospital and one woman subsequently died. A few minutes before the bomb went off, two newspapers received telephone calls telling of the planting of the bomb and of the time it would explode. This was possibly the most shocking act of sabotage in South Africa's history.

Vorster remembers: "When I got to the station, I found Hendrik van den Bergh and his senior officers there. We looked at the mess and I discussed the affair with them before I telephoned Dr Verwoerd. He was terribly shocked when he heard the news, but I gave him the assurance that we would have the man by midnight. He asked me how I could say this and I replied: 'Doctor, I live with my men and if they tell me that they will have the culprit by midnight, then I believe them.' I well remember how we stood on the station platform and that is where I really got respect for those police officers of mine. They started discussing possibilities, the pros and the cons of this one's involvement and that one's involvement. They asked each other could it be this man, or that woman. Then Hendrik van den Bergh said: 'Let's forget everybody and concentrate on John Harris'. And John Harris it

151

was. By eleven o'clock that evening I could telephone Dr Verwoerd to tell him that we had our man ... and that my officers had been right in saying that we would have him by midnight".

Van den Bergh recalls: "I told my chaps to arrest Harris and I went to our offices in Johannesburg to wait for him. As they were about to enter the door, I heard a shuffle and I heard somebody shouting about the abrogation of the rule of law. Two of my chaps brought Harris into the room and dumped him into a chair. I can remember standing in front of him and telling him:' I heard what you said about the rule of law. You are not in this office because of the abrogation of the rule of law but because of the application of the rule of law. You are going to help me apply the rule of law and you are going to account for your actions this afternoon. 'When I said that, the blood drained from his face and I told my chaps: 'Here is your man, take him away.' Then I telephoned John Vorster to confirm that it was Harris and that we had arrested him. The next morning I was at my office in Pretoria about 7 am. I had hardly opened one of the morning newspapers when one of my officers came in and told me that they had found all the materials for making a bomb similar to the station bomb at Harris's home ..."

That morning and afternoon, banner headlines told South Africa about the bomb. Vorster had made a statement: "The reckless and criminal explosion at the Johannesburg station this evening in the first place has to be seen as a deed of panic by an organisation which is known to the police ... we are faced by people without conscience and the full weight of the law will be applied to bring those who are guilty to justice[12]. "It was nothing more than a cold-blooded attempt to murder innocent by-standers[13]. The bombing was universally condemned by the Government, the Press, the Opposition and the Church. For weeks it was the main topic of conversation throughout South Africa.

But there was more to Vorster's activities as Minister of Justice. While the repercussions of the station bombing were still loud, down in the Eastern Cape the judiciary was preparing for the celebrations to mark the 100th anniversary of the establishment of the Eastern Cape Division of the Supreme Court of South Africa.

12. The Rand Daily Mail, 25/7/1964.
13. Die Transvaler, 25/7/1964.

152

The guest of honour would be the Minister of Justice who took another swipe at the liberals on his way to Grahamstown. He said that the police were closing in on the White people who were known to be the brains behind the current wave of sabotage and subversion in South Africa. The master-minds were White South Africans who shielded behind the liberals and who posed as liberals themselves. Amongst the liberals these people had found some very handy musket-bearers[14].

The celebrations were impressive and suitably reflected the heavy weight of history. South Africa's legal luminaries were there in abundance and Vorster brought sighs of relief (figuratively) to his audience when he said he was not in favour of changing the seat of the division from Grahamstown to the much larger city of Port Elizabeth, either then or in the future. He added that if things developed the way he expected they would, he would be able to recommend the suspension of the 90-day clause towards the end of the year[15].

Following the proceedings came lavish praise from Mr Justice A G Jennett, Judge President of the Eastern Cape Division, a man widely respected in the area and one who was certainly no Nationalist. He wrote after the celebrations: "My Dear Minister and Mrs Vorster, You both so endeared yourselves to the people here that you will find it difficult to pass through this town without interruption. My wife will be one of those who will stop you. She talks all day of your friendliness and kindness. For myself and, on behalf of this court, I can only say that I cannot find words to convey my deep gratitude. You have created a feeling of stability in this area and many practitioners in East London and the country districts have lost no time in expressing their gratitude. If you believe that my THANK YOU conveys even one half of the gratitude we feel, I shall be happy ..."

And while Vorster was battling with subversion, he took some time off to update South Africa's ponderous and archaic liquor laws. In their own way, the laws he introduced were almost as controversial to the people directly affected as was his security legislation. Nevertheless, the Liquor industry's mouthpiece, Wine, Liquor and Malt, had this to say of him in its July, 1964 issue: "We

14. The Cape Times, 28/7/1964.
15. The Eastern Province Herald (Port Elizabeth), 30/7/1964.

feel this is an appropriate moment to place on record the satisfaction and the gratitude of the great majority of those connected with the liquor trade and industry for the patience, understanding, accessibility and courtesy shown by Mr Vorster at all times to them in connection with his non-party legislation ..."

Shortly after this, Paul Sauer, veteran Nationalist politician, long-time Cabinet Minister and a sort of political elder statesman in the Party, wrote to Vorster. Sauer was a man of wit and insight. He was respected, even revered, in the Party. And he was a man who generally spoke his mind: "Dear John, thank you very much for your letter of August 16, I really appreciate it. I have a very high opinion of you, especially in regard to your future. You have, as a result of your action against subversive elements gained a fairly substantial reputation. Remember though: a reputation is easy to gain. The difficult thing is to maintain it. Be careful about what you say and do not say too much. Sometimes I am inclined to feel that you say more than is necessary. This can later lead to reproaches that you cannot implement everything (that you have promised). This is dangerous. Always keep something up your sleeve. I know you will not hold this little bit of advice against me because I would not have given it to anybody even if it is applicable. I would only have given it to somebody in whose future I had faith ..." The letter was signed: Your friend, P O Sauer.

Vorster remembers the letter well. How did he take Sauer's advice? "I appreciated it. Paul would never give advice unless it was genuine. He and I were very close ... he was a kind of political father to me. So I appreciated that he had bothered to give me advice and I tried to apply what he had said ...".

On October 9, speaking at the opening of a police station in Colesberg, Vorster said that organised sabotage and terrorism in South Africa had come to an end – thanks to the well-timed measures enforced by his department[16]. And, to a large extent, Vorster was correct. Van den Bergh had tremendously increased the effectiveness of the Security Police and Vorster had provided them with the security legislation they needed. If the communists and other subversives were not going to play according to the rules, then the Vorster/Van den Bergh axis would change the rules to give their men an edge.

16. The Pretoria News, 10/10/1964.

Looking back on that period, Van den Bergh insists today that he and his men never arrested anybody without just cause. "I never ordered the arrest of anybody without a factual case. Despite the fact that the 90-day legislation gave any commissioned officer the right to arrest suspects, I set up a special council of senior officers at my headquarters. Every request for permission to arrest anybody had to be referred to the council who would then make a recommendation to me. Every arrest had to be motivated and it had to be based on factual information. This applied to all arrests, with the exception of what we referred to as emergency arrests, when there simply was not the time to refer the whole affair to the council. In these cases, my instruction was that the facts – and I mean the facts – had to be on my desk the morning after the arrest. I told my men that I did not care whether they had to work through the night. But the information had to be at my disposal the next morning. I kept a tight rein on my chaps and I am quite satisfied that nobody was arrested wrongfully. Nobody was arrested without a case that could have been taken to court – and we took the vast majority of the people arrested to court ..."

Van den Bergh also claims that he never assaulted a prisoner in his life and that he constantly urged his men to follow his example: "I have never hit a man in my life. I told my men that they demean themselves when they assault anybody. Apart from this, if you hit a man then you admit to him that he is your superior. There are many ways to get information from people, no matter how unwilling they are. For instance, one of the people we arrested for sabotage would not say a word. He insulted his interrogators and made it quite clear that it was beneath his dignity to answer their questions. He really was getting under the skin of my chief interrogator, who came to me one day and said that he knew that this man would force him to lose his temper. I told him to calm down and that we would do something different. So I ordered a head and shoulders photograph to be taken of one of the accomplices who was being held in another jail. I got the Commissioner of Police to sign a blank police appointment certificate, I pasted the photograph in the appropriate place and then filled in the necessary details so that it would appear that the other prisoner had been a police lieutenant for some time. Then I told my chief interrogator to place the certificate in an envelope and attach the envelope to the inside of the dossier cover he was using. I then instructed him to rub the sides of the envelope so that the edges became frayed. Then I told him to practise until, feigning anger, he could slam the dossier shut in such a way that the appointment certificate would fly out and land on the side of the desk on which the prisoner was sitting.

"After much practice he said he was ready and that he could do just what I had ordered. He did it perfectly one day and the detainee quickly picked up the document, looked at it and, as my man tried to grab it from him, said: "Good god ... the bloody bastard. He is the leader of the gang and all the time he is a police officer'. We gave him a typewriter and he sat at it for two days setting out his whole story. When he had finished, we got one of the policemen who had penetrated his cell and who had in fact stayed in this flat for two months, to get him to sign his statement and swear an oath. When he saw this man, he almost fell over with amazement and said: 'Good god ... are you one of them too?' That was the kind of thing one did. When a man would not speak, you either persuaded him by the force of your personality acting on his guilty conscience, or you tricked him ..."

During discussion of this period of Vorster's career, I questioned him at length on his role as Minister of Justice, on parallels between his own internment and the detention he and his men meted out to other people. The discussion went like this:

Q: Did you have any hard feelings about your own detention?
A: Not really. By the nature of things, one remembers the pleasant things and forgets the unpleasant things in one's life. When I look back on Koffiefontein, I tend to remember the cameraderie, the jokes, the things which we had in common. You do not feel bitterness, only when some of the holier than thou chaps start criticising you for what you have done.

Q: Did you come across any of the policemen involved in your detention after you became Minister of Justice?
A: Yes, ever so many of them.

Q: Did you ever discriminate against any of those who were involved on the other side during the war?
A: No, never ever. I do not think I ever discussed it with anyone in the police force. That is, except for one police officer against

whom I had a very serious grudge. I do not want to mention the incident or his name because he is still living today. However, my feelings about him were such that I never greeted him on the occasions – and there were many – that I came across him after I went into politics. But, shortly after becoming Minister of Justice, I called him into my office and said: "Look, I want to tell you that I never greeted you before I took this position. Now that I am Minister of Justice, I will still not greet you when I meet you in private. However, if I meet you in public or in connection with my duties as Minister, I will greet you, I will treat you just as I would treat any other officer and you will have no complaints whatsoever about my attitude to you". Then he wanted to apologise to me and I said: "Look, I did not call you in here to extract an apology from you, I've just called you in to tell you what the situation is". And for years I treated him as courteously as I would treat any other police officer in public – but in private I never greeted him.

Q: And did you ever discriminate against him?
A: Never.

Q: Having been detained and interned without trial, how did you feel about having to do it to other people?
A: If you have got to do it, do it, but don't apologise for doing it. In all my political career, you have never heard me apologising or trying to shy away from responsibility. But that is what Harry Lawrence[17] and those guys did. They would not take the responsibility for what they did and they always tried to find excuses, to shy away from it instead of telling me: "We believed we had to do it in the interests of the State, and we did do it. So what". Had they done that, I would have respected them for it. In other words, if they genuinely saw me as a threat to the State and, according to their lights, saw the need to lock me up, I would have respected them for it.

Q: Are you saying that if the Government of the day identifies a man as a threat to the State then it is its duty to lock that man up, even without the benefit of a trial?

17. Minister of Interior and later of Justice in the Smuts Government.

157

A: If I see a man or a woman as a threat to the State and if there are valid reasons for not bringing that person to trial, then I must take them out of circulation one way or another. That is my responsibility as Minister of Justice and if I cannot take that responsibility, I must leave my job. If I do not want to carry out my responsibilities, then I must take my hat and go. But if I do accept the full responsibilities of the job, then I must do what I have to do without apologising.

Q: But what if you made a mistake?
A: Yes, unless I made a mistake. However, to this day I do not know that I made a mistake. I always made pretty sure before we acted against anybody. Right from the word go, I told my chaps that I did not want them to treat people they were holding as we were treated ourselves. Whenever it happened that people were not treated properly – and it did happen in a few cases – I never hesitated to take action.

Q: And presumably it happened in cases you were not aware of?
A: Yes, it may be so. But I would say that there was very little of this because I made it my business to know how people were being treated. I visited them in jail and in the police cells which Harry Lawrence never ever did. I visited the young students who were locked up. I visited them in Kroonstad and I even visited them in the Pretoria local jail. And I can tell you a good story about one of the chaps locked up in the Pretoria local. There was this attorney on the East Rand called Louis Baker[18]. He was a communist and I argued communism with him many a time when I still practised at the Bar. When I was appointed Minister of Justice, my old pals on the Side-Bar on the East Rand gave me a party and Louis came to that party. He was a likeable scoundrel and, during the party, I took him to one side and I said to him: "Louis, let me give you a tip ... take your wife and your kids and clear out of the country as quickly as you can. I know you can afford it because communism has made you rich ... you have defended so many communists at very good fees that you have become a rich man'. He asked me

18. Baker was sentenced to five years imprisonment during 1965 of having acted with the purpose of replacing the then South African dispensation with a dictatorship of the working classes.

158

why and I told him that, one of these days, my chaps were going to lock him up. So he said: "Do you think your pampoens[19] will ever catch me?" And I replied: "OK Louis, let's leave it at that". It was not long before my pampoens caught up with him and he was convicted in the Fischer case. One day I went to the Pretoria local jail for an interview with some of the students who were being imprisoned there. After speaking to them, I asked the officer in charge to bring Louis Baker to me so that I could speak to him privately. It was just an impulse on my part. So in came Louis Baker in his prison suit and he went as white as a sheet when he saw me. So I said: "Take a seat Louis" and he said: "John, did you come to see me?" I said: "Sure, Louis, close the door and sit down". I took out my cigarettes and offered him one. He asked me whether he could take two. I told him: "Man, Louis, take the whole box, they will never suspect that the Minister of Justice smuggled cigarettes into the prison . . . take the whole box". It was illegal for prisoners to have cigarettes and he was a bit nervous. He asked me what he should do with the cigarettes and I said to him: "Put the cigarettes down the front of your shirt. Nobody will be any the wiser because nobody will think that the Minister of Justice would give you a packet of cigarettes". So I gave him the cigarettes and he sighed and said: "To think that you warned me". I asked him whether he remembered the reply he had given me when I warned him and he said: "Yes, I remember. What a bloody fool I was!" Then he said that he just could not take it in prison and he asked me for remission of sentence, just for old times' sake. I asked him what the court had given him and he said he had been sentenced to five years. I told him that he would serve every day of those five years because I did not believe in remission of sentence for his kind of person. So we sat talking for a while and he told me how he longed to see his children. I told him that I knew how fond he was of his children but that prison regulations prevented children of under 16 coming to see people in jail. But I said that I would arrange for his children to see him on the following Saturday . . . and this was done. Before I left him, Louis asked me whether I would come and see him again. I said that I would if I ever got the chance . . . but I did not get the chance and Louis was released and he left the country".

19. Literally: pumpkins. An Afrikaans expression meaning, roughly, idiots.

Q: Back to detention without trial. You felt that if it was in the interests of the country, you would do it?
A: I never worried about it.

Q: Why did you ask Parliament for so much power in this regard?
A: I identified the threat and I took measures accordingly. Look, there was a communist plot to overthrow the Government and take South Africa by revolution and it was my job to stop it. It was my job to break the subversive machine in South Africa and, if the police did not have the powers they needed to do the job, then it was my duty to give them those powers. I promised them that I would not send them into the fight against communism empty-handed and I like to think that I kept that promise.

Q: You came in for considerable criticism at the time for taking excessive powers and for abusing those powers. In retrospect, would you have done anything differently?
A: No.

Q: Was this not the same way that you were handled, by people abusing excessive powers?
A: Except that I gave strict instructions that people were not to be treated as I and my comrades were treated. And I gave the police strict orders never to ill-treat women. Also I told them: Heaven help anybody who ill-treats a child.

Q: Were there any cases of ill-treatment brought to your notice?
A: Not that I can remember. But I do know that I acted quickly and firmly whenever any policeman misused the powers which I had obtained from Parliament. But this happened in only a very small proportion of the cases. It was unfortunate, but when you are dealing with revolution, it is unavoidable that a few heads will get broken. It is unfortunate, but you cannot avoid it. It was the price that had to be paid for preventing the revolution and for preventing the killing of thousands of people. It was a small price to pay, I think.

Q: What about the policemen who did exceed their powers, who did abuse their powers?
A: You get black sheep in all organisations, but there were very few of them in the South African Police Force. These chaps did a

26. *1970, photographed with Dr Hastings Banda, the Malawi President, at Libertas, in Pretoria.*

27. *Vorster and the Portuguese Prime Minister, Dr Marcello Caetano, on their way to a formal banquet in Lisbon in 1970.*

magnificent job. They worked day and night, they went without food and they went without sleep in order to defeat the communists. If it was not for them, we would not be sitting talking here today.

Q: But some people were assaulted?
A: Yes, because detainees can be obstreperous, I know that only too well.

Q: You mean you were like that when you were detained and interned?
A: Yes, chaps can be very obstreperous under these circumstances and policemen come to the end of their patience. They have a job to do and they are expected to bring results. They know that the future of the country depends on them ... they are not acting out of personal feelings of hatred or prejudice.

Q: What about the detainees who died in the cells, those who committed suicide?
A: This happened in a minute proportion of cases. Look, people do commit suicide in police cells and prisons the world over. But, while I was Minister of Justice, each and every case was investigated minutely and I went through the dossiers myself with a fine tooth comb.

Q: But was there not an inherent danger of a cover-up if you got the police to investigate their colleagues instead of allowing a judicial commission of inquiry into detention which was so often asked for by the Opposition in Parliament?
A: Naturally there are dangers. But I tell you this – and I have had a great deal of experience in this regard – that if you tell a policeman to investigate a crime of commission or omission on the part of another policeman, he will do it very thoroughly. I have not come across a single case where one policeman tried to cover up for another or tried to whitewash another. And everything I say in this regard applies to the prison service as well.

Q: Is it not that as Minister of Justice you had too strong a loyalty to these people?
A: Yes, I did have a very strong loyalty to them. But this loyalty was based on the merits of the people I had to work with and I

161

never glossed over their mistakes. Not once. And I regularly visited the prisons to inspect conditions. Whenever I passed through a town and I had the time, I would pay an impromptu visit to either the prison or the police cells, sometimes both.

Q: In a number of cases, there appeared to be prima facie evidence of the need for a full inquiry into either the prison service or the police treatment of detainees. Why did you consistently and vigorously refuse such an inquiry?
A: Because an inquiry was not justified. It would have been used as an opportunity to blacken the name of the police force and the prison service – unjustifiably. I just felt that the two services could deal with their own black sheep ... and they did deal with them. Because of this I did not feel that the whole prison service or the whole police force should be penalised for the activities of a few black sheep. To this day I do not know of a single policeman or prison officer who has neglected his duty when it came to investigating a colleague. They dealt very effectively with their own black sheep and no judicial inquiry was necessary.

Q: But would an inquiry not have cleared the reputation of the prison service or the police force if there was nothing to hide?
A: No, just the opposite would have happened. Our enemies had made it part of their deliberate policy to try to blacken the reputations of the police and prison services. The whole thing would have developed into a massive propaganda effort on their part which would have done a great deal of unnecessary harm.

And, with this as the basis for his thinking, Vorster stood by his men. But not all of them knew him sufficiently well to identify him when the occasion demanded. He remembers: "I was driving with my wife through the Eastern Cape when we came to Lady Frere. It is a small village as you know. It was tea-time and there appeared to be no café so I said to my wife: 'Let us go to the police station, say hullo to the sergeant and get a cup of tea out of him'. So she remained in the car and I went in and there was this big sergeant reading his newspaper, with his feet on the desk. I said good morning and he said: 'Good morning, what can I do for you?' I replied: 'Can you give me a cup of tea?' and he retorted quickly: 'What makes you think that I will give you a cup of tea ... do you think this is a café?' I tried to hide my amusement as I said, 'No, I

162

don't think this is a café but I do think that you might want to give the Minister of Justice a cup of tea'. The poor chap suddenly recognised me and said: 'Oh heavens!' I told him, 'Forget it … just make the tea'. He was so pleased to get out of the office and you never saw a fellow serve tea so quickly or eagerly".

On October 21, 1964, Verwoerd sent Vorster a hand-written letter enclosing a cutting from the Rand Daily Mail of the same day. Under the headline: SA seduced into political thuggery, the RDM quoted Mrs Jean Sinclair, National President of the Black Sash[20] who had told the organisation's annual conference in Pietermaritzburg the previous night that, in its 16 years of rule, the Nationalist Government had managed to prostitute the morality of an entire people and to seduce honest people into political thuggery. "The moral debasement of our people has been accomplished with such base cunning, with such calculated management of group psychology and the inherent weaknesses and fears of the human voice in society, that hardly a voice is now raised in protest. Each new infringement of our rights has met with less and less positive response until today it has become the silence of acquiesence …."

Verwoerd was furious and wrote to Vorster: "The enclosed cutting from the Mail contains, as I see it, blatant and extreme libel of a group of <u>identifiable people</u> (Verwoerd's underlining), that is, the members of the Cabinet. If this is right, then I think that Mrs Sinclair, as leader of the Black Sash, should not get away with it. She was the spokesman. Perhaps the RDM, as publisher, is also liable. If a member of the Cabinet should prosecute, I think the most suitable is the Minister of Justice because, later in the report, information is given about his department, so that, of the unnamed members of the Government, most of the light falls on him. I have underlined what appears to be libellous. Would you please get the legal advisers to go into this. If, due to the status of the people involved, high damages are awarded, it could break the Black Sash, because, after action by one (minister), all the others could start actions. It does not appear to me as just another political attack, or something that the courts would regard as a

20. An organisation of women formed to protest against the Government's abrogation of the rule of law. It later broadened its activities to include protest against the Government's racial policies and help and advice for people caught up in the web of the Government's legislation – especially the influx control legislation affecting Black people.

blow to be expected and accepted in the profession of politics, as part of the risk of vigorous battle. As far as I am concerned, this is a drastic libel without mitigating circumstances against a group of decent people of status."

The issue was a highly important one. If the Government had taken action and if it had won its case, it would have been able to cripple highly critical organisations like the Black Sash – and this might have been Verwoerd's intention. Cabinet Ministers would have slapped one libel action after another on their severest critics until criticism would have been watered down to the point of irrelevancy. Fortunately for the Government's critics, Vorster did not share Verwoerd's view. "I believed Verwoerd's reading of the law was correct, but I advised him and the cabinet against taking action because I felt that it was all in the day's game and that we ought to accept this kind of criticism without running to the courts. I believed then and I still believe today that if you enter the political arena you must not be able only to dish it out, but that you should be able to take it as well ..."

About this time, Mr Justice Irving Steyn wrote to Vorster thanking him for sentiments expressed when the judge's father, a former Member of the Provincial Council for Standerton, died. The judge wrote that his father had always had the highest regard for the Minister of Justice and that a few months before his death he had said: "I knew almost all of our Prime Ministers well – General Botha, General Hertzog, General Smuts, Dr Malan. Hans Strijdom and Dr Verwoerd. I think that General Hertzog, Dr Malan and Dr Verwoerd can be regarded as the founders of our nation. We are exceptionally fortunate that in the difficult times of the recent past that we have had a man like Dr Verwoerd at the helm. But this I want to say to you: If and when Dr Verwoerd should fall away, there is, fortunately for us, somebody who can take over immediately, somebody who might even prove the greatest of them all and that man is John Vorster". The judge wrote that he had quoted the words of his father as accurately as he could remember them, but what had made the deepest impression on him was the "almost prophetic" manner in which they had been delivered.

Prophetic indeed. Especially when it was considered that Verwoerd was at the peak of his career. He was Afrikanerdom's unblemished hero, the man who had given them the republic, the intellectual leader to whom all things seemed possible. The vast majority of Verwoerd's followers simply could not bring themselves to think of a time when he would not be there. And certainly there must have been very few Nationalists indeed who not only thought of a successor to Verwoerd, but who contemplated the treasonable idea that history might label his successor a greater man. The letter is pasted into the Vorster Press cutting scrapbooks, but Vorster could not recall it. When I read it out to him, his reaction: "Well, I'm damned. That was very complimentary of old Mr Steyn".

On November 30, 1964, Vorster announced that the 90-day clause of the General Law Amendment Act would be suspended on January 11, 1965. This announcement was generally welcomed, but the Opposition felt that it should be removed from the statute book completely. The Opposition's attitude was summed up by the Rand Daily Mail in a leader on December 1: "Mr Vorster's announcement indicates, we hope, that South Africa is nearing the end of a dark passage in her history. But the country still has no guarantee that the 90-day clause is done with. The Minister has often said that he can re-introduce it almost at a moment's notice at any time when he thinks it is advisable. There will be no relief from this threat until this pernicious provision is off the statute book. Only then will South Africa be able to talk about the rule of law and look the civilised world in the face again".

The newspapers reported on January 10 that the 90-day clause would be suspended, that 47 people still in detention would be charged the next day and that the remaining 26 would be freed. In Parliament on January 28 Vorster revealed that a total of 1095 people had been detained under the provisions of the 90-day clause during the 18 months in which it had been in operation. Altogether, 575 detainees had been charged with specific offences. Of these, 272 had been convicted, 210 had been discharged and 93 were still on trial or awaiting trial. A total of 241 detainees had given evidence for the State in criminal proceedings. Vorster also conceded that 26 people had been held under the 90-day clause for offences not connected with either sabotage or subversion – including robbery and murder, armed robbery and housebreaking and theft[21]. During the year, a total of 671 people were tried

21. The Daily News, 29/1/1965.

for contravening security laws. Of this number, five received death sentences, nine life sentences and eight sentences of 20 years imprisonment for sabotage. The vast majority of the convictions were for people who belonged to or who furthered the aims of a banned organisation – 285 received up to five years and 19 received prison senteces of between five and seven years[22].

Meanwhile, Abraham Fischer's rope had tightened. He was detained on July 9, 1964 under the 90-day clause, but he was released after three days. He was re-arrested on September 23, 1964 and charged with furthering the aims of the Communist Party. The charge-sheet alleged that Fischer and his co-accused aimed at establishing a "despotic system of government based on the dictatorship of the proletariat" in South Africa. Fischer was accused number one. However, he had just been granted a temporary passport to enable him to appear before the Privy Council in London in a case involving patent rights. Because of this, he was granted bail of R10 000. He won his case and returned to stand trial. Among the witnesses was Gerard Ludi, a secret police agent who had infiltrated the Communist Party. On January 25 counsel for Fischer, who was still out on his bail of R10 000, announced in court that he had found a letter on his desk from Fischer saying that the case's number one accused was absenting himself from the remainder of the trial; that he was going into hiding in South Africa in order to fight the policy of apartheid for as long as he could. Bail was estreated and the trial of the other accused continued. Fischer was recaptured on November 11. In May, 1966 he was found guilty of nine main charges under the Suppression of Communism Act and he was sentenced to life imprisonment. The judge commented that it was common cause that Fischer was chairman of the Communist Party in South Africa and that his activities constituted a very serious threat to the safety of the State. Fischer became seriously ill in prison early in 1975. After treatment in the H F Verwoerd hospital in Pretoria for cancer, he was eventually allowed to go to the home of his brother in Bloemfontein, where he died on May 8.

Vorster remembers Fischer and everything about him well, but, even now, declines to discuss exactly how he and his security men

22. The Survey of Race Relations, published by the South African Institute of Race relations, 1964, pages 84 and 85.

finally trapped Fischer and broke the Communist Party of South Africa. But he would say this: "Look, we knew that Fischer was our main target, that if you wanted to break communism in South Africa, you had to get Braam Fischer. But we bided our time until we had sufficient evidence on the party as a whole before we charged Fischer. When he was arrested for the first time, we deliberately released him so that he would think that we were bluffing, that we did not have sufficient evidence against him. Actually, we had all the evidence we needed, but we wanted to give ourselves some more time and lull the communists into a false sense of security. We appointed Gerard Ludi and gave him the job of getting into Fischer's cell and, in effect, getting the goods on Fischer. This he did very effectively. I read his reports over the years with tremendous interest. It was like reading a novel in instalments. I remember well one of the reports in which Ludi told of a lecture Fischer gave his cell on how to recognise a policeman. There was the policeman's haircut which he could never get away from, there was the way in which they polished their boots and the way in which they carried themselves. He said that a policeman could be spotted a mile away. Well, Ludi had posed very effectively as a ducktail, with all the accessories. And he sat there listening to Fischer tell them how to recognise a policeman. When it came to the trial and the time to call Ludi as a witness, Braam turned on one of his co-accused and said: 'Another one of those damned traitors'. He said this because, just before this, one of his followers, Piet Beyleveld had turned State's evidence. When the prosecutor asked Ludi what his occupation was, he said that he was a reporter on the Rand Daily Mail. Then the prosecutor asked him what his real occupation was and, of course, Braam was all eyes and ears. When Ludi said that he was a detective warrant officer in the South African Police, Fischer got such a fright that he dropped his note-book onto the floor ... he must have been thinking on how to recognise a policeman ...".

While Vorster was Minister of Justice, Fischer sent him several messages asking for permission for him to have newspapers: "He asked me would I please let him have newspapers because he had to keep up with the news of the world for the time when he took over in South Africa. He believed right to the very end that he would one day rule this country. I replied to him he would do better to read his Bible and worry about his soul because we would do all the taking-over that had to be done ... later on, when he was so ill, I made regular inquiries about him, but I did not interfere in my Minister of Justice's decision not to allow him to leave prison until very close to the end. I never interfere with these decisions".

To many people it seemed that Vorster was at the peak of his career. A columnist in the anti-government Sunday Chronicle[23] wrote of Vorster on March 28, 1965: "Mr Vorster is very popular with the police force and some officers describe him as the 'best Minister of Justice we have ever had'. Legal men who have met with him say that they have changed their opinion about him. They found him 'courteous and fair-minded'. He is known as a hard worker and has a thorough knowledge of his portfolio and of the problems of his officials. He is also one of the best public speakers in the Cabinet and gets more invitations to address Nationalist Party meetings than anyone else. The reason for this is easy to establish. Mr Vorster talks the way Afrikaners like Afrikaners to talk. He whips up their emotions if it is necessary and finds enough time to tell a few jokes to ridicule his opponents ... Mr Vorster rarely smiles, but his deadpan face makes the jokes even funnier ...".

Meanwhile, Vorster had been busy in Parliament with yet another controversial bill – the Official Secrets Amendment Bill in terms of which the Official Secrets Act would be widened to include police matters as well as military matters. The controversy had barely died down when Vorster introduced two new measures during the last days of the 1965 parliamentary session. And he had a surprise for everybody who thought he had exhausted his legislative shocks. The first measure – the Criminal Procedure Amendment Bill – gave the Attorneys-General the power to order the arrest of up to six months of any witness likely to give material evidence for the State in any criminal proceedings, if he was of the opinion that there was a danger that the witness might be intimidated or tampered with; that the witness might abscond; or that detention was in the best interests of either the witness or the administration of justice. The so-called "180-days Act".

Bill number two sought to amend the Suppression of Communism Act by giving the Minister of Justice the power to prohibit

23. Published in Johannesburg jointly by the Argus Printing and Publishing Company, and South African Associated Newspapers.

publication, should he deem this necessary, of any statement by any person (in South Africa or elsewhere) who advocated, defended or encouraged the achievement of any of the objects of communism. Afrikaans newspapers welcomed the legislation as a "mighty weapon against communism" while the Rand Daily Mail commented on June 7: "Mr Vorster's lust for power seems insatiable". The controversy was bitter and loud and so was the fight in Parliament. But Vorster stuck to his two new big guns and they became law in due course.

The New York Herald Tribune's highly respected Arnold Beichmann, provided a foreign view of Vorster. After a two-hour interview with the South African Minister of Justice, Beichmann wrote: "A large man, nearing his fiftieth birthday. Mr Vorster exudes power like some men exude money. He speaks quietly and sometimes inaudibly as he jiggles his horn-rimmed glasses across his lips. His words are accented with his native Afrikaans. He is a man who gives the impression that he is in full control and nothing can swing him from his course ..."[24].

By September 22 Vorster was at the Bloemfontein congress of the Orange Free State National Party where farmer delegates demanded full discussion of the law of assault as it affected farmers and their Black labourers. A congress resolution called for discussion because the position had become "untenable". One delegate said that farm labourers provoked farmers and then "when you give him a little slap, he runs off to the police and lays a charge". If the delegates expected sympathy from tough man Vorster, they were completely wrong. "The resolution is not entirely clear. I think the speaker was afraid to say what he meant, but I will say it. I issue many licences but one licence I cannot issue and that is for one man to assault another. I cannot do what the resolution asks me by implication to do. One general principle we must always maintain in all circumstances: nobody has the right to assault anybody else. Congress has my assurance that, if such assaults take place, I and the police will act accordingly[25]".

Living up to the promise he had made earlier – that he would seriously consider representations from parents whose children had been misled into subversive activities and subsequently

24. New York Herald Tribune, 1/8/1965.
25. The Cape Argus, 23/9/1965.

sentenced by the courts – Vorster confirmed on September 22 that Anthony Trew would shortly be released. Trew had been sentenced to four years imprisonment on November 11, 1964 for contravening the Suppression of Communism Act by furthering the aims of a banned organisation. Two years had been suspended and the jail sentence was due to end during November, 1966. Trew's father, General Secretary of the Automobile Association of South Africa, was granted an interview with Vorster in February and said afterwards that he was "deeply impressed with Mr Vorster's concern for my son and other misguided young men who had landed themselves in prison". Later Mr and Mrs Trew were to send the Vorsters a Christmas card, with a hand-written message: "It is particularly at this time that we remember how you assured happiness for our family. It is something we will never forget; even less will we forget the friendliness and courtesy you personally showed us".

Trew was released and flew to Oxford University on October 7 to resume his studies. Five days later, Mr R de Keller, father of David Guy "Spike" de Keller, wrote to Vorster: "I would like to convey to you, however inadequately, my very deep appreciation of your recent kindness to my son and myself. I feel honoured that you chose to impart your decision to me personally and both this and the merciful remission you have promised reveal the depth of your understanding as a father and your compassion as a Minister. My son is honoured that you spent so long with him and I believe his respect for you to be very real. He said it was a privilege to talk to you and I am sure he will have benefited from the experience. May I be forgiven if I pass on to you my son's final observation: 'He is as straight as a die, Dad'. I would like, on behalf of my son, to accept your offer to transfer him to Kroonstad, but would prefer the transfer be postponed until he has written his exam because I fear a move before then may be disruptive of his studies". In November, 1964, De Keller was sentenced to ten years imprisonment for sabotage. He was released in 1966. On December 3, 1965 Stephanie Kemp, a 23-year-old former part-time student at the University of Cape Town was freed a year before she had completed her sentence for contravening the Suppression of Communism Act by belonging to the banned National Committe for Liberation. One of the accused with Trew, her release also followed representations from her parents to Vorster.

Why did he do this? "I did not want kids rotting in prison, well knowing that it was grown-ups who used them for their own purposes. Ag, they were babes in the wood, Trew, De Keller Stephanie Kemp. They all played the game after their release, the only one who did not was Stephanie Kemp who later attacked me ... but that is life".

Vorster celebrated his 50th birthday on December 13. Good wishes came from all over the country, from the State President and Mrs Swart and from Dr and Mrs Verwoerd – and from the sport and entertainment committee at the Pretoria Central jail. Writing on behalf of the prisoners, the committee asked Vorster to accept a gift of a chess set and a chess board (the chess board remains in Vorster's parliamentary office, where he regularly plays with members of the parliamentary chess club). The prisoners wrote: "It is the firm conviction of the majority of us that, in both your personal capacity and your official capacity, you are working hard to form us South Africans into a lively, proud nation and that you provide our proud nation with its propelling force".

The 1966 parliamentary session, because of the coming General Election, was short and relatively uncontroversial. Vorster plunged into the election campaign with all his might, addressing meetings in the four corners of South Africa. The election was the expected triumph for the National Party. For 1966 the number of seats in the House of Assembly had been increased from 156 to 166. The Nationalists won 126, increasing their holding by 20 seats – leaving the United Party reduced from 49 to 39 members and the Progressive Party represented by Mrs Helen Suzman. A feeble challenge from the far right was all but eliminated, the Conservative National Party gaining only 936 votes and the Republican Party only 8 212. By contrast the Nationalists won 776 766 (or 58,6 per cent) of the votes cast in the election's contested seats, the UP received 490 941 (or 37,1 per cent) and the Progressive Party 41 065 (or 3,1 per cent). In a sense, the Nationalists' share of Parliament was out of all proportion to their share of the total vote. This is largely due to South Africa's constituency system aggravated by the fact that the law allows the delimitation commission to "load" urban constituencies by up to 15 per cent and to "unload" rural constituencies by the same amount. This means an urban vote is inevitably less valuable than a rural vote – and every one of the real rural seats went to the Nationalists. On a strictly proportional basis, the Nationalists would have held something like 97 seats, the UP 62 and the Progressive Party five.

The Nationalists were jubilant. Many thousands of English-speakers had voted for them – despite bitter controversies over the rule of law and the Opposition's repeated election claims of dictatorship, totalitarianism and the coming of a police state. In fact there is evidence to suggest that a large number of English-speakers had actually been highly impressed by Vorster's strong stand against subversion. Vorster was very pleased with the election result because he felt that it had completely vindicated his actions on subversion and sabotage – not to mention the fact that he was R15 richer. While Party workers in Nigel were going about the serious business of getting the faithful to the polls, a bit of fun was injected into the Nationalist operation with a competition in which people were asked to estimate Vorster's election majority (there was simply no chance that he would lose the election). Vorster took four tickets, one for himself and one for each of his three children. For himself, he estimated the majority would be 4 120 and for his children he estimated 4 000, 4 050 and 4 100 respectively. The majority in Nigel was exactly 4 120 and Vorster scooped the pool.

Apart from being the year of the General Election, 1966 marked the fifth anniversary of the coming of the republic. While there was speculation that 10 000 prisoners might receive remissions of sentence as part of the festivities, Vorster once again stepped deep into controversy. On May 11 his policemen served three banning orders on Ian Robertson, President of The National Union of South African Students (NUSAS), three weeks before Senator Robert Kennedy, of the United States, was due to arrive in South Africa as a guest of NUSAS. This action provoked an almost unprecedented outcry from the Opposition, while it generated noises of approval from Nationalist newspapers and from the Afrikaanse Studentebond (ASB)[26]. There were repeated and heated demands for the Government to prove its case in a court of law. And headlines flashed through the Opposition newspaper presses: Nation-wide Outcry, Country-wide Reactions of Shock, Scandalous says Helen Suzman, Move Against NUSAS May Bring

26. Literally: the league of Afrikaans students.

Direct Conflict With The State, Nation-wide Protest Storm, Ban is Part of Smear Campaign, 6 000 March in Protest, Student Ban "Brutal Act of Oppression", Challenge to Vorster Mounts, Student Leaders Seek Urgent Meeing with Vorster, NUSAS Plans Torch Vigil in Cape.

Vorster agreed to see a delegation of NUSAS leaders but, when he met them, he remained unmoved. He told them that Robertson had been banned in his personal capacity and not as the President of NUSAS and he refused to have Robertson charged. "Charge or Release" signs appeared throughout the country.

The next day more than 1 500 students at the University of the Witwatersrand cheered and jeered when one of the members of the deputation, Margaret Marshall, said that Vorster had told them that he was not a fascist in any sense[27]. On his arrival in Cape Town that afternoon, John Daniel, Vice-President of NUSAS, said Vorster had been "cordial but tough". In an interview with the Sunday Times on May 28, Marshall said Vorster had told them to disband NUSAS and to form a new student organisation which conformed to the South African way of life and which was all White. "This has confirmed our fears that further action is to be taken against NUSAS or its office-bearers ... the interview with the Minister made it quite clear to us that if any action is taken it will not be because we have acted illegally but because our views are opposed to his. He persisted in equating opposition to apartheid with opposition to South Africa. He told us repeatedly that we were unpatriotic and un-South African. He warned us once again to put our house in order yet he conceded that we had always acted within the law ...".

This then was Vorster's first direct confrontation with NUSAS. However, NUSAS had been under verbal attack for some time. On August 31, 1963, for instance, Vorster spoke at a Nasionale Jeugbond[28] congress and hinted of possible action against NUSAS. He said that progressive-liberalist ideas were taking root in certain universities amongst people whose parents where United Party followers. "I want to warn those parents, and I have every reason for saying this, so far as it concerns their children at

27. Rand Daily Mail, 27/5/1966.
28. Literally: The National Youth League. This was the National Party's youth wing. It replaced the old Junior National Party to which Vorster belonged.

certain universities, that they should ask what is going on with NUSAS and where it is leading the youth. It is high time this warning was given in the light of certain developments which will probably be revealed in the course of this year[29]". Two weeks later he was more specific, referring to NUSAS as a "cancer in the life of South Africa which must be cut out". Addressing about 300 Nationalists in Potchefstroom, he claimed that NUSAS had become the mouthpiece of the liberals and that it had also become tinged with communism. He could not say that every member of NUSAS was a communist, but he could say that every university communist was a member of NUSAS. An organisation in which communists had found a haven would have to be dealt with by South Africa – "I will reckon with NUSAS in my own time"[30].

NUSAS and Vorster were to remain bitter enemies for years. NUSAS remained one of the strongest critics of Government action and policies in South Africa. Each side attacked the other vigorously. And, when he thought it necessary, Vorster used some of his awesome powers against specific NUSAS leaders.

Not unpredictably, the Robertson banning was one of the major issues of the second, 1966 parliamentary session. It was raised vigorously by the Opposition who demanded the repeal of the ban. Vorster was told to charge or release Robertson. As in the past, the controversy raged but Vorster refused to budge a single inch. As far as he was concerned, Robertson was a threat to national security – and that was that.

If coming events cast their shadows before them, then two such shadows appeared within a few weeks of each other. On August 26 a tense, sombre Vorster told the House of Assembly that a group of terrorists had crossed into South West Africa. Two had been shot dead by the police and a number had been wounded, including eight men arrested by the police. A quantity of arms, including two machine-guns similar to those used by terrorists in Rhodesia had been captured. Vorster said he wanted to make it clear that SWA was dealing with an advance guard and that more such groups would try to cross the border in the future – "I say this because I want to be realistic and not because I want to create panic ..."[31].

29. The Sunday Tribune, 1/9/1963.
30. The Sunday Times, 19/9/1963.
31. The Cape Argus, 26/8/1966.

Exactly a week later, Chief Leabua Jonathan, Prime Minister of Lesotho, made a historic visit to South Africa, the first Black Head of Government to visit South Africa officially. After three-and-a-half hours of confidential discussion, Jonathan and Verwoerd issued a joint statement pledging mutual friendship and non-intervention in their respective countries' internal affairs. John Vorster was a interested observer – still unaware of the fact that he was witnessing elements of his own destiny.

On Monday, September 5, newspapers speculated about the major speech which Dr Verwoerd would make when he spoke during the course of the debate on the Prime Minister's vote. It was expected that Verwoerd would pay particular attention to South Africa's relations with its Black neighbours. It was also expected that he would deal with the issue of terrorism which had added a new and potentially dangerous dimension to the South African security battle.

The next morning, September 6, Vorster went to the offices of the Western Province Blood Transfusion Service where he donated his first pint of blood. He was doing this on the advice of a doctor who told him that he might be one of the few people whose low blood pressure could be relieved by regular donations of blood. Vorster was happy to try because low blood pressure was perhaps the only thing which even mildly blighted his life then. He recalled later: "Those years as Minister of Justice were my most turbulent in politics, but they were also the happiest years of my political career. I knew my job, I had the feeling that I was on top of my job. I got on well with the departments. I got on well with the judges, I got on well with the lawyers. The Secretary of Justice, the Commissioner of Prisons and the Commissioner of Police were all men who knew their jobs backwards and we worked very well together. General Keevy, the Commissioner of Police was the best policeman I have ever worked with, never flustered, always the same, nothing could put him off balance, always level-headed and he gave you the facts straight from the shoulder, whether you liked them or not. Hendrik van den Bergh was head of security. He is a go-getter and while there may have been plenty of criticism of him, he certainly delivered the goods at a critical point in South Africa's history. He had a good, cool head and this country owes him a great debt of gratitude. We all worked very well together as a team and the only bother in my life was my low blood pressure.

That is why I went to donate blood on September 6, hoping that this would be the end of my trouble".

In fact, it was the end of Vorster's trouble with low blood pressure. In possibly the greatest coincidence in South Africa's political history, the only possible physical handicap to Vorster becoming Prime Minister was eliminated as a mentally deranged parliamentary messenger prepared to kill Verwoerd – the man many Nationalists believed would rule for another generation.

Vorster may not have realised it on September 6 as he smiled for the photographers in the blood transfusion service offices, but destiny had finally caught up with him.

10 *Prime Minister*

South Africa's House of Assembly has seen much drama over the years. But nothing like the drama which played itself out on the afternoon of September 6, 1966 and which may just have changed the destiny of the entire country.

The House generally starts its daily sittings at 2,15 p.m. For a few minutes before the Speaker's procession enters the chamber, the division bells ring to summon members to their green leather benches. And during these few minutes parliamentary messengers are allowed into the chamber. However, once Mr Speaker enters the door, only members, officials and a few specially selected messengers are allowed in. Mr Speaker's throne is flanked by two special bays (each with its own entrance), one providing accommodation for Ministers' private secretaries and the other for senior government officials concerned with whatever debate might be in progress.

Generally the public galleries contain only a sprinkling of "outsiders", with most of the spectators made up of newspapermen, members' wives and a few diplomats. However, on September 6 the public galleries were packed because the debate on the Prime Minister's vote was in progress and Verwoerd was due to reply to his Opposition critics. This was due to be one of the highlights of the session. So, as the division bells rang on that fateful afternoon, the public galleries were packed. Most Cabinet Ministers' wives were already in position on their special benches, the seats reserved for the wives of members were full. The diplomatic bays were full, as were the special bays reserved for guests of the Prime Minister and the Speaker. The Order Paper for the day started with question time and many ministers were already in their seats, examining the answers to their questions for the last time. Verwoerd was sitting at his desk about to go through the papers on which his speech would be based. There was a definite air of tension, but this was only because everybody was waiting for an important speech, a speech which many observers believed would deal in detail with contacts with Black African neighbours and the new threat of terrorism on South Africa's borders.

Vorster was at his bench, one he shared with P W Botha, the Minister of Defence. The first question on the Order Paper was for the Minister of Justice and so Vorster reached for his glasses to take a last look at the typed answer before the Speaker entered. When he felt that his spectacles were not there, he asked Botha to lend him his glasses in the hope that they would be suitable. A little distance away, Frank Waring, Minister of Tourism, Sport and Recreation and of Forestry, was also looking down at the answer to a question. "I was practising the Afrikaans answer because the smart Alecks on the Opposition side always put the question to me in Afrikaans and then they would giggle loudly if I mispronounced a word . . ."

Mr Johann Theron, one of the House of Assembly Hansard writers was watching the floor, with members moving towards their benches, passing the odd comment on the way. He saw Dr Verwoerd come in, talking to the National Party's Chief Whip, Mr Koos Potgieter. Verwoerd sat down, and Potgieter took his seat immediately behind the Prime Minister. As Verwoerd sat down a man in parliamentary messenger's uniform entered the House from the lobby and moved to Verwoerd's bench. Then Johann Theron's eyes opened in shocked disbelief. "I could not make out what the man was up to, but he bent over Dr Verwoerd and raised his right hand high in the air, grasping a sheath knife. With his left hand he plucked off the sheath and he plunged the knife downwards. Dr Verwoerd fell back in his seat and remained sitting upright for a moment or two before slumping forward over the bench. Dr E F Fisher (United Party MP for Rosettenville and a medical practitioner) was first to reach Dr Verwoerd to render first aid. Then two men took over, trying to render mouth-to-mouth respiration . . ."[1].

Struggling with Botha's glasses, Vorster did not notice the messenger approaching Verwoerd. But, seated as he was almost directly behind the Prime Minister, he heard a scuffle and looked up. His eyes, too, opened in shock. "At first all that registered with

1. The Cape Argus, 6/9/1966.

me was the fact that Eben Dönges seemd to be involved in something. My first thought was that he had had a heart attack. Then I saw Dr Verwoerd slumped at his desk, with blood flowing from him. Only then did I realise that something had happened to him. Then I saw that Eben Dönges and Frank Waring were struggling with a man and I saw Aubrey Radford (M.P. for Durban Central) coming over from the Opposition benches. Things were not registering very well, but I can remember Willie Venter (National Party M P for Kimberley South) either stamping on the man or kicking him ... then it was all over. I remember, the bells were still ringing when it happened and all the members were not yet in the House".

Frank Waring, too, heard a scuffle. He looked up. "I saw this messenger with a dagger in his hand and Eben Dönges was on his back, struggling with him, but Dönges was not a strong man and did not have much effect. Then I realised that the man was stabbing Dr Verwoerd and I jumped up from my seat and rushed over. I grabbed the messenger by the neck and pulled him off Dr Verwoerd. However, his hand had already gone down again for the third time. The man stabbed at me as I held him and the knife sliced through my trousers, but without injuring me. I had fallen with my back on a desk and he was on top of me, still stabbing away. I tried to grab the hand with the knife, but by then, a number of other MPs had reached us, pulled him off me and took the dagger from his hand. It all happened in what must have been a few seconds. I remember seeing somebody standing on the man's hand and I thought at the time that this was a bit rough. I asked the chap afterwards why he had done this and he explained that the messenger was reaching for something in his pocket, which subsequently proved to be another knife. I can also remember the messenger calling out to us: 'You are a lot of bloody bullies'. I think the chaps would have torn him to pieces had the security men not taken him away. I was so busy that I did not even know that Dr Verwoerd was fatally injured. He was taken from the chamber and we were all numb from shock ..."

Meanwhile, Tini Vorster and Mrs Verwoerd were making their way to their gallery seats. They met at the door to the gallery, with Tini Vorster slightly in front. "As I was about to go in I saw the Prime Minister's bodyguard rushing across the floor of the house. I said to myself 'Nobody can go onto the floor of the House unless something drastic has happened'. Instinctively, I told Mrs Verwoerd not to go in and then I looked in and saw a scuffle centred on Dr Verwoerd. I just knew that something had happened to him. I told Mrs Verwoerd that something had happened to Doctor. I put my arm around her and we walked down the steps towards Dr Verwoerd's office. A number of people came into the office but nobody said directly what had happened. I knew what had happened but she thought it was just a temporary collapse or something and she said that she wanted to see Dr Verwoerd. She repeated that she wanted to see Doctor, that she wanted to go to Groote Schuur hospital and so the two of us went in the Prime Minister's car. At the hospital a lady doctor took us to the superintendent's office and on the way we met a dominee from Pinelands. Mrs Verwoerd walked a little ahead of us and I said to the dominee 'Please, don't leave us alone, please, you must tell Mrs Verwoerd what has happened'. Then Mrs Verwoerd was told that Doctor was dead. She was very calm and very brave and the two of us then went to their home and I waited with her until her son arrived from Stellenbosch ... I remember that earlier while we were in the car, she did not know that Dr Verwoerd was dead but she spoke of the fact that people came across stop streets in their lives and that this was a stop street in her life ..."

The "man in parliamentary messenger's uniform" was a messenger named Dimitri Stafendas who was later found to be insane and who is still being held in prison. While spectators fled from the galleries with horrified expressions on their faces, many of them crying, Vorster summoned the Commissioner of Police, General John Keevy. Keevy was there within minutes and Vorster told him to get Hendrik van den Bergh to take over the investigation. "We were gravely shocked and deeply concerned. We wanted to know as soon as possible whether the man was mad or whether this was an organised thing, so I sent for the man best qualified to get to the bottom of it quickly. Van den Bergh questioned him for 48 hours and I tell you that if a man does not break after 48 hours of Van den Bergh's questioning, then you know that he does not know a thing. Van den Bergh's diagnosis was that it was a one-man job and that Stafendas was not responsible for his actions ..."

About 3 p.m. the House reconvened, papers covering the blood on the floor. The Speaker, Mr H J Klopper, read prayers with a shaking voice. There was tense silence as the Leader of the House,

Mr Ben Schoeman said: "I have not heard officially from the hospital whether the Prime Minister is still alive. I do not believe he is. Therefore I wish to move as an unopposed motion that Parliament adjourns until reconvened by Mr Speaker".

South Africa was plunged into shocked mourning. Spokesmen for all political parties unanimously condemned the assassination. Tributes to Dr Verwoerd were made from both sides of South Africa's political divide. Ironically, it is to the Verwoerd Governments's most vigorous critic that one must turn for the most perceptive evaluation of Verwoerd, the politician. Writing in the Rand Daily Mail of September 10, the editor, Laurence Gandar said: "This was a man making his mark on the times because of an outlook which he, more than any other, symbolised and upheld in all its startling, abrasive unorthodoxy ... In his mind and in his speeches, the National Party's policy of baasskap refined and rationalised into the policy of separate development with vertical rather than horizontal lines of division. He visualised a series of ethnically-organised African homelands, sustained by border industries and gradually evolving into independent states which would one day enter a confederation of friendly, co-operating white and black states in Southern Africa. This was his grand design for the future. I have been amongst the many who have criticised this policy, but I recognised its political significance in that, at a time of continuing turmoil in Africa, Verwoerd came to be widely regarded as the one man who had a positive plan for South Africa which the Whites found acceptable and which seemed to them to be fair to the non-White as well ... The point was that he came to be recognised as the principal architect and driving force behind separate development. This was national policy, ostensibly endorsed at the polls and he was in full charge of it ... But it is in the sphere of foreign policy that Verwoerd made his most singular and personalised contribution. For, although he stood for a policy at home that ran completely counter to the main currents of world thought, he nevertheless had a lively sense of international realities and could judge with great shrewdness how far he could go and when to hold back. Early on, he managed to take South Africa out of the multi-racial Commonwealth and yet retain Britain's friendship. He was coldly critical of the United Nations, yet stiffly correct in his dealings with it. He confidently predicted the collapse of democracy in Africa and was proved largely correct. Racial disorders in the United States and Britain strengthened his belief in the incompatibility of White and Black living in the same society. At the same time, he was busy proving his point at the time of his death that separate White and Black states could enjoy friendly relations in Southern Africa. But it was for his handling of Rhodesia that he was seen at his skilful best. From the formal posture of neutrality, he gave enough help to Rhodesia to keep her going (thereby showing sanctions to be less then immediately effective) and yet not quite enough to provoke an open clash with Britain. He knew the risks but he was prepared to take them because of the high stakes involved and because he knew the strengths and the weaknesses of the parties involved, such as the United States, Britain, the African states and the United Nations ... Who is there to succeed him who will have anything like the same grasp of affairs or who can command anything like the same confidence and support at home ...?"

Who indeed. Once the shock of Verwoerd's assassination had lost its edge, speculation turned to a successor. On the day after Verwoerd's death, The Guardian in Britain accurately identified the two main contenders for the vacant post as John Vorster and Ben Schoeman. There was a great deal of speculation, some of it accurate, some hopelessly inaccurate. Quite clearly, Verwoerd had not identified any successor. This was confirmed by Dr A P Treurnicht, then editor of Die Kerkbode[2] who interviewed Mrs Verwoerd for a newspaper article in 1968. He quoted Mrs Verwoerd: "My husband did not name a successor or make any suggestions about one. He saw more than one possible successor. As far as Mr Vorster is concerned, I can bear witness to the high regard my husband had for him and for his outstanding competence. I can remember, for instance, one of our best-known singers telling my husband that she had heard Advocate Vorster's name mentioned as one of those who might come into consideration for the premiership. She asked my husband if this was true. He answered that Advocate Vorster was a very capable Cabinet Minister and that he was very definitely one of those men who would come into consideration for the premiership".

Just before lunch on September 7, when various groups in the

---

2. Literally: the Church Messenger. The official organ of the Dutch Reformed Church of South Africa.

National Party were beginning to work for their own particular choice of leader, Jaap Marais[3], the ultra-conservative Member of Parliament for Innesdal telephoned Vorster. "He asked me whether he and a few other members could see me very urgently about a very important matter. They said that it would be unwise to come to my office. Either I or they suggested that we should meet at my brother Koot's home. At any rate we agreed to meet there and to go there immediately. So we all met at Koot's home. Jaap Marais was the spokesman and they asked me whether I would be a candidate for the premiership. I said that I rather thought not, after all I was a very junior minister. Then they started arguing the case and I think it was Jaap Marais who pointed out that Verwoerd had also been a comparatively junior minister when he was elected to the premiership. After listening to them, I told them that my attitude was that if the caucus wanted me the caucus would elect me, but that I would not do a thing to gain election, I was not going to canvass anybody. In other words, I told them that if the caucus wanted me, I would agree to become Prime Minister, but that I would not push myself forward. A little after this meeting, Peet Pelser[4] came to me and said: 'Look John, all the chaps want to know whether you are eligible for election'. He spoke to me as a close personal friend and he told me that, as he read things, if I wanted to be elected, I could get the job. I told him that if the caucus wanted me, then I was eligible – but only on condition that I did not do anything about it myself. I have never pushed myself and I did not intend starting then".

Koot Vorster remembers the meeting in his study very well: "There was Jaap Marais, Gaffie Maree, Fanie Botha and Jan de Wet[5]. They wanted somewhere private and they asked me whether they could use my study. I went with them into the study

3. At that time Jaap Marais was MP for Innesdal and one of the most active and extreme of the Nationalist Members of Parliament. He was one of the four MPs who was expelled from the Party in 1969 for deviating from the official party line. He became one of the founders of the ultra-conservative Herstigte Nasionale Party (re-established National Party) shortly after this. Its first Deputy-Leader, Marais became the leader of the Party in 1977.
4. At the time MP for Klerksdorp and a close friend of the Vorsters. Pelser was also Deputy Speaker and Chairman of Committees in the House of Assembly. He was also to be Vorster's first appointment to the cabinet, as Minister of Justice. He remained in this capacity until 1974 when he retired.
5. Jannie de Wet later became Commissioner-General to the Indigenous peoples of South West Africa.

and I stayed there because I was extremely curious. Either they did not mind my being there or they were so intensely involved in what they were doing that they did not notice me. At any rate, I stayed and listened with great interest to what was said. Jaap Marais was the chief spokesman and he said to John: 'Oom[6] John: we want to plead with you to make yourself available for the post of Prime Minister because you are the only one who idealogically conforms to the ideas of the Afrikaner'. John said that he did not think that the older men would work under him as a younger man. They told him that they were convinced that the other Cabinet Ministers would. Jaap asked them whether they were convinced that he would make a success of the premiership and I remember him using these words: 'I would rather go down in history as the man who could have become Prime Minister than the man who did and who made a mess of it!' They said: 'No, you are the man to do it' and John replied, 'Well, if this is your idea, I will make myself available as a candidate, but I will do nothing to canvass support for myself. If the caucus wants me, then I am available'. They were convinced that John was the right man ... it was a very moving moment for me. I knew that I was listening to history being made".

Meanwhile, another group of people was also considering Vorster as a successor to Verwoerd. At the centre was Gert Bezuidenhout[7] a long-time friend of the Vorsters. "After Dr Verwoerd's assassination, I went to my office and sat down thunder-struck. Then we all went into the chamber and heard from Ben Schoeman that Doctor was dead. A little later I was in the lobby when one of our chaps came to me and told me that he had been called into the office of Omie van den Heever, Deputy Chairman of Committees, and that Omie was actively canvassing for Ben Schoeman. I was shocked because this was only about an hour after Dr Verwoerd's death. However, when I thought about it, I realised just how serious the situation was because there were something like 60 new Nationalist members who had been elected only that year and who knew nothing of Parliament and the qualities of the possible contenders for the premiership. I realised that these newcomers would be greatly impressed with Omie's status as Deputy Chairman of Committees and that this might

6. Literally: Uncle.
7. Gert Bezuidenhout left politics in 1972 to become Commissioner-General to the Lebowa Homeland. He died in 1977.

28. *With Sir de Villiers Graaff, Leader of the Opposition (left) and Dr Kurt Waldheim, Secretary-General of the United Nations, in Cape Town in 1972.*

Photo: Die Burger.

29. *Obviously happy, Vorster listens to the 1974 general election results with his wife at Libertas, Pretoria.*

Photo : Oggendblad, Pretoria.

30. As Chancellor of the University of Stellenbosch, Vorster was photographed with the Students Representative Council in 1974. On his left is his son, Pieter, who served as vice-Chairman of the SRC (like his father) and Primarius of the Dagbreek hostel (like his father).

affect their judgement when it came to selecting a successor to Dr
Verwoerd. I had not thought the thing out, but I was convinced
right then that John Vorster and not Ben Schoeman should be
Prime Minister ... everything I saw in Parliament, everything I
knew of the man, made me believe that he should be our next
Prime Minister – even though I had nothing whatsoever against
Ben Schoeman. I knew Vorster well and I knew that he would not
do anything positive to gain election. But I felt that something
should be done ..."

Bezuidenhout thought about things that Tuesday afternoon
and he thought hard that night. It was difficult because the
unthinkable had happened. Verwoerd had been killed and
nobody was certain yet whether it had been the beginning of an
organised series of events which would culminate in a general
uprising. The next day Bezuidenhout thought some more and, in
the afternoon, went to see Peet Pelser. "I told him what was
happening and I said that I was afraid that Omie would get a
commitment from these new MPs and that they would probably
stick to any undertaking they gave him to vote for Ben Schoeman.
Tactful as ever, Peet asked me who my candidate was and I said,
'There is only one man and that man is John Vorster'. Peet replied:
'Then surely you must ask him whether he is available? ... it is no
good having a candidate who is not prepared to be a candidate'.
Immediately I went to the telephone on his desk and phoned
Connie Mulder and Willem Cruywagen[8] and asked them to come
to the office. Together, we discussed the whole thing and decided
that before we could do anything, we had to get John Vorster's
consent ..."

Still in Peet Pelser's office, Bezuidenhout telephoned Vorster
and arranged a meeting for 5,30 pm at the Minister of Justice's
official residence at Savernake. "The three of us drove out there
together. We asked him to make himself available as a candidate.
He said that he was available, adding with a slight smile that Jaap
Marais had already asked him. I told him that we would keep him
informed of how things were going and he stressed that he was not
going actively to seek election. We drove back to Parliament and
collected a number of House of Assembly division lists because
these contained all the names of the Members of Parliament. We

8. Later to become Deputy Minister of Bantu Administration, a post in which he is still
serving.

185

could not get Senate division lists because we were not Senators so we used Senate hansard covers because the full list was printed on these. From there we went to Dr Mulder's home where our three families had gathered for supper. We were all shocked and subdued by what had happened ..."

After supper Bezuidenhout, Mulder and Cruywagen drove to the ridge overlooking the Carl Bremer Hospital. "I remember, it was a very clear night and we could see every light in Cape Town. For hours, until well after midnight, we asked ourselves why Dr Verwoerd should have been assassinated. But we decided that Dr Verwoerd was dead, that we had to look to the future, that the only logical successor was John Vorster and that there was work to be done. On the ridge we decided to draw certain people into a loose sort of committee that would report to me. Thirteen names were decided on and early on Thursday morning we phoned them and called them to a meeting in Connie Mulder's home[9]. Our list of names included the men who had approached Vorster the previous day. At the meeting we told the others what it was all about and all agreed that we had selected the right man for the job. They agreed to go along with us. We examined the lists of MPs and Senators and decided that there were certain people that we would *not* approach because we wanted to keep our operation as secret as possible. We felt that these people were so committed to Ben Schoeman that they would undermine our operation. Then we discussed the rest of the names and allocated a number to each member of the committee. This was done on a completely ad hoc basis. For instance, if Fanie Botha said he knew a man well, then this man's name would be added to his list. We decided that our chaps should not say anything bad about Ben Schoeman, that the whole thing would be done on a positive basis – and that basis was that John Vorster was the best man for the job."

9. The "committee of Thirteen" consisted of, Gert Bezuidenhout, Fanie Botha, then MP for Soutpansberg and now Minister of Labour, Willem Cruywagen, MP for Germiston, Jannie de Wet, Connie Mulder, MP for Randfontein and now both leader of the National Party of the Transvaal and Minister of Information and of the Interior, Willem Marais, at the time MP for Wonderboom but left Parliament when he was defeated as a HNP candidate in the 1970 general election, Daan van der Merwe, MP for Rissik and one of the NP's more conservative men, Andries Visser, MP for Florida, Jaap Marais, Chris Sadie, MP for Namakwaland and Flip de Jager, MP for Mayfair. Willem Cruywagen still keeps a list of the committee members in his wallet – after more than ten years.

The loosely-organised "Committee of Thirteen" started working almost immediately. That afternoon they met at Connie Mulder's home because a meeting in Parliament would have been too conspicuous. Bezuidenhout recalled: "At that first meeting all the members reported and I made my first assessment. It showed that 77 members of the caucus would support Vorster, about 57 would support Ben Schoeman, only 13 would support Dönges and there were 17 doubtfuls. You must understand that we never told people that we were campaigning for Vorster – except that, in the case of the newer Members, we decided that we would put Vorster's case vigorously. We saw to it that each man we approached saw at least two of our chaps so that we could be more or less certain that we knew exactly where that particular man stood ..."

By Friday morning, MPs and Senators were already beginning to get a feedback from their constituencies, from individuals, from prominent people and from their divisional committees. Bezuidenhout continued the story: "Everything indicated overwhelming support for Vorster. To us it was very clear that the man in the street wanted Vorster and that we were thus on the right track. Apart from this, as Members of Parliament and Senators spoke among themselves, it was clear that Vorster was getting the majority support and many doubtful Members began switching to him. In the Senate, for instance, we found right at the beginning that as many as 90 per cent of the members would back Ben Schoeman. However, by Thursday afternoon, as the Senators found out how the wind was blowing, many switched to Vorster. On Friday evening the Committee of Thirteen met again and we re-assessed the position. I sat down and wrote a letter to Vorster setting out the position as clearly as I could. I enclosed a list of the MPs who were for him, those who were against him and the doubtfuls. I took this letter with me when I left Cape Town for Pretoria the next (Saturday) morning to attend Dr Verwoerd's funeral".

Bezuidenhout gave me a copy of the letter, with a copy of the list he sent Vorster. He wrote:

"Dear John,

Attached find a list of names. The names preceded by a dot have promised you their support. Those with crosses are against you. The names followed by question marks are those we are not certain of and then there are a number of members who left before we could contact them. In Parliament, matters stand as follows:

	For	Against	Doubtful	Total
Senate	18	21	–	39
Assembly	73	36	16	125
	91	57	16	164

"It is being strongly whispered here that Minister P W Botha and Minister Jan Haak will support you. We have not yet managed to contact the following members but we are convinced that they will support you. They fall under the 16 doubtfuls: Giel de Wet, Wynand Malan, Braam Raubenheimer (Nelspruit), P C Roux (SWA), Hendrik Schoeman (Standerton), Nic Treurnicht. We believe that, of the 16, we can get at least 11 in favour of you. This will bring your total to 102. We are also hard at work in the Senate. We find some strong opposition. The boys are hard at work and, on Monday, they will all be at their posts to keep a watchful eye. My personal view is that it is going well, almost too well to be true. Our first canvass when Minister Dönges was still in the field showed:

For	Schoeman	Dönges	Doubtful	
77	57	13	17	165

After it began to filter through that Dr Dönges would not stand, almost all the members decided to vote for you. Your votes will definitely not be less than 86 and they might well go up to 109. Your friends – and you have many – will keep a tight rein and we are praying that you will become Prime Minister because we know that you and your wife, just like our previous Prime Minister, will sacrifice everything for our nation.

"Your election committee, if we can call ourselves this on the quiet, wish you strength and success."

It was signed: Your friend, Gert.

The attached list was interesting, reflecting as it did the Committee of Thirteen's assessment of the support for their Prime Ministerial candidate. When he showed me a copy of the letter and of the list, Bezuidenhout stressed that the list was "not definitive" and that the assessments in regard to some of the members of the House of Assembly may have been wrong. However, despite this reservation, the list makes fascinating reading.

Bekker, M J H (Potgietersrus) – For
Bezuidenhout G P C (Brakpan) – For
Bodenstein P (Rustenburg) – For
Botha H J (Aliwal) – Against.
Botha M C (Roodepoort) – For.
Botha M W (Jeppes) – For.
Botha P W (George) – Doubtful.
Botha S P (Soutpansberg) – For.
Brandt J W (Etosha) – For.
Carr D M (Maitland) – Against.
Coetzee B (Vereeniging) – For.
Coetzee J A (Kempton Park) – Doubtful.
Cruywagen W A (Germiston) – For.
De Jager P R (Mayfair) – For.
Delport W H (Port Elizabeth Central) – For.
De Wet J M (Karas) – For.
De Wet M W (Welkom) – Doubtful.
Diederichs N (Losberg) – Against.
Dönges T E (Worcester) – Against.
Du Plessis H R H (Kuruman) – For.
Du Toit J P (Vryburg) – Against.
Engelbrecht J J (Algoa) – For.
Erasmus A S D (Pietersburg) – Doubtful.
Erasmus J J P (Lichtenburg) – Against.
Fouche J J (Bloemfontein West) – Against.
Frank S (Omaruru) – For.
Froneman G F van L (Heilbron) – For.

Greyling J C (Carletonville) – Against.
Grobler M S F (Marico) – For.
Grobler W S J (Springs) – For.
Haak J F W (Bellville) – Doubtful.
Havemann W W B (Odendaalsrus) – For.
Henning J M (Vanderbijlpark) – For.
Hertzog A (Ermelo) – For.
Heystek J (Waterberg) – For.
Horn J W L (Prieska) – Against.
Janson T N H (Witbank) – For.
Jurgens J C (Geduld) – For.
Keyter H C A (Ladybrand) – For.
Knobel G J (Bethlehem) – Against.
Koornhof P G J (Primrose) – For.
Kotzé S F (Parow) – For.
Kruger J T (Prinshof) – For.
Langley T (Waterkloof) – Against.
Le Grange L (Potchefstroom) – For.
Le Roux F J (Hercules) – For.
Le Roux P M K (Oudshoorn) – Against.
Loots J J (Queenstown) – For.
Malan G F (Humansdorp) – Against.
Malan W C (Paarl) – Doubtful.
Marais J A (Innesdal) – For.
Marais P S (Moorreesburg) – For.
Marais W T (Wonderboom) – For.
Maree W A (Newcastle) – Against.
Martins H E (Wakkerstroom) – Against.
Mc Lachlan R (Westdene) – For.
Meyer P H (Vasco) – Against.
Morrison G de V (Cradock) – For.
Mulder C P (Randfontein) – For.
Muller H (Beaufort West) – Against.
Muller S L (Ceres) – Against.
Otto J C (Koedoespoort) – For.
Pansegrouw J S (Smithfield) – Against.
Pelser P C (Klerksdorp) – For.
Pienaar B (Zululand) – For.
Potgieter J E (Brits) – For.
Potgieter S P (Port Elizabeth North) – For.

Rall J J (Harrismith) – Against.
Rall J W (Middelburg) – Against.
Rall M J (Mossel Bay) – Against.
Raubenheimer A J (Nelspruit) – Doubtful.
Raubenheimer A L (Langlaagte) – Doubtful.
Reinecke C J (Pretoria District) – Doubtful.
Reynecke J P A (Boksburg) – For.
Rossouw W J C (Stilfontein) – For.
Roux P C (Mariental) – Doubtful.
Sadie N C Van R (Winburg) – For.
Schlebusch A L (Kroonstad) – For.
Schlebusch J A (Bloemfontein District) – Against.
Schoeman H (Standerton) – Doubtful.
Schoeman J C B (Randburg) – Against.
Smit H H (Stellenbosch) – For.
Smith J D (Turffontein) – For.
Steyn A N (Graaf Reinet) – For.
Swanepoel J W F (Kimberley North) – For.
Swiegers J G (Uitenhage) – Against.
Torlage P H (Klip River) – Against.
Treurnicht N F (Picketberg) – Doubtful.
Uys D C H (False Bay) – For.
Van Breda A (Tygervallei) – For.
Van den Berg G P (Wolmaransstad) – Against.
Van den Berg M J (Krugersdorp) – Against.
Van den Heever D J G (Pretoria Central) – Against.
Van der Merwe C V (Fauresmith) – Doubtful.
Van der Merwe H D K (Rissik) – For.
Van der Merwe P S (Middeland) – For.
Van der Merwe S W (Gordonia) – Against.
Van der Spuy J P (Johannesburg West) – For.
Van der Walt B J (Pretoria West) – For.
Van der Wath J G H (Windhoek) – Against.
Van Niekerk M C (Lichtenburg) – Against.
Van Rensburg M C G J (Bloemfontein West) – For.
Van Staden J W (Malmesbury) – Against.
Van Tonder J A (Germiston District) – For.
Van Vuuren P Z J (Benoni) – Doubtful.
Van Wyk H J (Virginia) – For.
Van Zyl J J B (Sunnyside) – For.

Venter M J De la R (Colesberg) – For.
Venter W L D M (Kimberley South) – For.
Viljoen M (Alberton) – Against.
Visse J H (Gezina) – For.
Visser A J (Umhlatuzana) – For.
Vorster B J (Nigel) – For.
Vorster L P J (De Aar) – Against.
Vosloo A H (Somerset East) – For.
Vosloo W L (Brentwood) – For.
Waring F W (Caledon) – Doubtful.
Wentzel J J (Christiana) – For.
Wentzel J J G (Bethal) – For.

Perhaps understandably most of the cabinet (in terms of the Bezuidenhout assessment which excluded Senators) were Schoeman men: Eben Dönges, the Minister of Finance, Nic Diederichs, the Minister of Economic Affairs, Jim Fouche, the Minister of Agricultural Technical Services and of Water Affairs, P M K le Roux, Minister of the Interior, Willie Maree, the Minister of Community Development, of Public Works and of Social Welfare and Pensions, Hilgard Muller, the Minister of Foreign Affairs, Ben Schoeman himself, and Marais Viljoen, Minister of Labour and of Coloured Affairs. For Vorster were M C Botha, Minister of Bantu Administration and Development and of Bantu Education, Albert Hertzog, Minister of Posts and Telegraphs and of Health, and Dirkie Uys, Minister of Agricultural Economics and Marketing and of Agricultural Credit and Land Tenure. Doubtfuls were P W Botha, Minister of Defence, Jan Haak, Minister of Mines and Planning, and Frank Waring, Minister of Forestry, of Tourism of Sport and Recreation. Ironically, Hilgard Muller and Marais Viljoen were later to become two of Vorster's closest associates.

Equally ironically, the ultra-conservatives – Jaap Marais, Albert Hertzog, Willie Marais, J J B van Zyl, H D K van der Merwe were behind Vorster to a man, believing passionately (and, ultimately, wrongly) that he would steer a more conservative course than Schoeman would have. Later Hertzog, Jaap Marais and Willie Marais led the ultra-conservative rebellion which led to the formation of the Herstigte Nasionale Party.

When I asked Vorster to discuss the list with me, he refused saying that he had only glanced at it that Saturday morning and told Bezuidenhout where he thought the list was wrong, especially as far as Ministers were concerned whom they did not contact and who gave Vorster their personal assurances of support. "I never paid any attention to it and I think that within hours it went out of my mind ... so there's nothing to say, really". Certainly nobody can say that being identified on the Bezuidenhout list as being against Vorster counted against anybody in later years. About the only "against" men who appeared promotion material – S L Muller, M P for Ceres, who became Deputy Minister of Justice, of Police and of Prisons and later Minister of Police then Minister of Transport, Dr Schalk van der Merwe, M P for Gordonia, who became Minister of Health, J G H van der Wath, Deputy Minister of South West African Affairs, who became Administrator of the territory – all made the grade under Vorster.

Also on that Friday, one of Vorster's other ardent supporters, Fanie Botha wrote:

"Dear John,

Consultations are taking place in a very good spirit. Out of the grand total, our man can command 93 votes. It is conservatively calculated on the basis that there will be two other candidates. If one pulls out, as rumour suggests, the position will improve even further. Greetings, Fanie B".

It had been arranged that Members of Parliament and Senators would gather at the new Transvaal Provincial Council building in Pretoria before Dr Verwoerd's funeral on Saturday. They would be given tea and lunch and they would then be taken to the funeral by bus. Bezuidenhout remembered: "When I got there, a car was waiting to take me to the Boulevard Hotel where the Vorsters were staying. In his room were De la Rey Venter (M P for De Aar-Colesberg) and Humphrey Du Plessis (M P for Kuruman). I handed Vorster the letter and gave him a brief outline of the situation. He had a very quick look at the letter and the list and he told me that we had marked as doubtful or as against him some people who had already offered him their support – so, you see, the position was even more favourable than we had anticipated".

Vorster himself remembers: "When Gert gave me the letter and told me how things stood, it looked as if I was going to get the vote in the caucus. I remember feeling scared of the responsibilities. But I said to myself that if this was what the caucus wanted and if this was what God willed, then I would try to give of my very best. Somebody had to do this job and, if the caucus wanted me, then I could not let the caucus down ...."

That afternoon, following the funeral, the Vorsters decided that there were so many people in and around the hotel, so much speculation and so many newspapermen that they would move to their home in Bryntyrion. Mrs Vorster explains: "Seeing all those people was a bit disturbing after the funeral. So we decided to open the house and stay there. We went there with Wessel Meyer, John's private secretary. That evening we went back to the hotel for dinner and the next day we arranged to have our boys, Pieter and Willem, who were at boarding school in Pretoria, home for the day. Elsa had come to Pretoria with her fiance and they were there as well. There was no food in the house and that morning the children went out to get some, with Willem taking his bicycle to get a loaf of bread and a pound of butter. Somebody bought us some meat ... I almost think it was one of the policemen who had been instructed to guard John. We really roughed it while we were there but it was much better than being in the hotel. I cannot remember what we spoke about while we were there, but I do know that I was not thinking at the time that John would be Prime Minister. It never really dawned on me until I got to Cape Town the next day. Perhaps it was that I was still so deeply moved as a result of Dr Verwoerd's death. You know I was with Mrs Verwoerd at the time and women feel more deeply about these things ...."

While "roughing it" in Pretoria, Vorster had a brief and ultimately profitable exchange with Mike Geldenhuys, one of the security policemen detailed to guard him[10]. Geldenhuys said to him at one stage: "Sir, it looks as if you are going to become our next Prime Minister". Vorster replied that it was all too soon to say what would happen in the National Party caucus room on Tuesday. But Geldenhuys insisted and Vorster told him "Look Mike, I'll bet you six golf balls that on Wednesday I will still be your Minister". Geldenhuys thought he was on to a good thing and so

---

10. Geldenhuys became Head of the Security Branch of the South African Police and, in 1977, was appointed Chief Deputy Commissioner of the South African Police.

he took the bet. Of course, Vorster knew by then that he would be Prime Minister and he also knew that one of his first actions would have to be a replacement for himself as Minister of Justice. This would be trusted friend Peet Pelser. But Vorster knew that he would retain the Police portfolio for some time after that. And so Geldenhuys lost the bet because he failed to appreciate the fact that while Vorster might never tell a lie, he often gets away with a great deal by phrasing his statements very carefully indeed.

On Monday, September 12, the Vorsters flew back to Cape Town. By then newspaper speculation had narrowed to Vorster and Schoeman. When the Vorsters arrived at their home, Savernake, they were greeted by Mrs Vorster's three sisters, Mrs Pelser and Mrs De La Rey Venter. They told Mrs Vorster bluntly "Look, you go up to your room Tini and forget about this house. We are taking over. You have no say in this house whatsoever". Mrs Vorster was not very well at the time and should have been in hospital, but her admission was postponed because of the funeral. She recalls: "Well, I let them take over. But I thought at the time: why all this fuss and bother? And it was only then that it began to sink into my mind that John could be elected Prime Minister the next day and that my friends were taking over my house in order to make things easier for me".

On Monday afternoon Beaumont Schoeman, then a reporter for the Transvaal Afrikaans newspaper, Die Vaderland[11] went to see both Vorster and Schoeman. He greeted Vorster and spoke briefly to him and then went to see Schoeman. Beaumont Schoeman tells the story of that meeting in his book "Van Malan Tot Verwoerd" :

"Schoeman's Private Secretary told me that Schoeman still had a visitor and that I should not go in immediately after the visitor left. He did not tell me who the visitor was but, after I had waited for about five minutes, the door opened and Cas Greyling, the M P for Carletonville, stormed out, head down and seeing nobody and greeting nobody. Greyling was one of Schoeman's chief agents. He was obviously upset at that moment and I realised that something had happened in the Minister's office which had upset him

---

11. Schoeman later joined the HNP and, amongst other duties, edited its journal, Die Afrikaner.
12. Published by Human and Rousseau, Cape Town and Pretoria.

tremendously. I waited in the Private Secretary's office for a few minutes more and then went into the Minister's office. My suspicions of a few minutes earlier when Greyling stormed out like an angry bull were confirmed by what I saw at that moment in the office. Schoeman sat behind the desk. He looked totally dumbfounded. His eyes were red and it looked to me as if he had been crying, even though I immediately recoiled from such a thought. We started talking about the tragedy of the previous week. Schoeman said that the wagon would have to continue on its way. Actually, the interview was finished, although I eagerly wanted to ask him about the following day's election. I was on the point of standing up to leave when Schoeman told me that, just before I came into the office, he had decided to withdraw from the election. This immediately explained Greyling's tempestuous mood. Naturally, my first question was what had made him take such a decision. 'Gossip', Schoeman answered with obvious bitterness in his voice. 'Gossip, even about my wife', he repeated. I did not dare to remain any longer"[13].

Later in the book, Beaumont Schoeman wrote that Cas Greyling had told him that, had Ben Schoeman remained in the race, he would have won by 11 votes. Well, Greyling may have believed this, but there were few others who did. By Monday afternoon, even before the news spread that Schoeman would withdraw, it was clear that Vorster would be the overwhelming winner. In fact that very afternoon, Omie van den Heever approached Gert Bezuidenhout and asked him to join him in his office for a cup of coffee. Bezuidenhout recalled: "We discussed the whole question of the election. I appealed to him – because I knew he was so close to Schoeman – to use his influence to avert a vote in the caucus. I pointed out to him just how overwhelming Vorster's support was and I asked him straight what he had found while he was in Pretoria for Dr Verwoerd's funeral. I asked him what the ordinary man in the street wanted and he immediately conceded that the man in the street wanted Vorster. He agreed with me that we should not vote on this issue ... in other words, even if he did not say so in as many words, he accepted that Ben Schoeman was a beaten man and that he should withdraw".

13. Ben Schoeman would not give me his own version of these events.
    He referred me rather brusquely to a book which he said he was writing and which would be published "soon".

The tension in and around Parliament on Tuesday morning was high as Nationalist MPs and Senators arrived for the crucial caucus meeting. Already a large crowd had gathered in Parliament Street. A big wooden stand had been erected opposite the steps leading to the main parliamentary entrance. It was crowded with foreign and South African cameramen and microphones were clustered together on the steps in preparation for the announcement.

That morning Willem Dempsey came in early from Stellenbosch. "I had not yet spoken to John about the premiership and the election. But I knew that I wanted him to become Prime Minister, not only because we were such good friends, but because I knew that he was the best man for the job. His office was in Marks Buildings at the time and his Private Secretary's office was a hive of activity, people coming in and going out. But all was quiet in John's office. I went in and he was sitting on a chair. I put my hand on his shoulder and said: 'John, you are going to become Prime Minister'. It was a very touching moment for me. He said: 'Yes, if it is God's will, then I will become Prime Minister'. I asked him whether there would be opposition. He said he did not know for certain but that he thought the decision would be unanimous. I think he knew at the time that Oom Ben was not going to stand. It was about 8,30 when I got to the office and I stayed there for about half an hour. We spoke about the old days, our days at university and we said to each other how we had never for one moment thought that this would ever happen to him. It had never occured to either of us that he would one day be posed to take over as Prime Minister. It was obvious to me that he had been deeply moved by the moment. After about half an hour, he said to me: 'Well, it is time I went across'. I watched him walk across the road to Parliament followed by security people. There was a lot of milling about, many people crowding the street but John walked very confidently and immediately people took notice of him. It was almost as if it was clear to them that he would become the next Prime Minister ... then I waited for him to come out again ..."

However, before leaving his office, Vorster had telephoned a firm of undertakers in Jamestown and asked them to put flowers on his parents' graves. Then he telephoned his sister Mona in Pretoria and told her what he had done. He said nothing about the impending caucus meeting but she knew from his request to have flowers put on his parents' graves that he was certain that he would be South Africa's next Prime Minister – because he had done the same at every important point in his career. Fresh flowers went on the graves when he was elected to Parliament, when he became a Deputy Minister and when he became Minister of Justice. Vorster explains: "I did it out of thankfulness and respect for my parents. Thankfulness for what they had done for me because I knew that I was no more and no less than what they made of me. They gave me the foundation upon which I could build. They provided me with the norms and the values that had guided me, that were guiding me then and which still guide me now. And then, naturally, I felt very close to my parents right then, as I did at every important point in my career. It was his closeness and my thankfulness which made me feel that they should somehow share the moment with me ..."

As Vorster crossed the road, he was reasonably certain that the decision would be a unanimous one – but not altogether certain. "I did not know for certain that Ben would withdraw. I went across the road fully prepared for a vote, even though I thought a vote would be unlikely. But, from what I had heard and from what my friends had been telling me, I was pretty sure that I would win if there was a vote".

At 10,30 am, the doors to the National Party caucus room on the fourth floor of the House of Assembly building closed. Senator T F J Dreyer opened the meeting with prayer and then Paul Sauer, Chairman of the Caucus and one of the most respected of the Nationalist parliamentarians, said he would first explain the election procedure before asking Mr Koos Potgieter, Chief Whip and MP for Brits to call for nominations. However, before he could outline the election procedure, Mr Schoeman stood up to say that he was not available for election. He explained that South Africa faced one of the most serious periods in its history and that it was absolutely necessary that there should not be the slightest suspicion of division in its ruling party. The new Leader and Prime Minister had to know that he could count on the support of all the Nationalist parliamentarians. A tremendous responsibility rested on the Prime Minister's shoulders and therefore he, Mr Schoeman, would serve him with advice and support. Throughout his brief speech, Schoeman was loudly cheered by a caucus still shaken by Verwoerd's death. Thereupon Mr S P (Fanie) Botha,

M P for Soutpansberg, nominated Mr Vorster, to be seconded by Mr G de K (Gaffie) Maree, M P for Namakwaland. There was no further nomination and Mr Sauer declared Mr Vorster unanimously elected. Immediately, Dr T E Dönges, Acting Prime Minister and Leader of the National Party in the Cape, Mr Jan de Klerk, Leader of the National Party in the Senate, Mr J J Fouche, Leader of the National Party in the Orange Free State, Mr W A Maree, Leader of the National Party in Natal, and Mr J G H van der Wath, Leader of the National Party in South West Africa, made short speeches congratulating Mr Vorster and pledging him support.

Speaking for the first time as Leader of the National Party, Vorster was obviously deeply moved by both the expressions of support and the knowledge of his new responsibilities. He thanked his colleagues for their confidence in him and he said that he would follow the same road prepared by Dr Verwoerd and his predecessors. As one man the caucus stood up and sang: Laat Heer U seen op hom daal[14] [15].

How did Vorster feel as the mantle of Dr Verwoerd was dropped on his shoulders? "It's very difficult to say exactly what I was thinking at that time. Everything happened so quickly that you did not have time to consult yourself to see how you felt. You had to make a speech in the caucus immediately and you knew that you had to go out right after that and face that huge gallery out in the street. As you know, the whole street was chock-a-block with people and television crews from the world over were there. You had to make a speech right off the cuff ... you were very moved, but there was not much time to think about anything".

At precisely 11,38 a.m. (according to a report in The Cape Argus of September 13), Senator Sauer, Mr Potgieter and Mr Vorster emerged, followed by Cabinet Ministers and other caucus members. The crowd cheered and, when the cheers had died down, the strains of the South African national anthem filled the street. Vorster listened with bowed head while his wife and daughter stood nearby, their faces bright with pride. Although there was obviously no doubt about the leadership issue, Senator Sauer asked Mr Potgieter to make the formal announcement.

14. Literally: Oh God, let your mercy descend upon him.
15. Die Burger, 14/9/1966.

Solemnly Mr Potgieter announced in Afrikaans: "The Honourable Mr B J Vorster has been unanimously elected as Leader of the National Party".

Facing the clustered microphones and the crowded street, Vorster paid his "humble tribute" to Dr Verwoerd and said that, with God's help, he would follow his predecessor's path. His voice heavy with emotion, Vorster said he believed in the principles of the National Party and in their full implementation "with all their consequences". He said he stood before them as a man who was small because he believed in God and that he, together with the other Nationalist leaders, would serve South Africa unanimously. Speaking in English, he said no man in South Africa's history had done more than Dr Verwoerd to bring English-speakers and Afrikaans-speakers together and he would do his utmost to promote national unity just as Dr Verwoerd had done. Pointing vigorously to the ground beside him, he said that, as far as the almighty God gave it to man to work out his own destiny, the destiny of South Africans would be decided "here" by South Africans. As soon as he had finished, MPs and Senators clustered around him shaking his hand. His wife and daughter rushed up to him and kissed him. Willem Dempsey watched from across the street and then went home, a lump in his throat as he thought of his old university pal shouldering the awesome burdens of the premiership.

Soon after this, Dönges, as Acting Prime Minister, Paul Sauer, as Chairman of Caucus, and Koos Potgieter as Chief Whip, went to State President Swart to inform him that Vorster had been chosen as the National Party's new leader. After asking the trio the traditional question. "Is the National Party the majority party in the House of Assembly?" – and offering them the equally traditional glass of sherry, Mr Swart asked his secretary to summon Vorster. This done, the State President asked Vorster to form a government and to advise him of the names of his cabinet members. Vorster said he would do this at a later stage. Then he left, to all intents and purposes Prime Minister of South Africa.

Throughout that first day as Prime Minister, Vorster was involved in a race against time. He had a great deal to do in his Minister of Justice's office before hurrying to the State President to see Peet Pelser, Minister of Justice, Prisons and Emergency Planning, and Louwrens Muller, Deputy Minister of Justice,

Police and Prisons, being sworn in. There were official photographs to be posed for and he had to prepare for his first appearance in the House of Assembly that afternoon. A short speech in the House and then off to an urgent cabinet meeting which took most of the afternoon. Immediately after this, he started work on his first speech to the nation over the South African Broadcasting Corporation's transmitters.

In Parliament he paid tribute to Dr Verwoerd: " ... some of us are mentioned in the history that is written, but it is only granted to a few of us to write history and that is what my predecessor, the late Dr Verwoerd, did in South Africa. Therefore, because I have to take the place of such a man, I am aware of my shortcomings and of my responsibilities ..." He explained at some length why he would retain the Police portfolio temporarily: " ... We are aware not only of threats but of positive action that has been taken in the past. I have been responsible for the portfolio for five years and as such I have woken up and gone to bed with all these problems in connection with the security of South Africa. It will be an impossible task, and it is an impossible task, for any successor, however able he may be, to read himself into all these problems and difficulties within a brief space of time or even within a matter of a few weeks. For that reason, in the first place, I felt, and in the second place, I am very strongly under the impression – and I do not apologise to anyone for having done this – that, for the time being and until we are again in calmer waters, I owe it to this House, to the people outside and to South Africa, our fatherland, in view of the experience I have gained and in view of the fact that this matter has been entrusted to me all these years, to take personal responsibility for the safety of the State ...". Perhaps conscious of the still-lingering sensitivity over his days in the Ossewa Brandwag and his belief then in an authoritarian state, Vorster added: "Mr Speaker, you will permit me to say something more. You as parliamentarians would like to know how I stand in regard to Parliament. In discussing this matter, I do not want to waste any words. I want to refer to what is on record, namely, what I said in the Honourable Senate in connection with my attitude to Parliament. I said that at the time because I meant it, because it is my belief. I have never said anything in which I have not believed. I believe in Parliament as an institution. I believe in the rights and privileges of members. I believe in the rights of minorities in this

Parliament and, as far as I am concerned, I shall at all times be the first to protect those rights. I believe in Parliament as an institution"[16].

Sitting only a few feet away was Joggie Victor, then Deputy Secretary of the House of Assembly. He told me: "I will never forget that day. I think the most difficult moment for him must have been when he stood up in the House in Verwoerd's place. For me the emotional tension of the moment was gripping in the extreme. I wondered at Vorster's ability to stand there in that highly-charged emotional atmosphere and to speak calmly, in full control of himself, without searching for words, without hesitating. What impressed me was that he did it in that same deep voice that he still uses when he has something important to say. Slow, deliberate, emphasising every word. It was not a speech, more like an announcement. But he did it in such a way that he impressed me tremendously".

After the cabinet meeting Vorster "wrote like the devil" in order to finish his address to the nation. "While I was busy Wessel Meyer came in and told me: 'I take it you remember that you must do the speech in English as well'. Well, in the rush, I had forgotten that I would have to make that speech in both languages so I got Arthur Claassen and Alf Ries[17] into my office. They translated as fast as I wrote. I should have been at the SABC's studios at 5 p.m. in order to make the two recordings. But I could not arrive there until about a minute after seven. I had to start recording the English version immediately and I just read out Arthur Claassen's translation without even having read it through. Fortunately the English version went on the air only about half a minute late. Then we did the Afrikaans version which was completed only a minute before it was due to go on the air at 8,30 p.m. I tell you, that was one of the most rushed days of my life ..."

In that first address to the nation, Vorster paid tribute to Verwoerd and said it would not be easy to step into the shoes of such a man. Meaning every word, he added, "I am aware of the responsibility, I am equally aware of my own shortcomings. I am, however, strengthened by the goodwill of the public, the knowledge that God's mercy is being sought for me in prayer and

16. Hansard, 1966, Volume 17, September 14, columns 2017 to 2019.
17. Claassen was then the head of the South African Press Association parliamentary team and Alf Ries was Die Burger's Political Correspondent.

the conviction that I will be supported by Him who determines and guides the ways of peoples and nations ...". After pledging that the Government would do everything in its power to protect the safety of the State, he said that he believed in separate development, in unity between English-speakers and Afrikaans-speakers in South Africa and in co-operation with other countries. He said: "We seek friendship from all in the knowledge that the only lasting friendship is the friendship that cannot be bought. We offer assistance where necessary in the knowledge that the only real help is that which does not violate the self-respect of the receiver or impair his honour. We stand before the world as a small nation which believes in the values of Christianity and civilisation. We ask little of the world. In fact we ask nothing which any nation does not seek for itself. We ask only that we be left in peace to work out our own salvation. We, the Whites, the Coloureds, the Indians and the Bantu are not only capable of doing so, but the peace and calm in South Africa is proof that we are, in fact, doing so. We ask in conclusion: Please accept that that which is our own is more dear to us than life itself".

Meanwhile, there was an air of quiet expectancy at Groote Schuur (literally, Big Barn), the stately old Cape Dutch mansion which Cecil John Rhodes, the arch-apostle of British imperialism and of capitalism, had donated to South Africa as official Cape Town residence of the country's Prime Ministers. A grieving Mrs Verwoerd had moved out the previous week. Included in her packing were the many gifts that had already arrived at Groote Schuur in anticipation of her husband's 65th birthday. Now the house and all its treasures stood prepared for the new occupants.

While Vorster had been busy in Parliament, Mrs Vorster was in the gallery watching. When he left the House for the cabinet meeting, she went home to Savernake to find that daughter Elsa and some of the family friends had already taken over, and that all the Vorsters' personal possessions had been moved to Groote Schuur. It came as a great relief to her that, on this exceptionally busy day, there was one problem which had already been solved.

Extensive coverage of Verwoerd's assassination and the appointment of his successor was given in foreign newspapers. Newspaper comment in Britain and the United States concentrated on Vorster's "toughness" and his alleged political extremism. The New York Times said that South Africa's Nationalists had flouted world opinion in the most dramatic manner possible by selecting Mr Vorster. "None of the other prospective successors to Hendrik F Verwoerd symbolises so utterly the Republic's oppressive racial policies and police-state laws . . .". The Financial Times: "Few people could have stepped onto the international stage with so unhappy a public image as the one adhering to the new South African Prime Minister. A man's past is always important in assessing his nature, but when he becomes Prime Minister, it is his future that counts". The Times, London: "Office changes the man. The highest office, assumed in a moment of crisis, can change him with surprising speed". The Evening Standard, London, reported: "Balthazar Johannes Vorster, South Africa's seventh Prime Minister, is a blunt ruthless, one-time Nazi sympathiser who lacks the vision that gave Verwoerd's bantustan policies a chance of success. At 50 he still tends to be narrow and sectionalist in his thinking and is still motivated by feelings of revenge for the treatment he received from the Smuts Government in 1942 when he was interned for his anti-war activities. His wit is wintry and if he has a lighter side to his sullen and obstinate nature, he has hidden it well".

Generally-speaking, the South African Press received the Vorster appointment favourably, although the Opposition Press expressed certain reservations. All wished him well in his attempts to deal with South Africa's problems.

After his broadcast to the nation, the Cape Times (September 15) commented: "There is no doubt that Mr Vorster has got off to a good start as Prime Minister; and his broadcast last night undoubtedly helped to establish a public image far more placable than of the stern devotee of security which has been current these past few years . . .". The Star's Gallery Correspondent recorded on September 15: "The age of Verwoerd has drawn to a close; the age of Vorster is just beginning . . . Mr Vorster is, of course, well-known in the House. The members opposite know him as a formidable guerilla fighter in debate, as an industrious minister, as a masterly tactician and as a cool-headed politician . . . Yesterday, for the first time, they saw and heard him as Prime Minister. It was not an occasion for rallying cries or chillingly earnest exhortations. It was a time to say simply and briefly on what path he intends leading South Africa. So Mr Vorster said little that was new. But what he said was perfectly appropriate to the time and place, said with deep conviction and without dramatics ..." The Transvaler reported on the same day: "Vorster's first actions as Prime Minister have been impressive".

How did the Vorsters feel about all this? All they can really remember is the tremendous rush of those first heady days. Mrs Vorster says: "Well, you really cannot describe your feelings. You were simply rushed off your feet, you hardly had time to think about what had happened and what would happen. There was simply no time. There was the Press and there were all those people who wanted to shake your hand ... naturally I was very proud of John and naturally I knew that he would do a good job because everything that he does, he does well ..." Vorster says: "It was all such a mad rush. In those first few weeks there was never a dull or an idle moment. Everything was upside-down and you simply had to get on with the job ... there was not time to think, no time to properly prepare yourself for the job. Politically speaking, you were living from hand to mouth. You had no rest, no sleep almost. It was work, work, work and still more work. And then there were the telephone calls, the letters, the telegrams, the requests for interviews from the thousands of people who wanted to congratulate you. To this day I am proud of the fact that these messages of goodwill came from all sections of our population, from English- and Afrikaans-speaking, from Black, White, Coloured and Indian. This is the kind of occasion when you really understand just how valuable a good wife is. Being Prime Minister is a two-man job and I continually thank God that I had and still have a wife who is a tower of strength ...".

Although he was prepared to let his name go forward as a candidate, Vorster knew that there would be problems. "I was totally unprepared for the job. I did not know what the job was all about. If and when I retire, I know that my successor will come to me from time to time to ask me how this thing originated and what was the background to that thing. I will be in a position to tell him, even the most confidential things. But I did not have that advantage. I had to start everything from scratch. For instance, that speech that Dr Verwoerd was going to make on South Africa's relations with her neighbouring states, if I only had a copy of that speech it would have helped me tremendously. By the very nature of Dr Verwoerd's premiership, so much was centralised in the Prime Minister himself that this made it extremely difficult for his successor. And then you must remember that I was a very junior minister. Eric Louw or Eben Dönges would not have been at the same disadvantage that I was because they were senior ministers ... and any Prime Minister talks more to his senior Cabinet Ministers than to his junior ministers ...".

But, prepared or unprepared, the Vorster era had begun – even though the beginning was marked with great scepticism about this dour new man's ability to fill the great Dr Verwoerd's shoes.

11 *The Early Years*

At his first cabinet meeting, Vorster told his colleagues plainly that he could not and would not try to be a second Verwoerd. All he could be was the first John Vorster. And many of his efforts in those early years were directed at proving himself the first John Vorster, at gaining mastery of the National Party machine, of slowly moving out of the shadow of Verwoerd. But the first few years of his premiership were dominated, too, by the need for a settlement in Rhodesia; the increasing need for a solution in South West Africa; the unhappy task of coping with a debilitating rebellion in the National Party; and Vorster's desire to show English-speaking South Africa that he had meant what he said on the steps of Parliament after his election as Prime Minister when he spoke of doing his utmost to promote unity between English-speakers and Afrikaans-speakers in South Africa.

Because of his parliamentary responsibilities, Vorster could not attend the funeral in Pretoria of his old Commandant-General, Dr Hans van Rensburg on October 1. While flags in Pretoria flew at half mast, a cortege which stretched for three miles followed Dr van Rensburg's remains to the cemetery on the outskirts of Pretoria. A small military guard of honour was present at both the church and the graveside and army officers acted as pall-bearers at the church. At the cemetery, the pall-bearers included M W Botha, MP for Jeppes, Professor C J de Jager, Professor G Cronje, Mr Justice J de Vos, Mr M S F Grobler, MP for Marico, Professor H M van der Westhuizen, Mr Justice J van Wyk de Vries, Mr Justice J F (Kowie) Marais, Dr P J Riekert, the Prime Minister's Economic Adviser, and Major-General H J van den Bergh, Head of the Security Police. Former members of the OB and the Stormjaers gave their distinctive salutes, standing smartly to attention. On the grave was a wreath of pure white flowers from the Vorsters.

Even though the funeral was only a faint echo of the bitterness of the past, the Vorsters' wreath brought considerable criticism from the opposition, summed up in a leading article in the Rand Daily Mail on October 4, 1966:

"Ever since the new Prime Minister was appointed, his old OB buddies have been popping up from their burrows and parading about with a new-found air of respectability. Their odious attachments are quietly being sanitised.

"The other day a group of them, members of the League of ex-Internees and Political Prisoners, flew to Cape Town and Mr Vorster entertained them at Groote Schuur. On Saturday, the late Dr Hans van Rensburg, the war-time Leader of the OB was afforded a semi-military funeral in Pretoria and flags in the capital flew at half-mast.

"For Dr van Rensburg's old comrades this was a sad occasion and it is understandable that even those who now hold high and responsible positions in the civil service should have wished to pay their final tributes. But it is far from fitting that several judges and a Deputy Commissioner of Police should have become involved in a ceremony which featured the Nazi-style salute of so controversial (to put it mildly) an organisation as the OB.

"It should not be forgotten what the OB stood for. It admired and backed Hitler. It gave encouragement to the enemy while South Africa was engaged in a long and bitter war. Some of its members committed sabotage. It advocated the abolition of Parliament and the introduction of one-party totalitarianism. That Major-General van den Bergh, the man responsible for the Security Police in South Africa should ever have belonged to such an outfit is bad enough. That he should be seen publicly giving its salute is downright disgraceful.

"Mr Vorster has assured the nation that he has changed since his internment days; that he no longer holds the anti-democratic views of the OB. Well and good. But he should be careful not to lend himself to their white-washing".

Two days later Dimitri Stafendas, Verwoerd's assassin appeared briefly at a specially constituted court in the Caledon Square police station in Cape Town. He was remanded for summary trial to the Supreme Court in Cape Town. On October 17 the court was crowded for what some newspapers had anticipated as the trial of the century. Neatly clad in a double-breasted suit and a light shirt with a maroon tie, Stafendas listened intently to both the evidence and the argument. However, Stafendas' guilt was never assessed.

208

Following medical and psychiatric evidence, the Judge President of the Cape, Mr Justice Andrew Beyers, found that Stafendas was mentally disordered and that he should be jailed at the State President's pleasure – in effect, an indeterminate sentence. The Judge referred to Stafendas as a "lunatic" and a man with a mind so diseased that he could not begin to find whether Stafendas was guilty or not. The Judge said he understood the feelings of revenge and retribution which arose among South Africans. However, if the court were to disregard the rule of law, Stafendas would have done greater damage to South Africa than had already been done. And so Stafendas went back to prison, where he remains to this day.

However, Stafendas was forgotton as Vorster prepared for his first National Party congress, the Orange Free State congress to be held in Bloemfontein. He was due to open it on October 25 with the traditional mass rally in the City Hall. By the time he started speaking, more than 3 000 people had gathered. They filled the hall to overflowing, they crowded the aisles and the platform and they clustered ten-deep around the doors and the windows. Outside hundreds more in short-sleeves and summer dress listened to Vorster's speech, relayed to them by loudspeakers. The Friend (Bloemfontein) recorded on October 26 that the crowd was even bigger than the one Dr Verwoerd drew to Bloemfontein when the 1966 general election campaign was reaching its climax. And it reported that the crowd cheered new man Vorster far louder and longer than it had cheered Verwoerd. Vorster did not disappoint his listeners. He hinted that South Africa might withdraw from the United Nations and he poured scorn on newspaper reports of dissent within the party – "The National Party has never been as united as it is now". The congress left no doubt that Vorster was supported by the overwhelming majority of the men and women who constituted the party machine and that his election by the caucus had accurately reflected the feelings of the party.

On October 26, Mr J A Fourie, Principal of the Afrikaanse Hoër Seunskool in Pretoria, wrote to the Vorsters telling them that their eldest son, Willem, had been selected as head boy for the coming year, 1967. Perhaps feeling the need to prove that this was not because of his parents, Mr Fourie explained: "This election is based strictly on merit and fixed pattern, in terms of which outstanding leadership qualities, outstanding behaviour, strong personality etc are the most important. You are to be congratulated on having a son who can match these high requirements. We have no doubt that he will fulfil all our and all your expectations".

Two days later, the United Nations General Assembly decided to revoke South Africa's mandate over SWA and to shift responsibility for the disputed territory to the United Nations. Even before this decision had been taken, the South African Foreign Minister, who had been attending the session, left New York for South Africa. Dr Hilgard Muller briefed the Prime Minister fully on developments when they met at Libertas on October 29 for a round-table discussion with 11 other Cabinet Ministers. By Monday, Vorster was on his way to East London to open the Cape National Party congress. Once again facing an enthusiastic and admiring crowd, Vorster said the UN decision was both ridiculous and impraticable – and his Government did not intend doing anything about it.

At the Transvaal congress a few days later, Vorster warned terrorists that he had instructed the South African Police to act against them as in times of war. He was wildly cheered by an audience which, as it had done in Bloemfontein, crowded the hall and spilled over into the passages and the environs of the building when he told them "We are prepared to meet the terrorists. They come to make war and to kill ... the Organisation of African Unity intends sending terrorists to South Africa but they will be meeting their death and that will be on the OAU's conscience". Almost as an aside during his speech he said that the National Party now stood stronger than ever before and he could not help smiling when he heard of a split in the party.

It fell to Dr Albert Hertzog to thank Vorster for his speech. He told the crowd with great apparent sincerity that, in John Vorster, South Africa now had a leader hewn from the same rock as the late Dr Verwoerd. South Africa's enemies sought in vain for chinks in the unity and solidarity of the National Party. "There are no chinks and there never will be any ... the party is solidly behind the Prime Minister. Mr Vorster, you have only to say and we will do. You have only to call and we will be right behind you ... it will never be necessary for you to look over your shoulder to see whether we are there". And yet, despite these sentiments, Dr Hertzog and his followers were already unhappy with their choice

210

of leader. They had hoped he would bring the party back from the "deviations" which they had already detected in Verwoerd's rule. But they had been disappointed and there were disturbing (to them) signs that Vorster might "deviate" even further. Already they were conniving within the party to force Vorster "back to the old road". Three years later, at the same congress, the rebellion would be pulled into the open. But, for the time being, Hertzog and his men fully supported the new Prime Minister: "Mr Vorster, you have only to call and we will be right behind you . . ."

Addressing the Rand Conference of the National Party on November 29, Vorster said that he would remain true to the old Voortrekker traditions when he met African leaders. "I will deal with them as the heads of their nations, no matter how small the nations might be or what the colours of their leaders might be. On this basis I will accept them and they must accept me.[1]" There were signs that the winds of change were blowing in Africa and that South Africa would eventually take her rightful place in Africa, not only to her own benefit, but to the benefit of all the African countries. "The road has been surveyed and the foundations have been laid by Dr Verwoerd for the bigger and leading role that South Africa will play in the future of Africa[2]". Although this speech made little real impact, it was important because it laid the foundations for the added dimension which Vorster would bring to the South African premiership: considerable contact with Black African leaders, even though this might lead to more disappointments than triumphs.

However, Vorster knew well – though he might have said nothing publicly at the time – that the fly in the ointment (to use the expression Vorster himself used when he spoke about the Rhodesian problem in public) remained Rhodesia; that Rhodesia remained the major obstacle to his ambitions for South Africa to take her rightful place in Africa. Thus he continually urged both Rhodesia and Britain to try to reach for a settlement. Soon after Smith left Rhodesia for his first round of talks with the British Prime Minister (the Tiger Talks), Vorster told a Nationalist rally at Heidelberg that he hoped they would succeed. An acceptable and realistic solution would be not only in the interests of Rhodesia and

1. Die Burger, 30/11/1966.
2. Die Transvaler, 30/11/1966.

Britain, but the rest of Africa and the western world[3]. But, the talks failed and, on December 6, Vorster said in an official statement that his Government did not believe it impossible, even "at this late stage", for agreement to be reached between Britain and Rhodesia if conditions were not insisted on which made such a settlement impossible. He said that he was sorry that Britain was referring the whole affair to the United Nations. "It must be emphasised that no-one's cause will be served by this and it must be foreseen that it will probably create interminable bitterness and damage ...[4].

Vorster's 51st birthday on December 13 coincided with the end of his first 90 days as Prime Minister. He played 18 holes of golf at Nigel in the glaring highveld sun, was guest of honour at a civic luncheon in Nigel and then at a braaivleis organised by the Town Council to mark his birthday. Speaking with even more emphasis then usual, he told the other guests that South Africa had always contended that the Rhodesian issue was a domestic matter between Rhodesia and Britain and that it was these countries that would have to find a solution to the problem. But he wanted to warn that the fact that South Africa had acted correctly should not be seen as a sign of weakness. The people who saw this as a sign of weakness were making a big mistake. South Africa would not yield to outside pressure to change its standpoint[5]. The speech was splashed in the British Press.

The next day Vorster went on holiday and, for all practical purposes, this ended one of the most dramatic years in South Africa's political history.

The ever-perceptive Laurence Gandar wrote in the Daily Mail: "Much has been written about the impact on South Africa of Dr Verwoerd's disappearence from the scene, of the removal of so dominating, so aloof, so seemingly omniscient a figure and his replacement by someone so different in intellect, temperament and style. Yet the remarkable thing is how quickly the country adjusted itself to the change, how little, in fact, was changed. All that can be said is that the trends and tendencies already under way developed more readily and openly under the new Prime Minister. He himself has uttered no new thoughts and given no new twist to

3. The Rand Daily Mail, 2/12/1966.
4. The Daily News, 7/12/1966.
5. Die Burger, 14/12/1966.

212

the policies laid down by his predecessor. What he has done is to introduce a more humane and relaxed touch to the premiership and the importance of this is that it is helping its own way to drain some of the strain and rigidity out of the body politic. Here was Mr Vorster, thrust into the highest office in the land at a moment of great complexity and anxiety, addressing the country over the radio in calm and measured terms, taking up his onerous duties with conspicuous calmness, then going off to play his regular round of golf, cracking his jokes at dinners and meetings and being much photographed in informal family surroundings. It all seemed very re-assuring, not the least because the Prime Minister was no longer a remote superman, taking all the nation's decisions in his remote ivory tower, but a down-to-earth chap, prepared to listen to other people ...[6].

Two days later, sitting in London, David ("Spike") de Keller, the young man who had been released from prison on Vorster's orders, wrote: "Dear Mr Vorster, This letter is long overdue but I thought that Christmas was perhaps an appropriate time in which to express my deepest gratitude to you. Sir, my parents and I are deeply indebted to you for your compassionate understanding and generosity shown to us. I would like to congratulate you on your election as Prime Minister – your integrity should be an example to everyone in South Africa and I am sure you will continue to display compassion in human situations ..."

On December 20, at the Prime Minister's holiday home at Oubos in the Eastern Cape, the Vorster's celebrated their 25th wedding anniversary. There was no fanfare, only a deep consciousness of the total communication and the total mutual trust which had brought them where they were, and which would be needed so much in the stormy political years ahead.

That year the Vorster's Christmas cards included greetings from Ladybird and Lyndon B Johnson, from Harold and Mary Wilson – and from David ("Spike") de Keller.

At 10.45 a.m. on January 10, 1967, Lesotho's Chief Leabua Jonathan walked into the South African Prime Minister's office for the second time in four months. Instead of a smiling, cherubic Verwoerd, he was received by Vorster, his usually stern face softened by one of his rare smiles. Two hours later Vorster was

6. The Rand Daily Mail, 17/12/1966.

host at a small lunch in a private room at Cape Town's smartest hotel where Jonathan was the guest of honour. And while they were toasting each other at lunch, a joint communique was released to the Press. It said: " . . . We met in a spirit of goodwill and our discussion, which was both friendly and frank, ranged over a wide field on bilateral problems and international affairs of common concern. On fundamental issues we found ourselves completely in accord, more specifically on the fact that differences in political philosophy are no bar to fruitful co-operation. We both firmly believe in peaceful co-existence on the basis of equality, mutual respect and non-interference in another's domestic affairs. We agree that our two countries should remain constantly vigilant against the dangers of international communism . . ." At the luncheon, Chief Jonathan briefly thanked Vorster. Warmed by the hospitality, by Vorster's reception of him as an equal and by some of South Africa's best. wines, Jonathan said expansively: "Our meeting in Cape Town was really historic, not only for the future of our two countries, but also for the future of Africa. Indeed, it is a milestone on the road to international co-operation . . ."[7].

Milestone it certainly was. However, in the years that followed Jonathan deviated considerably from these sentiments and commitments as he tried to exploit international hostility to South Africa and as he tried to consolidate his personal power. Also, he tried to achieve respectability among the OAU nations. Despite the fact that he turned to South Africa in 1970 for help in organising his security forces after he siezed power when facing certain electoral defeat, Jonathan believed he could get more by posing as a victim of South African racism than by co-operating with his neighbour.

But the communique did provide the key to Vorster's approach to Africa itself: "We agree that our two countries should remain constantly vigilant against the dangers of international communism". In the seventies, Vorster would use growing Black suspicion of communist imperialism to divide Africa into those countries which might co-operate with him and those which would not. He then concentrated on those with a deep suspicion of communist motives to achieve, in terms of African realities, some spectacular contacts.

7. Die Burger, 11/1/1967.

214

In the House of Assembly on February 8, the issue of sport was raised for the first time under Vorster's premiership. Mr P M K le Roux, the Minister of the Interior, told the Assembly: "I am prepared to say that the new Prime Minister, like his predecessor, will be just as unbending as a rock. But, within the framework of the policy, we will try, on the most carefully considered basis, to achieve the greatest success"[8]. Little did Mr le Roux know then just how much the framework would be stretched to accommodate more and more sports concessions – concessions which led to increasing inter-racial contact in sport and to the steady elimination in the late seventies of inter-racial sports barriers. Nor did Mr le Roux know then that it would be the sports policy which would finally provoke the ultra-conservative rebels into an open confrontation with the National Party leadership at the Transvaal congress in 1969.

Addressing his first rally in the Cape Peninsula on Friday, February 17, Vorster told an enthusiastic crowd at Parow that it was the National Party's task to lead South Africa to the fullest possible participation in the international world. He repeated during his speech that South Africa could and would fulfil its role in the world, in spite of differences in domestic policy and in spite of the problems that would occur from time to time. The Cape Argus political correspondent commented the next day: "The few thousand Nationalists who went to Parow last night to listen to the Prime Minister heard a new voice telling them that a new phase had been reached in South African politics ... the part of his speech that dealt with international politics was positive, constructive and forceful in its overall tone of friendship and goodwill ... recent prognostications that Mr Vorster would see his chief task as Prime Minister as the resolution of South Africa's international problems were confirmed ...". His colleague on The Star commented on February 25: "It is slowly becoming clear that Mr John Vorster's Government has set itself the laudable objective of abandoning the cry of the earlier Nationalist regimes which seemed to be for the world to stop so that they could get off. He is showing every sign of waiting to get back on, and to make concessions in the process ...". In Die Burger of the same day, political columnist Dawie wrote: "Those were weighty words

8. Die Burger, 9/2/1967.

delivered by the Prime Minister in Parow ... on the surface they were in direct conflict with the 'laager mentality' so frequently ascribed to the Afrikaner in general and the Nationalist in particular. Here we have an appeal and a challenge to move out into the world, to look outwards, to become involved, to seek our national salvation in participation instead of in separation ..."

Apart from anything else, the speech was seen at the time as a firm indication (whereas the Le Roux speech in the House of Assembly was only a hint) that the first area in which Vorster would try to combat isolation would be in the field of sport. Immediately after the Parow speech speculation that the Party was preparing for the "further development" of its sports policy gained momentum. On Tuesday, February 21, 1967, newspapers informed their readers that Vorster had discussed details of the new sports policy with members of the Nationalist parliamentary caucus. Nothing official was said at the time, although intense speculation continued for weeks afterwards. A few weeks later, addressing a big Nationalist rally at Oudtshoorn, Vorster said that traditional international sports links which had been built up over the years should be maintained for South Africa: South Africa's young people were entitled to this. On the other hand, it would be foolish of South Africa to attempt to make sports ties with countries like the West Indies, India and Pakistan because this could give rise to unpleasantness out of which no good could come. It was important to differentiate between internal and external sport. Internally the National Party had only one policy and that policy was that the different race groups should exercise and administer sport separately. When it came to international sport, he would discuss this in further detail at a later stage[9].

Meanwhile, within the National Party itself, the underground rightist groups were frantically discussing the whole issue of sport. With their chronic thin-end-of-the-wedge thinking, they believed that if even one Black or Brown person played against a White in South Africa, this would be the beginning of the end of apartheid, the beginning of racial integration, the end of the White Man in South Africa and the complete disappearance of the Afrikaner, his culture and his traditional way of life. By now it was clear to them that Vorster was their enemy number one and slowly the moves to

9. Die Burger, 6/3/1967.

try to get rid of him began. In one sense, the ultra-conservatives were right: the new thinking on sport would lead to more and more concessions over the years as the Government struggled to reconcile National Party policy with the demands of the late Sixties, the early and the late Seventies. And, as it tried to retain South Africa's sports ties, more and more apartheid barriers were removed from the sports' fields.

The Government's sports policy and all the changes that were made over the years would be the subject for a lengthy book. At first the Government differentiated between "domestic" and "international" sport. Then the term "international" was broadened to include sport between the different South African "nations", then between the different race groups. Meanwhile, in certain sports – such as tennis and athletics – Black and Brown South Africans were allowed to compete in "mixed trials" for representative South African teams. Further concessions were made which allowed (in certain sports such as soccer) Black teams to play White teams. Finally, by 1977, Black and Brown sportsmen and women were playing with White South Africans on a limited basis. The sports policy was complex and frequently contradictory (at least to Vorster's opposition). But the result was the steady elimination of the barriers between sportsmen and women of different colours. The whole process might have taken place too slowly for many of Vorster's critics; but it certainly generated considerable tensions within the National Party itself and even verligte[10] Nationalists concede that, in the early years, Vorster was moving as fast as he practically could.

About the same time Fate, an overseas journal claiming "fantastic reality", discussed the new South African Prime Minister's horoscope. "His horoscope shows the sun well aspected in the sign of Sagittarius, the moon in Pisces in conjunction with the planet Jupiter. The chances are that he was born in the morning hours and that his horoscope has either a Scorpio or a Capricorn ascendant. According to all reports Mr Vorster has a reputation for ruthlessness. In the past he has been responsible for internal security in South Africa and for the implementation of the apartheid policy. There is nothing in his horoscope to indicate the megalomania of a Mussolini, Hitler or Napoleon. In fact the

10. Literally: enlightened.

factors which immediately spring to the eye are (a) his is basically a very flexible, versatile, adaptable temperament, he is probably now Prime Minister because of an opportunist streak which enabled him to think and move quickly at a time of crisis; (b) he has a very definite ability to put his ideas and personality across in a very attractive way. His horoscope shows the moon and Jupiter very closely conjoined and this favours his becoming very popular with the South African people. Don't therefore underestimate Mr Vorster in the political arena. He has a very good chance indeed of consolidating his position successfully in South Africa; he is an adroit politician who manoeuvres with considerable skill ... it would be foolish to have too many preconceived ideas about Mr Vorster. He is a quick-witted, highly-intelligent man who seems likely to win his way into the hearts of the South African people and gain their loyal support. His is not obviously the horoscope of a dictator. Basically, his is a very different outlook and personality from that of Dr Verwoerd. This will become apparent towards the end of 1968 as the imprint of his personality on South African policy begins to be felt".

More history arrived in South Africa in the form of three Malawi Cabinet Mininsters who had come for a seven-day goodwill visit after initial and fruitful contact between South Africa and Malawi. On March 13, they met Vorster and five of his Cabinet Ministers and at noon they signed a trade agreement with South Africa. After further meetings with the ministers and visits to the Transkei, Johannesburg and Pretoria, they left for home amidst speculation that there would be further African delegations visiting South Africa in the forseeable future.

On April 15, the sun broke through the autumn clouds over Stellenbosch for the wedding of Vorster's daughter, Elizabeth, to a well-to-do Orange Free State farmer, Andre Kolwer. The wedding was simple, but the bride wore, in the words of one reporter, "a magnificent gown of pure white silk over pale pink ...". Amongst the guests were the Vorster's own two wedding attendants, Flooi du Plessis and Flip la Grange, and also Willem Dempsey.

As a result of Vorster's Republic Day broadcast on May 31, newspaper headlines suddenly began to reflect the word "outwards". He told the nation that he believed South Africa's greatest problem was her attempt to eliminate friction between the

218

various population groups – including friction between individuals, nations and states. On South Africa's relations with the outside world, said Vorster, the time had come for "a united outward movement". It was not his intention to try to build Rome in a single day, but he would slowly and systematically try to establish good relations with neighbouring states in Southern Africa and with nations to the North – as saner attitudes prevailed[11]. In fact foreign affairs dominated the 1967 parliamentary session and Vorster's image was bright. The Pretoria News commented on June 16: "The session of Parliament which ended yesterday will be remembered mainly for two things: the Prime Minister Mr Vorster's success in providing himself with a new political image and the strong emphasis that was placed by members of all parties on South Africa's position in international affairs ...." Sir de Villiers Graaff, the Leader of the Opposition, conceded reluctantly that Vorster had undoubtedly made an impact on the public, but he remained untested and Graaff did not believe that "this leopard has changed his spots"[12].

Mrs Helen Suzman, the lone representative of the Progressive Party shared none of this mild enthusiasm for Vorster. At a report-back meeting in her constituency on June 28, she said that the implementation of apartheid was now being carried out with greater ruthlessness than ever before by the tough, young Nationalists with whom the Prime Minister had surrounded himself – "But Mr Vorster has a shrewd understanding of public relations. Without really having altered basic policy one iota, he has managed to create a favourable image of himself as a much more modern and enlightened Prime Minister than his predecessor. He is certainly less aloof than Dr Verwoerd, who was not given to playing golf, meeting the Press and making witty after-dinner speeches ...". The Prime Minister's "concessions" on sport revealed nothing really radical; the past session of Parliament had not revealed any change and the freedom from unrest which the Government claimed was proof of the acceptance of its policies by non-Whites was not approval but acceptance under duress.[13]

Meanwhile, there had been more rumblings in the National

11. The Star, 1/6/1967.
12. The Star, 15/6/1967.
13. The Star, 29/6/1967.

Party. By now Professor Wimpie de Klerk, of the University of Potchefstroom,[14] had coined the words "verlig" and "verkramp"[15] and the two factions within the Party became known as "verligtes" and "verkramptes". Indirectly the different factions sniped at each other and it was becoming increasingly clear that Vorster would soon have to deal with a major conflict within the Party. But Vorster was reluctant to see all this. On his return from what could only be described as a triumphal visit to South West Africa, he issued a brief statement which he hoped would put an end to the childish squabbling among his followers: "The present quarrel in the ranks of Afrikaners is not only unsavoury and everybody who takes part in it unworthy, but it serves no purpose – it just creates confusion amongst our people at a time when we in South Africa simply cannot afford this. I am glad, on my return to South Africa, to establish that, with a few exceptions, the members of our Party did not become involved nor did they show any inclination to become involved. I sincerely hope we have seen the end of a holiday episode that has not brought glory to any of its participants or profited our cause".

Strong words. However, Vorster hoped that by speaking out at this stage he would be able to stop the rot. Partly he was misled by the 'verkramptes' protestations of loyalty whenever they were confronted with the allegations against them or when Vorster or the other Nationalist leaders called for motions of loyalty in one Party formation or another. Vorster explains: "In view of their continued protestations of loyalty, I, as Party leader, had to accept these declarations, no matter how I felt deep down. Naturally I hoped that they were being sincere and I gave them the benefit of the doubt. However, deep down, I suppose I knew that the time would come for a showdown. But I also knew deep down that I would choose my own time and place for that showdown. But, genuinely, at that time I accepted their declarations of loyalty because I wanted to accept them. When it became clear that they

14. De Klerk is now editor of Die Transvaler and is continuing with the campaign for change in the Party's policy which he started while at Potchefstroom.
15. While verlig means enlightened, verkramp means – more or less – cramped, narrow-minded. Following De Klerk's use of these words, verlig has been used to mean progressive, enlightened while verkramp has come to mean narrow-minded, ultra-conservative, resistant to change. Both words are now part of South Africa's general political vocabulary.

were disloyal, then I acted . . . all I can say about this eagerness of mine to accept their declarations of loyalty is that I fought one civil war with my fellow-Afrikaners – and I did not want to become involved in another. But, when it was forced on me, I met it head-on . . ."

Die Burger, however, refused to accept the Prime Minister's assessment of the whole affair as a "holiday episode". Like other verligte voices in the National Party, it saw itself ranged against ruthless verkramptes who were trying to push the Party further and further towards the right. Irrespective of what Mr Vorster had said, they (and others) had declared war on the reactionaries within the Party and they would continue that war.

On August 11, Vorster took a trip back in time to Koffiefontein. He had been invited to address a Nationalist rally there and he took the opportunity of revisiting the site of the old internment camps. The buildings had gone, their places marked only by the concrete slabs which formed the floors of the huts. The whole area was overgrown with trees. Vorster took one look and turned to the party with him: "Look at it now . . . this is what happens when one is away – they neglect the place like this". At his side as he walked through the camp site was his daughter Elsa who plied him with questions. He visited the bakery from which the internees had dug a tunnel and he looked around the place which had been his home for so many months.

There was a holiday atmosphere in Koffiefontein (population 4 000) that day. Vorster told the schoolchildren who met him on his arrival that morning that they need not go back to school. Most of the shops and businesses in the town closed for the afternoon so that bosses and workers alike could attend the meeting. Long before the rally was due to start, the people of Koffiefontein and the surrounding area started drifting towards the site of the rally. Early in the day the streets had been sprinkled with water to keep the fine dust down. Flags spanned the streets and many of the buildings were decorated. Apart from the emotional overtones of the visit, the speech was an important one because Vorster dealt at some length with the situation in the Party. He denied that there was either dissent of confusion in the Party. He denied vehemently that there was an imminent split in the Party, but he conceded that there was a "certain irritation" among some people. And he warned people not to look for "liberalists" in the National Party.

He defended Afrikaans-language newspapers which had become the target for a verkrampte attack (although, in many cases, it was the verkramptes reacting to newspaper attacks on themselves) and he attacked Mr S E D Brown, editor of the South African Observer[16], and spokesman for South Africa's lunatic-fringe rightists. The National Party, Vorster said, was conservative but it was not stagnant. South Africa lived in a changing world and it was the Party's duty to lead the country in this changing world, no matter what the stoep-sitters[17] said. South Africa could only keep its enemies at bay by moving "outwards".

To political observers, it was clear that Mr Vorster was turning his back on the verkramptes in the Party and committing himself to change, even though the change might be far too slow for almost all of his Opposition critics.

After making considerable impact in Durban at the Natal National Party congress, Vorster moved to SWA where he opened the SWA National Party congress. The opening meeting had been preceded by considerable newspaper speculation about a major speech and a new deal for SWA. So it was not surprising that almost 2 000 anxious South Westers crowded in and around a Windhoek hall to hear his speech. Vorster told them legislation was being prepared which would more closely link SWA with South Africa, more fully integrate the SWA and South African administrations. He stressed that this was not "incorporation" and that the planned action was fully in keeping with the letter of the original mandate. The legislation would re-arrange powers in such a way that certain powers which belonged to the central government and which were currently exercised by the SWA administration, would go to the central government. The congress later gave its unanimous backing to the Government's as yet undisclosed plans for the territory, thus giving Vorster what amounted to a blank cheque for the future. Among the Whites, the

16. The South African Observer was the mouthpiece of ultra-conservative English-speakers in South Africa. It had, and still has, connections with ultra-conservative groups in other parts of the world, especially the United States of America. At one stage, the editor, Mr Brown, was a National Party favourite because of his support for National Party policies. However, as he identified himself with the rightists in the Party and started accusing Vorster of "liberalism" and the "betrayal of the White Man", he quickly became identified as an enemy and was consequently shifted out.

17. Literally: those who sit on the stoep. In Afrikaans it is used to refer to arm-chair critics.

most serious fears at the time appeared to centre on whether this would interfere with SWA's rather liberal liquor laws ...

Subsequent developments in SWA show that at some stage Vorster changed his course and, instead of drawing SWA closer to South Africa, started working hard for the territory's "self-determination" and ultimate independence. Questioned on this, Vorster replied by pointing to a statement in the government-published Survey of South West Africa for 1967 which said quite clearly that it was the people of SWA who would decide on their own future. He told me his whole strategy on SWA was two-fold: to get the people in the territory to realise that they would have to take the initiative in solving the "SWA question" and to buy time for this process to be completed. "There was a time when the people of SWA did not care much for their future. To them it was the job of the South African Government. They were not concerned one iota about their future or where they had to go or what they had to do. So it was my task to educate them to their responsibilities and to keep the wolves off their backs while this was happening. I have always accepted that SWA has a special international character. There is just no getting away from it and it would have been foolish to incorporate SWA into SA in view of the position the territory occupied in the international scene. ...".

Vorster's next date of any importance was in Grahamstown, in the middle of the Eastern Cape's British settler country, where both he and his wife were due to lay the foundation stones for the impressive 1820 Settlers' National Monument on historic Gunfire Hill overlooking Grahamstown on Settlers' Day, September 4, 1967. It was a strange setting for this ex-Koffiefontein internee who had so single-mindedly fought against British interests during the war. The crowd of more than 1 500 people consisted mainly of descendants of the early British settlers. They gathered atop Gunfire Hill against a backdrop created by the flags of Scotland, Ireland, England, Wales and South Africa. On the hilltop, a guard of honour was drawn up consisting of kilted members of the First City Regiment. The whole area and the whole ceremony reeked of the English culture in which this area had been steeped ever since 1820. But the changed times were re-flected in the bilingual programme, in the fact that the Anglican Archbishop of Cape Town blessed the foundation stone and Dominee W A Landman, of the Dutch Reformed Church, pronounced the benediction. And by the presence of Vorster – determined to show the people of Grahamstown that, while he was fiercely determined to preserve his own culture, he was fully prepared to honour another.

Speaking bare-headed beneath the blazing sun, Vorster paid high tribute to the settlers and said that both English-speakers and Afrikaans-speakers had taken root in South Africa. They wanted to grow and they wanted to stand together. Despite the differences of the past, they had come to a new understanding because they realised South Africa was the only home for both sections; and because they knew that there was room in South Africa for both sections. "I take pride in what belongs to me – my Voortrekker heritage – and you take pride in what belongs to you. But we both take pride in what belongs to South Africa"[18].

Vorster's speech made a great impact on the people of the Eastern Cape and of the country. It was summed up in a leading article in the Rand Daily Mail on September 5: "Yesterday was no ordinary Settler's Day. At Grahamstown, an impressive array of dignitaries, as well as hundreds of descendants of the 1820 Settlers assembled to pay homage to the memory of these pioneers in a ceremony which was as colourful as it was moving. It was an occasion to which Mr Vorster rose admirably with one of the finest public addresses he has made. This was a true Prime Minister speaking, an Afrikaner leader whose tribute to the English-speaking section and its contribution to South Africa could not have been more generous and more gracious. It was also an example of how adaptable Mr Vorster can be for only a fortnight ago he gave encouragement to a move to eliminate the Union Jack from the centrepiece of our National Flag ..."[19].

Vorster remembers the occasion well. "That was an important speech because it was my first act as Prime Minister as far as the English-speaking section was concerned. Naturally, I had to declare myself, as it were, to them on that occasion, and declare myself in such a way that there could be no misunderstanding whatsoever about my sentiments and my intentions. In a sense, I had an advantage because, coming as I did from the Eastern Cape,

18. Eastern Province Herald, 9/9/1967.
19. As it happened, nothing came of the flag issue. The whole matter appears to have died a natural death, although the move to give South Africa a new flag could be revived at any time.

224

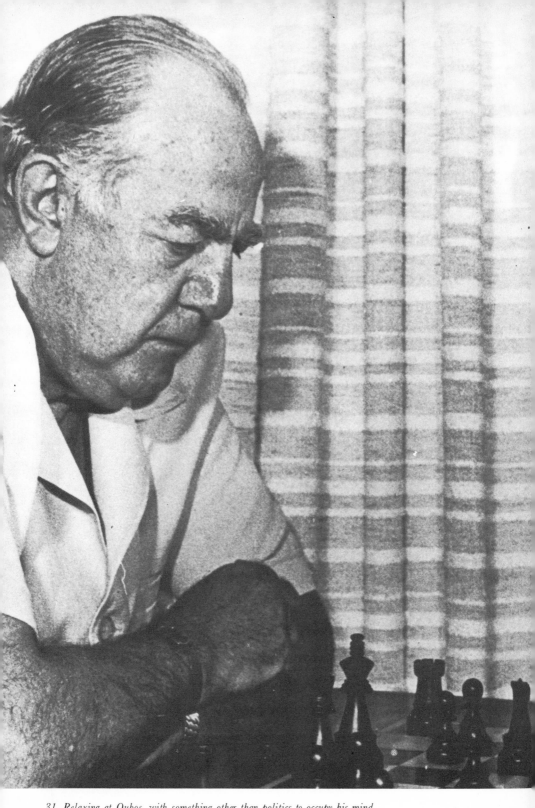

31. *Relaxing at Oubos, with something other than politics to occupy his mind.*

32. *Oubos, 1975 – reading a cowboy book.*

33. *Photographed at Oubos in January, 1976 with Ivor Richard, the British Ambassador to the United Nations, who came to talk to Vorster about yet another possible Rhodesian settlement package.*

Photo: The Argus, Cape Town.

34. *In deep conversation with the Mayor of Cape Town, Mr Tyers, and Sir de Villiers Graaff,
the Leader of the Opposition, at a function in the Cape Town City Hall.*

Photo: Nasionale Koerante, Cape Town.

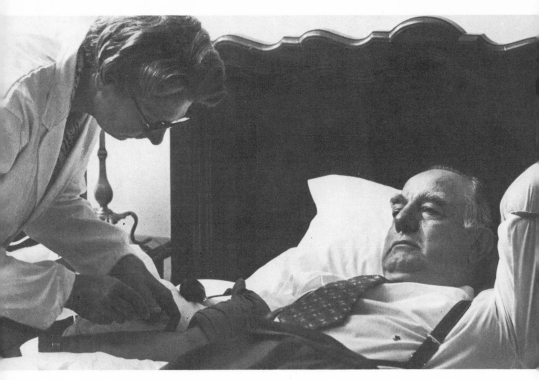

35. Vorster photographed at Groote Schuur, in February, 1977 after giving his 50th pint of blood to the Western Province Blood Transfusion Service.

I was only too well aware of the contribution the English-speakers have made to South Africa. My tribute to them was a genuine one, not motivated by political expediency. I would like to think that I got my message across and that it was taken as a genuine message, a message from the heart. I looked on their memorial in exactly the same way as I look on the Voortrekker Monument. In a sense that memorial is the English-speakers' Voortrekker Monument and I wanted them to know that I respected the monument to their pioneers just as I respected the monument to my own ... I could think myself into their position and I hope my speech on that day conveyed this to those who were there ...".

But perhaps the most important public function of these early Vorster years was still to come – the Transvaal National Party congress to be held on the emotional first anniversary of Verwoerd's death, to be held in Pretoria, the focus of all the ultra-conservative agitation against a man who had allegedly and almost blasphemously "deviated" from the "Verwoerd line". Before the public meeting which marked the congress opening, about half of the 1 000 official delegates had watched Vorster place a wreath on Verwoerd's grave. Emotions ran high as both delegates and Prime Minister prepared for the event. For Vorster the occasion was important because, apart from the need to provide Nationalists with the kind of inspiration that would pull them out of the simmering internal squabbling, there was the need on this anniversary of Verwoerd's death to show that he (Vorster) was his own man.

For occasions such as this, the Pretoria City Hall is almost intimidatingly impressive. The walls are punctuated by bunting and by National Party and South African flags. Banners proclaim the mottoes of previous Prime Ministers. Hertzog's "South Africa First", Malan's "Believe in your God, Believe in your Nation, Believe in Yourself", Strijdom's "The Struggle Continues" and Verwoerd's "Build Your Own Future". The hall itself is packed. People crowd the doorways and the aisles. Crowds mill around outside. On the lavishly-floral stage sits the might of the National Party, the Cabinet Ministers, the deputy ministers, the top party functionaries and their wives. The lovely organ plays and the audience sing the songs to which Nationalist Afrikanerdom has gone to battle for generations. There is steel in the air. The central aisle is lined with young people, each carrying a South African flag which is raised to provide a canopy under which the Prime Minister and his entourage walk as they enter the hall. At the same time the audience sing Die Lied van Jong Suid Afrika[20]. This is drowned by a deafening standing ovation as Vorster reaches the stage and turns to wave to the crowd. They stand solemnly and sing: Laat Heer U seen Op Hom Daal[21]. There is a prayer, a string of too-long preparatory speeches and then another massive standing ovation as Vorster stands up to speak.

With slow diction and great emphasis he tells the silent, expectant crowd how September 6 cut deep wounds into every South African heart, how the day started with the wreath-laying ceremony at Verwoerd's grave. His voice rising slightly, he tells them that it was on this day that they had gathered in order to continue from the point where Dr Verwoerd's work had ended; in order to serve the Party to which Dr Verwoerd had dedicated his life; in order to show that the ideals of the National Party remained both strong and alive. His voice still humble, his diction still slow, he thanks the Party for its support during the past year and pledges anew his loyalty to the Party.

The tempo quickens, the voice rises. "Now Mr Chairman, you have asked me to give you a motto. I want to do it tonight. You have said that one does not know how much time you are allotted to complete a task. We know this is so and I thought about it in relation to the motto I must give you. You said we were involved in a struggle for our survival. This is true, but we are fighting for more than our survival, much more than that. We are a pious nation, we established a party in faith and we carried it forward in faith. Even in the dark days when we could not see, we had faith that we were on the right road. We did all this because we believed that we had been destined to do this. And if I give you a motto tonight, then it is this: "Fulfil Your Destiny ..."

This is a statement from deep within the closet of Vorster's conviction and the audience rise like one man to cheer and cheer again. From this point onwards "Fulfil Your Destiny" will be hung with the other Prime Ministerial mottoes at the National Party's important functions. Sometimes it will be hung alone. But there

---

20. Literally: The Song of Young South Africa. A song which has become something of an anthem for the National Party.
21. Literally! "Oh God, let your mercy descend on him".

can be no argument: Vorster the Prime Minister has finally "arrived".

He continues to tell his audience that the cornerstones upon which the structure of the National Party has been built were: prosperity, freedom, security and peace. His voice rising, the tempo of his deliberate delivery quickening fast, now Vorster raises his hand, one finger pointing, to emphasise his points. The audience cheers loudly, sometimes standing for a wild ovation which interrupts the flow of the Prime Minister's oratory. Switching easily to his own accented but generally excellent English, Vorster gives great emphasis to his determination to see to it that both the English and Afrikaans cultures receive equal treatment. He repeats the kernel of the message delivered earlier in Grahamstown and he says: "That is how I spoke to my fellow English-speaking South Africans. That is how I feel and that is the spirit in which I have led the National Party for the past 12 months – and that is the spirit in which I will continue to lead the National Party ..." And he refers to an earlier speech by the Minister of Foreign Affairs in which Dr Hilgard Muller had said South Africa might soon have to arrange for diplomatic relations with countries in Africa. Vorster tells his audience: "Without going into any details, I want to tell you that the first step in this direction is much closer than most of you people think".

When the speech finally ends, the audience stands for an ovation that lasts for almost two minutes. Vorster is clearly the master of the National Party of the Transvaal, despite the increasingly active and bold attempts to undermine his authority, to polarise the Party and to force out the verligtes.

Thinking back on that speech, Vorster recalls that the motto, "Fulfil your Destiny" came to him on the spur of the moment. "Jan de Klerk was chairman of that meeting and right towards the end of his welcoming address he made mention of the fact that all previous leaders had given the Party a motto and the congress was looking forward to receiving mine. Frankly, I did not give the question of a motto a single thought until Jan de Klerk mentioned it and the motto I did give came from me absolutely spontaneously. It came from right within me as I tried to give the spirit of my whole outlook on life ...".

Then on to Brakpan, the town into which he had moved as a young and penniless ex-detainee in 1944 to start his new life and to provide a base for his political ambitions. The occasion was a special meeting of the Brakpan Town Council, called to confer the freedom of the town on its honoured former resident. The council ceremony ended with a speech by Vorster which rocked South Africa and the international community.

The Rand Daily Mail reported the next day: "The Prime Minister, Mr Vorster, made two startling announcements in Brakpan last night. He revealed that members of the South African Police were active in Rhodesia in the fight against terrorists. He stressed that only policemen had gone to Rhodesia and that they had gone there with Rhodesia's approval. Mr Vorster also said that a Russian spy had been arrested in South Africa. This was the first Russian spy to have been picked up in South Africa and Mr Vorster promised to give further details this weekend". Mr Vorster added that this was not an attempt to interfere with the Rhodesian situation because South Africa still regarded this as a matter for Britain and Rhodesia exclusively. However, the South African policemen had been sent to Rhodesia in order to combat South African terrorists who were trying to reach South Africa through Rhodesia (at this time, both Mozambique and Angola were still in Portuguese hands and the Botswana Government did not want to become involved in any way with the military battle against South Africa). Mr Vorster said that when it became clear that these terrorists were not individuals but a concentrated force, it became clear that South Africa had to act. "It became clear to us that we could not sit still and wait until they arrived here. It became clear to us that we must fight where we were allowed to fight ... For that reason the Government decided, with the approval of Rhodesia, to send our people there to take up their posts in the front line. This decision has been implemented recently". Vorster added that the British Government had been informed of South Africa's actions[22]. The Brakpan crowd roared its approval and within hours the first telegrams of congratulation poured into Vorster's Pretoria office. While the impotent British Government planned a "strong protest", South African newspapers generally approved of the Prime Minister's actions – the English-language newspapers much less enthusiastically than their Afrikaans-language counterparts.

22. Rand Daily Mail, 15/9/1967.

228

The British protest was made on September 14 by way of a note delivered by the British Ambassador in South Africa, Sir John Nicholls, to the Minister of Foreign Affairs. It said South Africa had no right to enter Rhodesia without Britain's permission and it demanded the immediate withdrawal of South African security forces. The South African Government politely refused and the policemen stayed there until Vorster decided it was time for them to come back[23].

On the first anniversary of his succession to the premiership, Vorster spoke frankly of the needs and problems of prime ministerial office to Dagbreek en Sondagnuus (the story was printed on September 17, 1967). "A task such as this requires a great deal of mercy, goodwill, a great capacity for work and a sense of humour. If you do not have these things, you can forget about it. And then you must do your best to retain your natural domestic happiness and your family relationships. In other words, you must try to reconcile your domestic responsibilities with your governmental responsibilities so that you do not neglect either of them ... what takes a great deal of getting used to is that you have little or no privacy. This applies to everything, even holidays. One misses it tremendously. Apart from the fact that you have so little privacy, there are so many demands on your time because of the position you fill ..." And he had something to say about general political philosophy and the attitude politicians should adopt. "To young politicians, I give the advice which I followed myself – I remained true to this policy all the years that I was a back-bencher – and that was to adopt the attitude that it was my Government that was governing and that it was my Party's leaders who were appointed by my Party; that it was the Government's task and function to implement the policy of the Party and to protect the Party leaders against attack, no matter from what quarter. I never saw it as my task to push forward policy, either in Parliament or outside. A person can never become a good leader unless he is also a good follower. No leader chooses himself. He is pushed forward by his own people to fill that position. One must take into account the fact that all people never place emphasis on the same aspects of a question and that all people at all times will not necessarily

23. The South African Police were withdrawn from Rhodesia in 1975 as part of a Rhodesian peace initiative.

emphasise a standpoint equally strongly. One must take into account that each person has his own personality and individuality. What is of fundamental importance is that all people, while they might feel the same over basic matters of principle, do not necessarily have to think alike over the details. For the rest, it is the attitude with which you act and the loyalty that arises from your actions which are important to me. In other words, the two most important principles in politics are firmess and loyalty".

In a nutshell, this statement contained Vorster's whole attitude to politics and it provided the guidelines – right ones or wrong – for his later action against his "rebels". He already knew that he was going to take different routes to Verwoerd's to the same objectives and that his brand of leadership would be vastly different from Verwoerd's. So he was preparing the way, conditioning his followers for the changes that were taking place and that would still take place. He was to repeat similar statements often during the months ahead as he and his lieutenants struggled first to contain the ultra-conservative rebellion and then excise the rebels.

One controversy remained for 1967 – and that controversy broke over Vorster's head because he attended, as Prime Minister, the unveiling of a monument to Dr Hans van Rensburg, the Ossewa-Brandwag Commandant-General. The monument over Dr van Rensburg's grave near Pretoria was an impressive affair with a granite column surmounted by a torch which was ignited as the monument was unveiled. Addressing a crowd of about 400 people, Vorster said bluntly: "There are people who take offence because we are here today. There are petty people who resent the fact that I am here today in my present capacity ... but we are standing here today at the grave of a man and I have never been ashamed to stand at a grave of a man ...". Vorster said the happenings of the war years were part of history and they belonged to history, just as the OB did, and he did not want to refer to them that day. However, if it was not for the tight discipline which Dr van Rensburg exercised in those years, then the history of South Africa would probably have been different. He said that none of the people who had served the late OB leader could say they were sorry that their paths crossed his. He was a loyal, highly-cultured and gifted man whose true role in South

Africa had been much misunderstood and would only be seen in its proper perspective by history. And Vorster used the opportunity to warn Afrikaners that they could not afford a repetition of the war years, that they could not afford the luxury of division within their own ranks.

The United Party was furious. So were many of South Africa's English-language newspapers. The Rand Daily Mail wrote in a leading article on October 10: "While insensitive behaviour of this kind is not entirely unexpected of Mr Vorster, the really interesting question that arises is to what extent the bannings, house arrests and detentions without trial which he has largely fathered in South Africa, stem from the Koffiefontein syndrome that is still so plainly present in his make-up ...". The Star commented on October 9 before the unveiling: "There are men now on Robben Island[24] or in exile who would raise their eye-brows in slightly amused approval if they knew that the Prime Minister of South Africa is to devote his public activities on Kruger Day to unveiling a monument to the former leader of the Ossewa-Brandwag, Dr Van Rensburg. They will feel that the wheel of history has only to make another turn before somebody equally exalted will be doing the same for them ... Mr Vorster's loyalty to his old comrades and his old leader is understandable. But he is now the leader of a parliamentary democracy and his official appearance at such an occasion seems improper, even shocking".

Reminded of this criticism, Vorster reacted sharply, despite the passage of almost ten years. "These people (who criticised him) know nothing about loyalty, nothing about feeling for people, nothing about friendship. Koffiefontein had nothing to do with it whatsoever. Dr van Rensburg was my friend. He was a good friend of mine and I was proud to have been associated with him. He was a man in every sense of the word, a man you could have gone to war with, a man you could have followed to the ends of the earth. I was there because he was a friend of mine and the fact that I was Prime Minister had absolutely nothing whatsoever to do with it ... as for the criticism from the Opposition and its newspapers, it left me absolutely cold".

24. Robben Island is a small island a few miles from Cape Town on which are imprisoned a number of people convicted of essentially political offences.

On October 23, Vorster met Ian Smith in Pretoria. The next evening, speaking in Brakpan, he underlined the attitude he would follow through thick and thin over Rhodesia: "It is my honest conviction that it is essential for the stability and prosperity of Southern Africa as a whole that the Rhodesian question is solved"[25].

In December, South Africa formally exchanged Ambassadors with Malawi and the Sunday Times commented rather optimistically on December 17: " . . . what Malawi can do today, Zambia may well wish to try tomorrow".

And thus ended 1967. Vorster had, during the course of the year, showed himself as his own man. He was certainly a very different Prime Minister to Dr Verwoerd. This was apparent to all those who had worked with Verwoerd and who now worked with Vorster.

Frank Waring, who served in both the Verwoerd and the Vorster Cabinets[26] discussed with me the differences between the two Leaders. "Verwoerd was a man who would listen, ask you questions and show that he knew a great deal about your portfolio. But then he said: 'This is what we will do . . .' and that was that. Verwoerd wanted to make all the decisions. Verwoerd was a very strong character and he dominated the cabinet completely. However, I must say that, even in this atmosphere, Vorster showed himself as a man of ability and decision. Verwoerd was so overwhelming and dominating as Prime Minister that it was simply inconceivable that the time would arrive when he was not there . . . so it was an almost superhuman task John Vorster was presented with when he had to step into Verwoerd's shoes. In addition, there was Ben Schoeman who was still obviously sore about the fact that he had to make way for Vorster in the race for the premiership. However, Vorster always treated Ben with the greatest consider-

25. Die Burger, 24/10/1967.
26. Frank Waring was a staunch, but conservative, member of the UP and its MP for Orange Grove from 1943 to 1954 when he broke with the UP along with a number of other conservatives. He continued as MP for Orange Grove until the 1958 General Election which he did not contest. In 1961 he contested the Maitland constituency as an independant, losing to the UP's Tony Hickman. In 1961 Verwoerd made him Minister of Information and in 1962 he re-entered Parliament as Nationalist MP for Vasco. From 1966 until his retirement from politics in 1972 he was MP for Caledon. His cabinet posts included Information (1961 to 1966), Tourism (1963 to 1966), Forestry (1966 to 1968), Sports and Recreation (1966 to 1972), Tourism (1966 to 1972) and Indian Affairs (1968 to 1972)..

ation even on occasions when, had I been Prime Minister, I would certainly not have acted as Vorster did. Soon after he took over he made it clear to the cabinet that he was relying on his ministers. Each minister would have the responsibility for looking after his own portfolio. Vorster would not hand down decisions, he would listen to his ministers, question them, make suggestions . . . never give orders. While Verwoerd was largely a dictator, Vorster brought us back to true cabinet rule and true cabinet responsibility. Vorster never said 'You are wrong.' He always said 'Don't you think you should consider this or that, don't you think you should do it this way'. Verwoerd made you feel you were a child, Vorster did just the opposite . . .".

His wife, Joyce, a controversial woman in her own right, chipped in: "I think the differences could be summed up by the experiences I had of both of them. I remember wanting to ask Verwoerd whether I could do something. He said he could give me five minutes of his time. He spoke to me for 40, telling me why I could not do whatever it was that I wanted to do. He talked me blind. Verwoerd assumed you would never argue with what he had to say. He said, in effect 'This is what is going to be. I have explained it all to you my girlie, but you must understand that this is the law.' Vorster was different. At a dinner he told me that something I had written was very foolish, very stupid and that I had made a bad error of judgement. I replied, in effect, that that was how I saw the issue, tough luck. But he did not pursue the dispute; he did not continue arguing with me. He had given his viewpoint rather bluntly and he had heard mine. He treated me like an adult . . .".

Frank Waring went on: "While Vorster left no doubt as to who was the Leader of the National Party, he tackled the difficult transition stage with great skill and tact. Remember he had inherited Dr Verwoerd's cabinet, that cabinet had gone through a very traumatic experience and it was now being chaired by one of its most junior members. As far as I, and many of my colleagues, was concerned his status grew with every cabinet meeting. Even when I felt that, had I been Vorster, my patience with Ben Schoeman would have been tested to its limit, Vorster took it all in his stride until Ben must have realised that he had under-rated Vorster and that he should accept Vorster's leadership fully . . . which I really think he did do".

A senior civil servant who worked closely with both Verwoerd and Vorster summed them up: "Verwoerd was like an electronic computer. Feed in the right information and, inevitably and quickly, he would make the right decision. And, having made the decision he would get up from his chair and march straight to his objective. He would not check to see if there was a door he could go through. If necessary he would march straight through the wall. The major problem with him was when somebody else had fed him wrong information which he accepted as fact – especially in the field of economics. Then it took hours and days and weeks to extract the wrong information and replace it with the correct information. You would have to argue every inch of the way. In a sense Vorster is the same. Feed him the correct information and, invariably, he will take the correct decision. But then he stops and looks around to see how he can reach the objective. If there is a convenient door, then OK, he will go through the door. But, if not, he may walk out of the door behind him, go to the building next door, climb up on the roof, backtrack, through a window, over a wall and on to his objective. All of which means that it is very difficult to judge Vorster on his earliest moves which may in fact be in the opposite direction to his objective ... but he reaches the objective inevitably – with less trauma to those associated with him than the Verwoerd practice".

Obviously growing increasingly perturbed about the rising Opposition speculation about disunity in the National Party, Vorster reacted to Opposition taunting in the House of Assembly during the No-Confidence debate in <u>February</u>. "As Leader of the National Party, I can say that there is not a single member of the National Party in the House of Assembly who does not fully endorse the Party's policy, in all its scope, with all its consequences and also as it has manifested itself under my leadership"[27]. While Vorster was telling the truth, some of the men who had given the assurances in yet another one of the motions of confidence that had been placed before the caucus in an effort to smoke out the dissidents, had not.

Later in the month Vorster considerably reshuffled his cabinet. In the reshuffle, Hertzog lost the portfolio of Posts and Telegraphs. Most newspapers speculated that this was a sign that

27. Die Burger, 7/2/1968.

he was on his way out, that the reduced status meant that his role in the subversive group within the National Party had been indentified and that this was the first step of Vorster's action against him. But, Vorster contends that this is not so. "You more or less had the message that Hertzog was involved in the subversive group, but you still gave him the benefit of the doubt. Basie van Rensburg had to come into the cabinet[28] and, after considering various possibilities, I felt the best way was to give him Posts and Telegraphs. I took the portfolio away from Hertzog, not because I wanted to act against him, but because I wanted to create a position for Basie ...".

Meanwhile the sports policy slowly "evolved" and the Nationalist dissidents stepped up their activities. The National Party celebrated the twentieth anniversary of its accession to power in South Africa and Vorster had further talks with the Rhodesian Prime Minister Ian Smith – and the relationship between the two men was still an extremely warm one.

However, the dominant feature of the South African political scene remained the broedertwis[29] in the National Party. The dissidents were careful not to attack the Prime Miniter or his policies directly. They cleverly sniped at the verligtes and only indirectly hit at Vorster. They avoided one confrontation after another believing that it was better to try to convert the National Party from within than to try to fight it from outside. By now it was clear even to Vorster that the showdown would have to come. By now he realised that there WAS disloyalty in his Party and, to a man of his background and convictions, this was possibly the most unforgivable of all political sins. However, he felt that the disloyalty was confined to a relatively small group of people and his strategy would be eventually to force the break, but to to make the break as small as possible.

Hertzog would have to go. Vorster called Hertzog to Libertas in Pretoria and asked for his resignation so that Hertzog could leave the cabinet quietly in the major reshuffle that Vorster already had in mind. Hertzog refused and Vorster had to ask the State President to use his powers to end Hertzog's cabinet career which

28. Basie van Rensburg, then MP for Bloemfontein East and Leader of the National Party in the Orange Free State, he served as Minister of Posts and Telegraphs until his death in 1970.
29. Literally: quarrel between brothers.

had spanned ten years. Thus the State President wrote to Hertzog on August 9 telling him he would be removed as a minister from August 12. This was a bitter pill for Hertzog but he had to swallow it. At the same time, it was the signal that Vorster was now on the warpath in earnest. Just as he had shown single-mindedness of purpose when he had to battle with subversion of the Nationalist Government, he now showed that single-mindedness of purpose in dealing with the rebels in his own Party. Vorster may have taken a long time to accept that there was rebellion in his Party. But when he did accept battle, he held the initiative – unlike the luckless United Party which later became involved in broedertwis of its own. Unlike Vorster, the leader of the UP, Sir de Villiers Graaff, allowed the disputes between the Johannesburg-based "Young Turks" and the more conservative party establishment to eat his party away. He allowed battles to rage across the entire party machine and accepted one papering-over operation after another. But Vorster now pounced whenever he was given the opportunity. The moment rebelliousness appeared, he took the appropriate action, always attempting to goad the reluctant (as they had become by then) rebels into a final showdown. However, the rebels managed to duck and weave and to remain in the Party because, as one top Nationalist told me at the time, for a splintering off there has to be a party machine which wants to get the dissidents out (which was the case of the National Party) and there had to be dissidents who wanted to get out (which wasn't the case).

So when the executive of the Transvaal National Party met on August 12, 1968 they unanimously expelled from the Party six young Nationalists who had written so-called "smear letters" attacking Vorster and his policies. But still the "big boys" remained out of reach.

Meanwhile Vorster had travelled to the small Orange Free State town of Heilbron to address a Nationalist rally. The rally was held on the local rugby field on August 18. It was attended by more than 2 000 people, many of whom had travelled hundreds of kilometres to be present at the gathering. A brisk breeze sang through the stands and ruffled the grass while the Prime Minister made another landmark speech in the best Vorster tradition: blunt, direct and to the point, down to earth, a combination of humility and confident determination. As always, Vorster spoke

236

with great determination. As always, he spoke the language of ordinary men – and he declared war on the "super Afrikaners" who were undermining the National Party leadership.

One of his first points at Heilbron was: "It is absolutely imperative that the leader of a political party should know where he stands with his followers, but it is even more important for the followers to know where they stand with their leader ... I know where I stand with you, the Nationlists of the Orange Free State, and it is my privilege this afternoon to tell you, straight from the shoulder, where you stand with me and where I want to go ...".

He spoke of his own leadership. " ... every Prime Minister in any country, not only South Africa, has his own specific problems and in most cases, if not in all cases, the problems with which he must cope differ from the problems of his predecessors ... and he has his own specific approach to these problems because he is the man who has to solve those problems. All that he has in common with his predecessors is that all of them were members of the same political party and all of them were bound by the principles of that party. But, Mr Chairman, I have noticed that it is fashionable to make comparisons, so let me say very clearly: Methods which may have been valid in Dr Malan's time or possibly in Mr Strijdom's time can no longer be valid in 1968 because circumstances have changed radically since those days – and it is a foolish Prime Minister who does not take changed circumstances into account. I must apply the National Party's policies and its principles in the light of the changed circumstances in which I find myself".

On English-speakers, he said: "I want to say very clearly in very plain Afrikaans: There are people who argue that we (the National Party) have become big and strong and that we no longer need the English-speakers. Mr Chairman, I want to say to you that as long as I am Leader of the National Party, I will not cheat the English-speakers who endorse the principles of the National Party, who give South Africa their love, who give their loyalty to South Africa. And if there are people who think it is good politics to do this, then I reject it with contempt. And if there are people who think I must do it, then I refuse to do it – AND IT WILL NOT BE DONE BY THE NATIONAL PARTY".

Then came the crunch. "Mr Chairman, I have said that a leader must know where his followers stand, but that it is very important that the followers should know where the leader stands. I have told you how I see things. If I am right, then I expect the loyal support of every follower – and I am aware of that. Mr Chairman, what stands in the way of the building of the South African nation is a bunch of jingoes on the one side ... and now, suddenly, a bunch of super-Afrikaners on the other side. And then, Mr Chairman, there is a bunch that is sitting on the fence and they have been there for a long time. I think the time has come for them to make a choice. More than that I do not want to say, except to say that there will come a time when I will make it possible for them to choose!"

Vorster had set the stage for a showdown. But the rebels were reluctant. They kept low during the "information congress" of the 12 Pretoria constituencies. They kept just as low during the Transvaal congress, despite attempts to draw them into the open. Nor were there signs of dissent at any of the other party congresses which followed. However, nobody was fooled. It was just a question of time before the showdown took place.

On October 13, Vorster addressed a Nationalist gathering at Ladysmith and told his audience that he welcomed the Gibraltar talks between Ian Smith and the British Prime Minister. It was obvious that a solution would be in the interests of the whole of Southern Africa. He stressed once again that the whole affair was a matter between Rhodesia and Britain and added: "I certainly have never nor will I in the future try to dictate what the solution is. I have said it all along and it will always be South Africa's standpoint that we do not interfere in other countries' domestic affairs. I have said it before and I stress it again that we in this country fervently pray that there will be a solution to the problem. I have been asked before whether South Africa has offered advice. My answer is: Yes, we have offered advice but we have never tried to dictate ... Mr Smith and Mr Wilson must work out a solution for the well-being of both countries and Southern Africa"[30].

Since that statement, there have been many attempts at a Rhodesian solution and many allegations that Vorster has twisted Ian Smith's arm in the process. Vorster vehemently denies this. "I have done what I can to work for settlement in Rhodesia, to bring parties together, to give advice. But I have never twisted Smith's arm. I have never given him an ultimatum. I have never urged him

30. Sunday Express, 13/10/1968.

238

to do anything which he did not want to do or which he did not stand for. I could have exerted all the influence in the world (on Smith) had I said to him: OK, if you do not do what I say, then we cut you off. But I never did that. What influence I may or may not have exerted was based on knowing more of what goes on in the outside world, having better contacts with the outside world, knowing what is the reality of the situation. What I have done at all times was to point out alternatives to Smith, to point out what the various courses of action were and what the consequences of any one of these courses of action would be. But I have always said to him that the decision was his. In the process, I made it clear to him what the limitations of our own resources might have been. If anything, my influence on Rhodesia has been the influence of the cold water reality ... Ian Smith can never say that I tried to force him to do anything – and I do not think for one moment that he will say that".

On November 5, 1968 Mr J A Fourie, principal of the Afrikaanse Hoër Seunskool wrote to the Vorsters: "You are heartily congratulated with the election of your son as Head Boy of this school. Truly an exceptional distinction to have two sons achieve this honour, one after another. The election is done by the boys and the teachers and is based on merit; the candidates must have a strong personality, etc. Pieter has a fine potential and may he still give you and his school great satisfaction".

On January 19, the Sunday Times published the result of a national public opinion survey conducted for them by Market Research Africa, one of the leading market research firms in South Africa. In the survey, adult White South Africans of both language groups, from different economic levels and from different parts of the country, were asked which word they would choose to describe the job Vorster had done as Prime Minister. Eighty-two per cent of all those questioned thought Vorster had done either an "excellent" or a "good" job of the premiership. A total of 11,9 per cent thought he had done an "average" job, the rest thought he had done a "poor" or "very poor" job. Of Afrikaans-speakers, 92 per cent thought he had done an "excellent" or a "good" job. Observers commented at the time on the "remarkably high proportion of English-speaking South Africans who admire Mr Vorster as Prime Minister".

Speaking in the Senate on March 4, Vorster vigorously

239

committed himself – once again – to working towards the unity of English-speaking and Afrikaans-speaking South Africans. He said there was only one way in which the two groups could really work together in South Africa and that was by respecting one another, by understanding one another and by each section retaining its identity, language, culture and traditions. This was the spirit that reigned in the National Party. He repeated the statement he made in Grahamstown and said with some emotion, "This is my creed . . . this is what I believe in". Because certain Afrikaners had suggested that the National Party was strong enough to do without English-speakers, he had said at Heilbron that for as long as he was leader of the National Party, English-speakers would not be cheated. "And I repeat this again today, the English-speakers are coming and they will come to the National Party in ever-increasing numbers – AND THEY WILL NOT BE CHEATED". At the same time, he said that he did not see English-Afrikaans nation-building only in the context of the National Party. People did not have to belong to the same political party to be good South Africans. He was determined to build a nation, irrespective of party political loyalties. He added: "of course there are patriots and there are better patriots – and one can be a better patriot in the National Party".[31].

This whole question of "national unity" was and still is almost an article of faith for Vorster, despite the fact that his verkrampte critics were right in their view that the National Party could retain power without the support of English-speakers. In fact Vorster probably concedes more to English-speakers than their electoral support warrants. In the days of his battle with the rebels in the Party, he certainly risked a great deal by emphasising his determination not to "cheat" English-speakers. Partly this is a product of his own background, his upbringing among English-speakers in the Eastern Cape and partly it is a product of his acceptance that most English-speakers in South Africa are as committed to the country as the Afrikaans-speakers are.

Smith visited Vorster again on March 8 for discussions about Rhodesia, shortly after publication of a constitution which the Rhodesians claimed was a "world-beater".

Speaking at Malmesbury on March 21, Vorster confronted the

31. The Cape Argus, 5/3/1969.

240

36. Meeting President Kenneth Kaunda in Zambia during the famous "bridge talks" in 1974. Watching is Dr Hilgard Muller, the South African Minister of Foreign Affairs.

Photo : Argus Africa News Service.

37. *A sight Vorster never thought he would ever see – a Zambian with a poster near the hotel where Vorster lunched with President Kenneth Kaunda in 1974.*

Photo: *Argus Africa News Service.*

38. *Vorster with his old university friends in 1967. From left to right: Flooi du Plessis, Flip la Grange, Vorster, Willem Dempsey.*

39. Vorster never writes out his speeches. He uses a few scribbled notes such as these.

verkrampte dissidents in the National Party in the strongest terms. He said the National Party was quite strong enough to fight on two fronts. At the same time, he hit at the "verligte" Party newspapers. And he announced that he would hold talks that Monday with the representatives of the different Nationalist newspapers' managements in order to straighten out relations between the newspapers and the Party[32]. He also told the more than 3 000 Nationalists who attended the meeting that he could not accept, the United States "friendly suggestion" that he should receive "unconditionally" a United Nations representative to discuss the question of SWA. However, South Africa was prepared to hold discussions with a representative of the UN's Secretary-General on matters of interest affecting South Africa's relations with the world body, but she was only prepared to hold these discussions on the basis of no prejudice to her own position[33].

Vorster's next step in the field of security was the creation of the Bureau for State Security (which the Opposition and the English-language newspapers quickly dubbed BOSS, to the annoyance of both the Bureau and the Government). For the first time in the estimates of expenditure an amount appeared under the Prime Minister's vote: Secret Services: R4 063 000. At the same time the Department of Defence budget for "Secret Services" shrunk from R790 000 to R39 000 and the Police vote for the same service increased from R412 000 to R1 218 000. Vorster was creating a South African CIA which would, *inter alia,* take over foreign intelligence from the country's Military Intelligence service. During the debate in the House of Assembly, Vorster conceded that there would be a dramatic increase in expenditure on secret services. Given the threats which South Africa faced, the money was little enough to pay for the country's security. Security services in South Africa had worked under an umbrella or co-ordinating organisation, but this organisation had not worked as successfully as it should have done and a new organisation was required.

Hendrik van den Bergh, who had been selected as the next Commissioner of the South African Police, was appointed Head of the Bureau and Security Adviser to the Prime Minister. What few people realised at the time was that Van den Bergh's major

32. The Rand Daily Mail, 22/3/1969.
33. The Star, 22/3/1969.

241

function would be the creation of contacts in Africa and the establishment of lines of communication between Pretoria and African capitals – lines of communication which would have surprised most South Africans and flabbergasted more than one Black African leader.

But still the major preoccupation was the increasingly obvious rebellion in the National Party. Again there were moves to flush the rebels out. Again they ducked, choosing to remain in the Party rather than fight it from outside. For instance, on May 20 Vorster made a statement to Die Burger saying that the recent differences in the Party had been unanimously resolved at a caucus meeting that day. Dr Hertzog had now accepted and endorsed the Party attitude on a controversial speech he had made on Calvinism and in which he had implied that English-speakers could not be trusted with the maintenance of White civilisation in South Africa. Dr Hertzog had also agreed to counteract the confusing and incorrect impressions which had flowed from his speech. Dr Hertzog had stated unequivocally that he rejected the people who, sheltering behind his name, were then planning a new political party.

However, Hertzog, ultimately, did not "counteract the confusing and incorrect impressions" which had flowed from his speech. Clearly the confrontation was at hand, and all eyes were focussed on the series of National Party congresses that would be held in the months ahead, especially the Transvaal congress due to be held in the Pretoria City Hall in September.

During this congress, Mr Ben Schoeman, leader of the Transvaal, asked the congress to vote on four resolutions, each covering a point on which the dissidents had criticised the Government. This obviously caught the verkramptes unawares as they were asked to express full confidence in the Government's policy on immigration, relations with other African states, co-operation with English-speaking people, and sport. There was ostensible unanimity on the first three resolutions, but not on the fourth. Of the more than 1 000 delegates to the congress, 11, including Albert Hertzog, voted against the resolution. Seven, including Jaap Marais, abstained from voting. The names of all these people were recorded and it was stated that they would have to "explain" their positions to their respective divisional committees.

One thing was quite clear: with the enthusiastic help of Ben

Schoeman, Vorster had finally managed to isolate the hard core of the rebels. Apart from anything else, their whole performance at the congress was so unimpressive that a number of the fence-sitters quietly fell off on the Vorster/Schoeman side.

After speaking for more than an hour at the official opening of the Orange Free State National Party congress in Bloemfontein, Vorster announced that there would be an early general election during the first few months of 1970. This decision had been taken because of the actions by the National Party rebels which had given the impression overseas that the National Party and the Nationalist Government were unstable. The election would provide an opportunity to show the world just how strong and stable the Government really was.

Within weeks of the Transvaal congress, both Hertzog and Marais were expelled from the Party in the Transvaal. The same fate befell Mr Louis Stoffberg, MP for Worcester and the lone Cape rebel. Mr Willie Marais, MP for Wonderboom, resigned before he, too, was kicked out by the Transvaal machine. On October 24 a mass rally was held in Pretoria and the next day the Herstigte Nasionale Party (an attempt to capitalise on Malan's old Herenigde Nasionale Party's HNP) was formed with Dr Hertzog as its leader and Mr Jaap Marais as its deputy leader. More than 1 000 delegates from different parts of South Africa attended the congress which was marked by the driving enthusiasm and fanaticism which was once the hallmark of the National Party itself. Enthusiastically they set about preparations for the election. Confidently the HNP predicted that it would give the "Vorster Party" the fright of its life.

Perhaps with less enthusiasm, but certainly with equal determination, the National Party prepared for the election. Its sole objective was the annihilation of the HNP. This became clear during the 1970 parliamentary session and it became even clearer during the election campaign which followed. If anything, the National Party swung to the right in terms of its election rhetoric as it tried hard to prove to its voters that it was still the true representative of Afrikaner nationalism. This preoccupation with the HNP and this determination to prove that the Party had not departed from traditional Nationalist paths, probably cost the National Party a considerable number of English-speaker votes, and this was reflected in the overall election results. However, the National

243

Party achieved its main purpose, the virtual annihilation of the HNP.

When the election results were released, the National Party had lost nine seats to the United Party. However it regained the four seats occupied by the HNP men when Parliament was dissolved: Innesdal, Wonderboom, Ermelo and Worcester. Of the 78 HNP candidates, all but three lost their deposits. The National Party gained 54,86 per cent of the overall votes in contested seats (down from 58,6 per cent in 1966), the UP gained 37,53 per cent (up slightly from 37,1 per cent) the Progressive Party 3,46 per cent (up from 3,1 per cent) and the HNP a devastatingly low 3,59 per cent.

Despite the loss of seats to the United Party, Vorster was glad that the election had shown that the HNP would never be more than an irritation and that, if he continued carefully, it was unlikely that he would have to become involved in another debilitating and saddening fight with his fellow-Afrikaners.

Thus ended Vorster's early years as Prime Minister. The 1970 election marked a watershed in his career as Premier. In a sense, the fight with the HNP, the realisation that he had had to contend with subversion in his own Party, and that in the van of that subversion were men such as Jaap Marais and Willie Marais who had formed part of the deputation which had asked him to stand for the premiership, left Vorster a sadder but a wiser man. And probably also a more cautious man.

With the HNP disposed of for all practical purposes, Vorster could now give his full attention to the problems of the country. But the early years had already shown quite clearly what his major preoccupations would be: A Rhodesian settlement, a solution in SWA, English-Afrikaans unity, improved relations with Africa, the fight against international isolation, and the maintenance of the security of the State.

In the years that followed, he moved on all these fronts and on some of them he moved spectacularly. Added in later years was a new constitutional deal for Indian, Coloured and White people, a move away from race discrimination and a greater willingness to accept domestic change. But that is another book in itself.

244

12 *At Random*

With the narrative over, my notes still contained a mass of information on Vorster, on his attitudes, his opinions and his beliefs. And they contained some anecdotes which either did not fit into the narrative or which came after 1970. However, they do provide valuable insights and so I am including them in this the penultimate chapter.

First, Vorster's views on his political contemporaries. While he would speak freely about his adversaries, he was reluctant to give his views on the leading figures in the National Party.

Sir de Villiers Graaff, until 1977 the Leader of the Opposition and the Leader of the United Party. "Looking objectively at Graaff, I would say that he has everything a leader requires – except leadership. This assessment is based not only on my own judgements but also on the talk of his followers and his ex-followers. You cannot have leadership without political acumen and political sense. You can have the best body in the world, but, if you do not have ball sense, you cannot play the game effectively. Graaff is well-qualified. He is a lawyer and, when it comes to politics, I think lawyers have a definite advantage. He is presentable. He does not lack the means to pursue his political ambitions. He comes from a respected family with a political back-ground. He was very well received when he started in politics ... What more do you want? But the trouble with him is that he can speak with the same intensity on Newcastle Disease amongst poultry as he can on republicanism or any other emotional issue on which he feels strongly. That is a decided disadvantage. Admittedly, Graaff's speeches read better than they sound but, unfortunately, the voters do not read you, they listen to you. My personal dealings with him leave nothing to be desired and we have got on very well together. He is a charming and an honest man and, frankly, no Prime Minister could want a better leader of the Opposition".

Mr Japie Basson, MP for Bezuidenhout and stormy petrel of opposition politics[1]. "Quite frankly, I do not like the man so everything I say about him is prejudiced – I must admit that very frankly. I think he is an opportunist and, quite honestly, I do not hold with opportunism of any kind. There is an old English saying: 'Ever ready to hurt but afraid to strike.' That typifies Japie Basson as far as I am concerned. In a certain sense, perhaps Japie has too much political acumen, and this may account for his opportunism. He certainly knows his way about politics, but he reads the signs wrongly. He read them wrongly in 1959 when he left the National Party and he has read them wrongly on a number of occasions since then. In 1959 he believed absolutely that the National Party was due to fall, otherwise he would not have left."

Mr Radclyffe Cadman, MP for Umhlatuzana and from 1977 the Leader of the Opposition and of the New Republic Party which replaced the United Party. "He has an incisive mind, he is a good debater and he can sum up a situation accurately and quickly. But he has not got the forcefulness of Mr Douglas Mitchell[2]. And if the leader of a republic-wide party has to come from Natal, then he must be very forceful indeed. If I may put it that way, I think he is insular of mind. He is certainly a very good man to have in a party, but I cannot see him succeed as a leader."

Mr Vause Raw, MP for Durban Point and one of the Opposition front-benchers. "A bluff, hale and hearty chap, a good fighter to have on your side. But not serious enough, although at times he pretends to be very serious. Very often, listening to him objectively, you get the idea that he does not really mean what he is saying, that it is just for the record, that it does not really come from the heart ...".

Mr Lionel Murray, MP for Green Point and another Opposition front-bencher. "I think of him as the man who has missed the boat. Very presentable, very able. But he just seems to fall short when he has to take up a particular standpoint".

Mrs Helen Suzman, for many years the sole representative of the Progressive Party in the House of Assembly, now one of the Progressive Federal team. "We came to Parliament together. I

1. See note 11, Chapter two.
2. MP for Natal South Coast from 1948 to 1974. Mitchell was a fiery and outspoken politician who was Leader of the United Party in Natal for 25 years.

246

would say this of her: <u>I have a high regard for the way in which she has preserved her femininity and the way that she dresses. She is always smart, she is always neat</u>. I do not want to mention names, but we have had some women who have been just the opposite in Parliament. Her politics I consider decidedly dangerous for South Africa and my own view is that she has rendered great disservice to South Africa. However, ignoring her political views, she is a good parliamentarian – if she was not, she would never have achieved her present status. She can put her case very well indeed, except that she tends to exaggerate. But then, some people might very well say the same of me. She is too obsessed with certain ideas and, as she gets older, she becomes more and more frustrated because she cannot get her way".

Mr Colin Eglin, Leader of the Progressive Federal Party and MP for Sea Point. "As a backbencher in the old United Party, he was a very able man. When he came back to Parliament in 1974 as Leader of the Progressive Party, I thought seriously that he would make a great impact on Parliament. He has not made that impact and I am inclined to think that Helen Suzman cramps his style in the same way that a possessive mother cramps the style of her kids. He does not impress me as a man with great leadership qualities – and here I am talking of his activities in the House of Assembly because I have no knowledge of what happens in his Party. In the House he has fallen far short of my expectations".

Mr Harry Schwarz, one-time Leader of the United Party in the Transvaal and the Leader of the "Young Turk" movement which tried to change the UP. Now a leading member of the Progressive Federal Party and MP for Yeoville. "Far too impulsive, far too full of Harry Schwarz. But able, very able, and a hard worker."

Dr F van Zyl Slabbert, MP for Rondebosch and another leading member of the Progressive Federal Party, a man many of the PFP members see as a future leader. "Well, when he stood for Parliament, you will remember that the Opposition newspapers raved about him, spoke of him as a future Prime Minister and that kind of thing. If that is so, then that future is very, very far off indeed. I get the idea that being a back-bencher in a small party with limited time for debate in Parliament is steadily killing Van Zyl Slabbert politically. It means that he has very little scope because he has so little time for debate and it is difficult to judge his abilities in Parliament – and it is in Parliament that a political leader or a potential political leader must stand the real test of leadership".

And Vorster's thoughts on *Parliament* itself. "Parliament is a harsh taskmaster. It does not pass over anybody or anything and if you land in the parliamentary mill, you are ground very fine indeed, unless you have the qualities to make the grade. And those qualities are very difficult to describe. What makes a politician? One might as well ask: What makes a woman? Some women have IT and others do not. And the same might be said for politicians. Some have that indefinable IT and others do not. You cannot sit down and list the qualities. I have seen chaps go to the Bar with a mediocre academic record and I have seen them make a tremendous success. On the other hand, I have seen chaps who graduated with honours go the Bar and get absolutely nowhere. Parliament tends to weed out people, not necessarily the good people from the bad people, of course, because I have seen some good men go under and some bad guys come out on top. To illustrate the point, a farmer friend of mine in the Orange Free State tends to sleep rather late in the morning – unlike almost every other farmer I know. However, he is a very good farmer and he does exceptionally well. One day his neighbour came to him and said: 'Jurgen, I can understand many things. But this thing I cannot understand: our ground is the same because my farm is next to yours, the climate is the same, we grow the same crops and we run the same stock, I get up long before sunrise and I work myself near to death while you only get up when the sun is high, and, yet, your farm progresses while mine goes backwards'. My friend replied: 'Oom Piet, that is so. The difference is that when I do leave my bed, then I am awake man'. This is what Parliament is all about. When you stand up there to speak, then you must be awake. Personally, I do not write out my speeches ever, except when I am dealing with a highly technical matter or when a section of the speech must be worded very precisely indeed, possibly because it is meant for overseas consumption. I do not write out my speeches because I feel that I will be a total flop if I do. Rightly or wrongly, when I stand up in Parliament, I want to argue the case. I think people who listen to you, in Parliament and at political meetings, want to hear argument. It is a sacrifice enough for people to come to political meetings and, good heavens, if you still have to give them a sing-song speech read from a piece of paper instead of a full-blooded political speech, you are letting them down badly. In any case, this is my nature, I put my points down on a piece of paper and then I proceed to argue the case just as if I was in court ...".

On retirement. "Candidly, if I come to the conclusion that my going would not harm South Africa and it would not harm the National Party, then I would go tomorrow. And when I am out, then I am out. Some boxers have come back, but most have made an awful mess. Some politicians have come back and made quite a success of it, but they are few and far between. Once I retire, I would like to think that I have retired for good. I would not like to hang like the proverbial millstone around my successor's neck. When I do go, I would like an opportunity to tell people how they should treat my successor. I would like to tell them to treat my successor in the same way as I would have liked to have been treated – and people did not always treat me as I would have liked them to. I will not in any way try to name a successor or influence the selection of a successor. Dr Malan, unfortunately, tried to impose Havenga on the National Party, and that was wrong. It was wrong in the moral sense, in the practical sense, in the political sense ... in every possible way. This sort of thing is bad tactics, bad politics. And it is unfair. I will just drop out. Naturally, I will take a keen interest in what is happening. Politics, after all, is right there in one's blood and it stands to reason that you cannot suddenly become apolitical overnight. But it also stands to reason that I will avoid public statements. I know only too well just how complex things are for a Prime Minister and I know only too well that, in many instances, he is the only man who has all the facts. And you cannot comment with justice on any action of his unless you, too, have all the facts. Apart from this, you must accept that any man who reaches the position of Prime Minister is not an absolute fool and that he always has good reasons for taking a certain step, even though his action might appear foolish to an outsider. I have plenty of experience of this kind of thing and I know how often it is that you cannot always say to people, even those closest to you, why you did this or that or why, in a given set of circumstances, you took a particular step. Because I know this so well, I also know that I must not lightly judge my successor".

On the people who influenced him. "People always ask you whether anybody in particular has made a mark on you, whether you have modelled your own career on another's. But, if you do consciously mould yourself to your conception of another person, then you are ersatz, artificial, and you do not amount to a damned thing. As you go along, you pick up impressions, you learn from people. I have learned from all sorts of people, from leaders, from backbenchers, from ordinary men in the street, from constituents, from political adversaries. But the moment you consciously try to mould yourself to any pattern, you begin to fail. All my leaders have been extremely important to me and I have learned a great deal from each of them. But I say this: You are, after all, a product of all the influences which have come to bear on you and admittedly some influences have been heavier than others. But if you have your own strong character, then these influences will affect you differently to the way in which they will affect others. You will be, in effect, your own kind of man ...".

On his concept of Southern Africa. "You ask me what I am trying to do for Southern Africa, what I envisage for Southern Africa. Let me say firstly that peace is of the utmost importance because peace is the foundation for the development of any area. But you want more than peace, you want the normalisation of relations so that there can be trade between the various peoples and the various nations, so that the under-developed nations can benefit, so that there can be a really prosperous sub-continent consisting of politically-independent countries working closely together in the economic field. For myself, I am not very interested in unions or commonwealths or that kind of formalised thing. It might still come in this area and I suppose there are people who feel stronger about this sort of thing than I do. Perhaps if and when the normalisation of relations comes about, people will turn their minds to some kind of formal relationship. If this happens, well and good. However, my objective at this stage is to try to bring about peace and a normalisation of relations. This is the first objective. My concept of Southern Africa does not involve a very definite set of borders ... let me say I am thinking of the countries south of the equator. They form a natural region and I think the time will come when escalating transport costs mean that, in order to survive, countries will have to buy from the nearest market because it will also be the cheapest market – and we are so obviously the nearest and the best and, in the long term, the cheapest market for Southern Africa.

250

"When it comes to political systems, I say that I can live with any form of government as long as my internal affairs are not meddled with and as long as that government does not create trouble within my own country. Naturally, one would prefer to have a system of government of your own choice on your borders, but I can live with any form of government. To some extent we are co-existing successfully with the Mozambique Government even though it is Marxist – or says that it is Marxist. But, back to the future, there is no point in building castles in the air. The future must be left to the people who are in power then, if I might continue with the building analogy, in a sense, in seeking the normalisation of relationships, I am clearing the site so that it will be available for others to build on. Once there is normalisation of relations, I think the problem of future relationships will take care of itself. One thing I know is this: The whole area lends itself well to a closer relationship because the different countries complement each other so well. I know that it will be difficult to achieve the close relationship I envisage because you are dealing with people of different cultural insights, people of different backgrounds and with widely differing levels of education and development. But I believe that it can be done. All that it will require is a degree of responsibility and clear-sightedness on the part of the leaders of the area ...".

On Chief Leabua Jonathan, the Prime Minister of Lesotho. "When first I met Jonathan in 1967 we had a very friendly discussion indeed and we both held out high hopes for good relations between our two countries. We revised the customs union agreements in a way that very definitely favoured Lesotho. You leant over backwards in order to help Lesotho – and Botswana and Swaziland – develop. In fact the revised agreement was a deliberate attempt to be as generous as possible. But Oliver asked for more and Oliver is never satisfied once he has tasted the good life. Now Jonathan has found that by raving against South Africa he can raise money in different countries. With him it is a question of money. There can be no other acceptable explanation for the way he has turned his back on us. For instance, there is the question of water from Oxbow. Jonathan was under the impression that we just had to have that Oxbow water. But Oxbow was not economic and there comes a limit to what we will pay. So Jonathan pushed too far – and I think he realises this today".

On Malawi's President Hastings Banda. "Banda stands out as a man with an opposite approach to Jonathan's. He started from the standpoint that his people are not rich, that Malawi is not a rich country and that it has a considerable backlog to catch up on. And he acted accordingly. First of all he set about bringing stability and discipline to Malawi. He inspired his people to work hard, to build their country up from the bottom. As a result, Malawi today is a country which is developing steadily. I respect this and I respect greatly Banda's attitude. And, because of this, Malawi's chances of getting assistance from South Africa are so much greater. It fits in with my own political philosophy on Africa, which is quite clear. Our aim is to help people help themselves. This is what has impressed me about Malawi. We helped Malawi and she is now helping herself – and very impressively so. Lesotho is just the opposite. Jonathan wants to start at the top. He wants the money to come flowing in. He does not want to start at the bottom and provide the really lasting foundation for development".

On Sir Seretse Khama, President of Botswana. "I have only met Khama once and that was when he came to pay his respects to me and to thank me for having him in hospital here[3]. We are not over-fond of each other – that stands to reason. But we get on well. I think Khama is a man with his feet on the ground. He realises that he has got to build up his country and that development must come from within, that you cannot develop a country simply by taking hand-outs like Lesotho has done over the past couple of years. Botswana is obviously the most strategically-placed Black country in relation to South Africa and I realise that there must be tremendous pressures on Sir Seretse. But I think he has been relatively level-headed about it all and I think he takes the interests of his own country very much to heart. Also there is a level of real democracy in Botswana which is absent from most other African countries".

On Swaziland. "By tradition, we have always had friendly relations with Swaziland. I have never met King Sobhuza but I have met the Prime Minister and a number of ministers. We got on well. I find Swaziland a country which does not want to blow itself up like a frog. And that is the difference between countries like

3. Sir Seretse Khama visited South Africa on a number of occasions for treatment for liver and heart complaints.

Botswana and Swaziland on the one hand, and Lesotho. Lesotho has developed delusions of grandeur."

On Portugal and its then African provinces. "I was in Portugal in 1970 to meet Caetano and I had three days of discussions with him. It soon became clear that there was a fundamental difference in our outlooks in that I believed in separate development and ultimate independence for Black peoples while this appeared anathema for Caetano and Portugal. However, we had a great deal of common interest which made high-level discussion both necessary and rewarding. I found Caetano a typical Professor of Law and he impressed me more as an academician than as a politician. Throughout the discussions I had with him, I sensed something that I simply could not put my finger on. Then at the state banquet in my honour – a very glittering affair at the Little Versailles (The Queluz Palace) – he sat opposite me. There were about 15 ministers and top government officials at the table and Caetano turned to me and suddenly said from across the table:. 'Of the 15 you see here, 12 are my former students'. Then it suddenly struck me that his was not a cabinet. It was a Professor and his students running the country. And it became clear to me that the relationship was not one between a Prime Minister and a cabinet, but between a student and professor. And this is wrong, obviously wrong. My own relationship with my Cabinet Ministers is to give them the responsibility and then to allow them to exercise it. I am not there to run any minister's portfolio, although naturally, one keeps an eye on them and one keeps in constant touch with what is happening. It is the minister's responsibility to conduct everyday affairs. If you think a minister has done wrong, you first ask for all the particulars from that minister because you cannot judge until you have all the particulars.

"When it came to the question of independence for Portuguese territories like Mozambique and Angola, I never actually suggested that Caetano should give them independence. However at that stage Caetano was greatly perturbed about our intention of giving self-government to Owambo because he believed that it would influence the situation in Angola and because it ran contrary to his own concept of what should happen in Angola and Mozambique. You must not forget that Portugal, a small European country, set great store by these two vast tracts of African land. When it came to the future of Portugal in Africa, I think that, in my own mind, the writing was already on the wall. But it is like a very sick man. You know he is sick and you are almost certain that he is going to die, but when he does die, it always seems to take you by surprise. And this is how the Spinola coup and the subsequent events in Portugal and its African provinces affected me. This despite the fact that it had gradually dawned on me that the longer the wars in both Mozambique and Angola carried on, the worse the situations in those territories would become. This fed into my own thinking and it naturally affected my planning and policies. All this meant that I knew that I would have to live with independent and possibly even hostile states on my borders. That is why South Africa adopted the attitude that she was not interested in who formed a government or in what kind of a government it was. She was only interested that it should be a good government".

On the appointment of Cabinet Ministers. "Basically, it is not for a Prime Minister to pull somebody up, it is up to his contemporaries to thrust him forward. If you see that his contemporaries have thrust a man up, if you see that his contemporaries listen to him with some respect in the caucus and in Parliament, then you must keep your eyes on him. And if you see that he proves himself in the House – always the ultimate test, in my opinion – then you know that you have cabinet material on your hands. Another important point is that a Prime Minister – any Prime Minister – can only bring in a very limited number of people from outside the political machine. Mostly because you owe it to the people who have been prepared to work through the machine to allow them to pick the fruits, but also because a man or a woman simply cannot make a success of a political career without having gone through the machine. Naturally there are exceptions, but they are few and far between. Speaking generally, perhaps I can best illustrate it with this story: Think of a Prime Minister as a gardener. He is confronted with a number of plants and naturally there are some plants which he favours and which he might water secretly during the night. But when it comes to picking the fruit, he must pick the best fruit. And it will happen that some of the plants he has watered secretly during the night do not bear fruit or their fruit is unsuitable. So he must leave them alone. And just as naturally, some of the plants that he has not watered will bear fruit in large measure – and he must pick that fruit, whatever his feelings might

254

be. It does not offer you much, if any, personal choice. The Prime Minister must promote those people who have been thrust upwards by the political process. It is a mistake, in fact, to make cabinet appointments a personal issue and I have tried to avoid this at all times. It is not one's personal interests that count but the interests of the country and of the party."

On the leadership of a political party. "In the first place, you must do the very obvious: You must lead. You must lead in caucus, in Parliament and outside Parliament you must give a lead to your people. But, as I have so often said, no leader must ever get out of sight or out of earshot of his followers. And he must never try to lead from behind. Your followers expect that in all fields, but especially in the caucus where the most intimate matters are discussed, that you should give them a clear lead. A man who cannot give a lead in the caucus will find that his party slowly disintegrates. I would like to think that I am giving a lead and that I am keeping the correct distance between myself and my followers. And I like to think that I know where I am going. On this point, there is this current parrot-cry "change". Everybody wants to change things. Everybody wants the Prime Minister to make change. But what kind of change? Change from what to what? These people never stop for a moment to think of the full consequences of their cries for change. As I have said, I like to think that I know where I am going and that I know what my objectives are. I have already said that the National Party is not stagnant and I say now that it will make the changes that are necessary in order to reach its objectives. But those changes will be made in an orderly fashion and according to a definite pattern and strategy. When it comes to objectives, my first objective is to safeguard the identity of my nation – and by my nation I mean those Afrikaners and those English-speakers who feel the same and who identify themselves with each other. Secondly, I do not want anything which will lead to the position where the political power over your own people passes out of your hands. Finally, one wants to see peace, prosperity and order for all the peoples of the country. I think these are my main objectives and I think it is fair to say that everything I have done or that I have tried to do is rooted in these objectives".

On Africa. "I grew up believing that we Whites have a mission to fulfil in Africa, that we have a duty towards Africa, that Africa has

255

been good to us, that Africa is our mother, that Africa, having been good to us, deserves something from us in return. I am being honest and sincere when I say that I believe that we have a duty towards Africa. Naturally, at the same time, you want to do your level best to get your own people accepted by Africa, accepted as an African people with every right to be in Africa, as opposed to the here-today-gone-tomorrow idea of the colonialists. I believe that we have as much right as any other nation to be in Africa. But I also believe that we have a duty to Africa. We must try to be of use to Africa, to give guidance, advice, expertise. After all, there is a great deal that we can give to Africa. We are the only White people, call it technologically developed people if you wish, that have come to terms with Africa. This makes our technology, our expertise that much more valuable because it is of Africa itself. It is not expertise developed in Europe and then transplanted to Africa in the hope that it can be adapted to African people and African traditions. It is not a coincidence that my people are called Afrikaners, that we called our language Afrikaans. We are Africans, we are of Africa and to my last day in politics I will strive to have us accepted by the people of Africa ...".

And then there are a few stories which tell much about Vorster.

The Parade, Cape Town: "I have always been a great Parade man. Before I was Prime Minister and people were less concerned about my security and that kind of thing, and when I had the time, I used to go to the Parade regularly. There were interesting people to see and there were interesting things to buy. In the process, I became very friendly with an old couple, Mr and Mrs Stokes, who had a stall on the Parade. And when I went to the Parade, I always sat down to have tea with them – and a long chat. Suddenly on a day after I became Prime Minister, I said to myself: 'John, it is time that you visited the Parade again, just by yourself, just as it was in the old days.' So I told my chief security chap that I wanted to go to the Parade, on my own, that I wanted to walk about the parade all by myself. He said: 'Yes Sir'. And that was that. The two of us went down to the Parade and I told him: 'Alwyn Conradie, you just go and lose yourself, I do not want to see you again during the next hour-and-a-half'. And I thought to myself: At least I am alone again, just as I was in the days when I was still the Minister of Justice when I never had a bodyguard, when I always went just where I wanted to go. Still in this frame of mind, I had not gone 20 paces when I saw a man whom I recognised as a policeman in plain clothes. I called to him and asked: 'What are you doing here' and he replied: 'Sir, I am investigating a crime'. I asked: 'Since when do police officers investigate crime on Cape Town's Parade on a Saturday morning dressed in a safari suit?' He just smiled at me rather sheepishly. Another 20 paces or so and I recognised a second policeman. I promptly asked him whether he, too, was there to investigate a crime on the Parade on a Saturday morning. He said: 'Yes sir' with a huge smile on his face. So I knew that I was not alone, that all of them were there, and that I would probably never really be alone for as long as I was Prime Minister.

"But anyway, what could I do, and so I went to the Stokes' stall and we had tea sitting on boxes – those were the only seats. I had a lovely chat to Mr and Mrs Stokes about this and that until a Coloured minister of religion approached me and asked whether he could speak to me. In parenthesis, one of your big problems as Prime Minister is that everybody recognises you and now with television it is going to become even worse. However, I told him that I had all the time in the world to talk to him. We gave him a box to sit on and the two of us talked for about half an hour or so. It was a very interesting conversation and when I looked up I saw that there was a whole group of people standing around listening to us.

"The Coloured minister wanted to talk to me about separate development and how he saw it. It was one of the most positive expositions of the policy of separate development that I have ever heard. It was not a question of asking me for anything. He made three points: Firstly, he told me how proud he was to go to a post office and talk to a postmaster who was one of his own people. Secondly, he said how proud he was to patronise a service station belonging to one of his own people. Thirdly, he said how proud he was to go to a good-class restaurant run by one of his own people. When we had finished talking, a man broke through the circle around us, introduced himself to me and said that he was a passenger on board a ship now anchored in the harbour. He asked me: 'Sir, please tell me, are you the Prime Minister of South Africa as these people around you say you are?' I replied, 'Yes sir, they tell me that too'. And he looked just a little put out, saying: 'By heaven! If I arrive back in Britain and tell people that I saw the Prime Minister of South Africa sitting on a box on the Parade in Cape

Town talking to a Coloured man, they will tell me that I am a liar. And if I tell them that I went up to the Prime Minister of South Africa, introduced myself to him and talked to him, then they are going to call me a bloody liar'. With that, he shook my hand and strode off, back to his boat ..."

Driving in the Kruger National Park. "Got a letter the other day from a chap. It was a short letter: 'Sir, would you kindly settle a bet I took with a friend of mine that I saw you driving your wife in the Kruger National Park and that it was only the two of you in the car. He said I was a liar and I bet him R10 that it was so'. So I wrote back to him one line only: 'Tell your friend to pay'. You see they (the security people) never want me to drive my own car – and driving my car is a great luxury for me. So when we get into the Park, I tell the security chaps to get into the car following me and I drive myself. This is the only place that they will allow me to drive my own car in and I think that is the thing I miss most about being Prime Minister is the fact that I cannot drive my own car ..."

Meeting President Kenneth Kaunda[4]. "I flew in early that morning and, at the appointed time, I walked over the bridge with Hilgard Muller, Brand Fourie[5], Hendrik van den Bergh and Johann van Rooyen[6] and maybe two or three other chaps. There were literally thousands of Black people on the other side of the bridge and I heard a British reporter saying to a chap standing next to him, 'I still think he has not got the guts to walk in amongst the crowd on the other side'. Well, we walked across the bridge and we were met by Mark Chona[7]. He showed us into a Mercedes 600, which is much smarter then my own Mercedes, and off we went. As far as I was concerned, they could have driven me to Timbuctoo. We stopped in front of a hotel in Livingstone where there was a crowd of hundreds of Black people and a few White people. The whole route from the bridge to the hotel was lined by thousands of Blacks waving banners with slogans like 'Vorster is a Statesman' and

4. The meeting was a product of a 1974 joint Vorster/Kaunda initiative to arrange talks between Rhodesia's Prime Minister Ian Smith and Bishop Abel Muzorewa of the African National Congress. Vorster provided the venue for the talks in the form of South Africa's presidential White Train (the State President's train which is used for top dignitaries). which was parked on the Victoria Falls bridge between Zambia and Rhodesia.
5. Secretary of Foreign Affairs.
6. Vorster's chief bodyguard.
7. Special adviser to the Zambian President and one of his closest and most trusted associates.

cheering loudly. Well, I hardly thought a year ago or so that I would ever get this kind of reception in Zambia, but my thoughts were cut short by our arrival at the hotel where President Kaunda and his ministers were waiting for us. I got out of the car, he greetd me very warmly and then introduced me to his ministers. All around us were photographers, television cameramen and cheering Black people. We went into the hotel, tea was ordered and the first thing Kaunda said to me was: 'I am told, Mr Prime Minister, that you tell a very good story about Amin. My ministers and I have been waiting for this moment to meet you and to hear the story from your on lips'. I had made up the story myself and I thought it was a very good one so I told them: 'Mr President, the story goes like this: Having elevated himself to field marshal, Amin thought it was time to change the name of his country and he decided to change it to Idi. He gave all the necessary instructions and all the necessary documents were drawn up for the change. However, before the gazette making the change legal was due to come out, one of the few wise men left came to him in great haste and said: 'Mr Field Marshal you must stop this notice immediately. We can't possibly change the name of Uganda to Idi'. So Amin asked: 'Why not? Is Idi not a beautiful name? Is Idi not the name of the strongest and most bemedalled man in Africa? Why can't we change Uganda to Idi? 'And the wise man replied: 'No, Mr Field Marshal, there is nothing wrong with the name Idi, but it has only come to my notice today that there is a country in the world called Cyprus'. Amin asked: 'So what?' And the wise man replied: 'Well, Field Marshal, they call the people of that country Cypriots ...' Well, I tell you I have never seen people laugh so much in my life. Kaunda almost cracked his sides laughing. He enjoyed it so much that later in the day he suddenly asked me to tell him the whole story all over again.

"Well, after I had told him the story about Amin for the first time, he asked me whether he could tell me a story as well. I agreed and he told me the story about Van der Merwe and I growing up together. The story goes that our ways parted and I did not see Van for many years. Then we met again and he told me that he was farming in Zambia, a good country with fertile soil and a good government. He asked me what I was doing and I said that I had become the Prime Minister of South Africa. He wasn't impressed and said, 'Oh well, John, where I come from, we make the Natives do that work'. We all laughed and I asked Kaunda where he had heard the story. He said he had heard it from Sir Seretse Khama and I responded, looking at Kaunda, 'Well, here's one Native I think is doing a good job'. And we all laughed again. Then we started talking business, went back to the bridge where I said my piece and Kaunda said his piece.

"When we came out of the coach, I asked him: 'Mr President, when last were you in Rhodesia?. He said he could not remember, but he thought it was in 1961 or 1962. So I said to him: 'Let's go and look at the place'. He replied: 'Okay, with you I will go anywhere'. So off we went to the Rhodesian side to the great consternation of the security men. We got into a car – I don't know whose car it was but I rather think it was Ian Smith's car – and we drove off with assorted security men rushing behind. I told Kaunda that the General Manager of the South African Railways had a coach at the Victoria Falls station and that we should go and have tea there. He seemed to be enjoying himself enormously and we sat talking for about an hour while Kobus Loubser[8] served us with tea. Then it was time for us to cross to the other side again for a lunch in Livingstone at which I was the guest of honour. Kaunda asked me to say grace and I said it in Afrikaans. The whole affair was very friendly and I enjoyed it greatly. After lunch I rested for a while in a suite that had been reserved for me. Then we all went back to the train and while the parties directly concerned were discussing their affairs, Kaunda and I talked for a while – about the Rhodesian problem, about our own relations about this and about that. I must say we got on very well together. Later we went back for dinner at the hotel on his side. I had dinner alone in my suite and then back to the train where Kaunda and I talked again until about 11,30. Then I said to him: 'Mr President, I am sorry, I must go now'. And I left, went to the airport and flew back to Pretoria".

\Discussion with African nationalist Duma Nokwe. "When I was at the Bar in Johannesburg in the early '50s, Duma Nokwe, Secretary-General of the African National Congress, was also an advocate. One day I invited him to come to my chambers and I said to him: 'Nokwe, I want to talk to you, not as a White Man to a Black Man, not as an Afrikaner Nationalist to an ANC leader, but as an advocate to an advocate. I want to ask you a question and a great

8. General Manager of the South African Railways and Harbours Administration.

deal – as far as my attitude to you is concerned – will depend on your answer. What I want to know from you is why you decided to come to the Bar. In all fairness, I want to say that before you answer, I decided to become a lawyer because I thought that it was a reasonable living, but also because I wanted to serve my people by entering politics as a lawyer. Was it the same with you?' He answered me: 'No, I'm not interested in people, I'm interested only in governing this country – and we WILL govern this country one day'. So I said to him: 'If that is your attitude, then I have nothing further to say to you. If that is your attitude to your people, then I don't want to talk to you and I am going to tell you now that you are going to land in trouble one day'. With that he left – and he did get into trouble[9]. You see, there was this basic difference between us. He wanted power, with me it was a question of serving my people. And today it is still a question of serving my people..."

---

9. With twelve other people Nokwe was sentenced to a year's imprisonment in terms of the Unlawful Organisations Act for furthering the objects of the banned Pan Africanist Congress in 1961. However, the next year an appeal against both the judgement and the sentence was upheld in the Supreme Court. He later fled the country.

13 *The man and his family*

On the morning of September 13, 1966, just before his election as Leader of the National Party and thus Prime Minister of South Africa, Vorster telephoned his sons at their boarding school in Pretoria. He told them what was due to happen and added: "Remember, no matter what might happen today – keep your feet on the ground". And it was appropriate that, as he reached for the pinnacle of his political career, he should pass this message to his sons. Because if the Vorster family has a motto, then that motto reflects their determination to keep their feet on the ground, to remain "ordinary" people, to retain their friends, to live their lives as fully and as naturally as possible – despite high office and political success which had taken the family from a modest home in Brakpan to a ministerial residence in Pretoria and, ultimately, to Libertas and Groote Schuur, the official homes of South African Prime Ministers in Pretoria and Cape Town respectively.

It is the thread that runs through the assessment of Vorster the man by his old university friends. Says Flooi du Plessis: "He has not changed in the slightest since the days at university and he has kept all his friends through the years. I cannot think of a single friend that that man has lost. If I had to sit down now and list his qualities, the very first that springs to mind is his dependability. He is a dependable man and that is why I cannot conceive that he will ever turn his back on those Afrikaners who are loyal to him; and that is why he has never turned his back on a friend. He is tremendously loyal, both to his beliefs and to his friends. Dependability, loyalty, ambition tied to the concept of service and a great sense of history. These are the things I believe make Vorster tick. When I say he believes in being of service, I mean that he tries to do everything as well as he can. By a sense of history, I mean that he sees himself and he must be seen in the context of Afrikaner Nationalism. I think the basis of John's beliefs is still Afrikaner

Nationalism and, from what I know of him, I cannot see him except against the background of Afrikaner Nationalism. It is what gives him his drive, it is what motivates him. And I think that if ever Afrikaner Nationalism disappointed him, this would break his heart ...".

Flip la Grange says: "Throughout the years he has changed not a bit. He is the man we knew at university ... and he has not lost a single friend in all those years in spite of climbing up the ladder from a university first-year to Prime Minister. What are his most outstanding characteristics? Well, I got to know Vorster very well and I tell you he is the first person I would ask to come with me if I had to go to war. In other words, he is a man that I could trust through thick and thin – as a person, as a friend and as a Party man. As far as I am concerned, he is absolutely honest, absolutely reliable. He is a life-time friend who has been the same to me over all these years. He is a leader, nobody who knows him can deny that. He is tremendously loyal and he has a tremendous sense of duty".

And Willem Dempsey: "Vorster has not changed one jot or tittle. He is the same friendly man he was at university. Of course, the cares of high office weigh heavily on him. Apart from this he has not changed at all: and the same holds good for that wonderful wife of his. She is the same person she was when we were all at university. He is a man of great integrity, a man with a great sense of duty, a man who has never lost a friend ..."

Vorster indeed, remains true to his friends. One of his closest university friends was a young man named Amandus Scholtz who graduated from the University of Stellenbosch and eventually served in Johannesburg as psychological inspector of schools. However, he died in his early thirties and was buried at Ventersburg in the Orange Free State. While in Johannesburg, he would visit the Vorsters' Brakpan home almost every weekend. So, whenever Vorster passed Ventersburg, whether it was on offiical business, whether he was on his way to Parliament or on his way home, he would stop at the cemetery and doff his hat to his old friend. Vorster explains: "He was a wonderful chap, Amandus. We were very close and so it was a natural thing for me to say hullo to him every time I passed Ventersburg. I have not been past the town by car for almost 15 years now, but when next I pass, I will pay my respects again."

The views of others close to Vorster are:

"As long as he is convinced that he is acting in the interests of the country, nothing and nobody can put him off his stride" – Koot Vorster, brother[1].

"John Vorster is a man of absolute and unimpeachable integrity. He walks only one road and that is the straight road. He also believes that one must work hard for every cent" – The late Gert Bezuidenhout, an old friend[2].

"John is the most even-tempered man I know , he is the easiest man to live with. In all our years together, I have never heard him raise his voice once ... you know John doesn't show his feelings like other people, he does not get upset, he does not get agitated ..." Tini Vorster.

"Everything he thinks, does or says, he thinks does or says because he has first thought about it. I do not for one moment think that he will ever say something that he does not mean ... there is too much at stake for him" – Willem Vorster, son[3].

"He is a very impractical person. For instance, he cannot fix an electric plug, he cannot change a tyre, he cannot fix a leaking roof, he knows absolutely nothing about what he refers to as 'machinery'" – Elsa Kolwer, daughter.

"He does not act from ulterior motives. He acts according to what he thinks is in the best interests of the Afrikaners and the South African nation. Now I think he is misguided and that his priorities are absolutely wrong ... but there is no doubt whatsoever about the man's genuineness or his integrity" – Kowie Marais, who is now totally opposed to Vorster politically.

Discussing his father, Willem Vorster says: "My father's philosophy, which I think he applies very widely now, is the same as the philosophy he applied to his children. He will let you do a thing after having given you the necessary advice. Then he will wait until you have bumped your head before he intervenes. But he will never prescribe to you."

This attitude is confirmed by many of the Cabinet Ministers and senior officials who have worked with Vorster. He does not tell

1. Cape Argus 13/9/1966.
2. Beeld 18/9/1966.
3. Most of the Vorster children's references to their parents come from a South African Broadcasting Corporation programme, broadcast on the Afrikaans service during 1976. It was titled "'n Man soos my pa" (A man like my father).

them they are wrong. He does not tell them: "Do this, do that." He makes suggestions instead – as he explains himself: "As Minister of Justice, I never issued orders. My way of dealing with a situation was to say to the head of a department: 'Don't you think you should try this or that? Don't you think this way will be better? Should you not think about doing it another way?' I have found that you get far better results doing things in this manner. Making suggestions is far better than giving direct orders. You must not throw your weight around. Nobody likes or respects a man who throws his weight around. Nobody co-operates with anybody who throws his weight around. I remember being told a story about a Cabinet Minister who served many, many years ago. I won't mention his name, but the story goes that there was a file on his desk which he had not attended to for a very long time. Ultimately the head of the department said to him that the matter was extremely urgent. The minister replied: 'Mr Secretary, nothing in this office is urgent unless I say so'. Well, that sort of thing just does not work out. It is completely at odds with the philosophy that I have applied and which I contine to apply. I take the viewpoint that departmental heads are experts in their fields and that Cabinet Ministers are supposed to be experts in their fields as well. When a decision has to be taken, I first hear out the experts. Once I have heard the experts, then I do not hesitate to come to a decision. And when I have come to a decision, then I put it to the minister by way of a suggestion or by saying: 'I think we should do this ...', never by way of a direct order. As Prime Minister, you want to run things so that your ministers feel free to come to you at all times to discuss matters with you ..."

Though Vorster is not afraid to take a decision, he very rarely takes a snap decision. While decisions – even on vital matters – came easily to Verwoerd, who was utterly convinced he was right, Vorster takes his decision-making responsibilities very seriously indeed. He agonises over important decisions. "Important decisions take a great deal out of one. For instance, many a time when people think that you are taciturn or perhaps they might even feel that you are unfriendly, then it is because you are rolling things around in your head, constantly weighing up this thing and that thing ..." And, behind almost every decision is a balance sheet. "That is always my approach to a problem. As a lawyer this is the obvious approach. In all your decisions, in everything in which you are involved, it is a question of sorting out the pros and the cons, taking a hard look at them, assessing them, re-assessing them, taking the decision and then translating that decision into action. But that is what politics is all about – weighing up the pros and cons. Naturally, you do not take your decisions easily, you apply your mind to them as fully as you can. However, there are occasions when you are under such pressure that you do not have the time to work out a balance sheet in your mind. There are times when you have to rely on your political instincts, your feel for politics. Let me say outright that I have relied very heavily on my political instincts on a number of occasions and, on balance, I think that I have come out of these decisions on the right side. I think I inherited my instincts in politics from my mother who was very seldom wrong when she relied on her instincts – and, when I refer to my mother, I am referring to instincts in a much broader field than politics".

Even though, sitting behind his desk, Vorster exudes power, I accept it when he says "I am here because I want to serve my people. I am not here because I enjoy power or the exercise of power. As I have said so often – to you as well – a person cannot eat power. It is a fool who lusts after power. I never have. I have certainly used power and I will continue to use power in the interests of the country. But I do not think that I have tried to advance either my own or my Party's interests by the exercise of power. And when I one day walk out of that door and retire, I will not miss power for one single moment . . . that I can assure you".

But, while power as such may hold few attractions for him, he loves and enjoys politics – especially debating an important issue in the House of Assembly. He once told me that the things he enjoyed most in life were: speaking in Parliament, arguing a case in a court of law and cross-examining a witness. But what stimulates him most is speaking in Parliament. "Frankly, every time you get on your feet to speak in Parliament it is a whole new experience in itself. It's stimulating, it's exhilarating, it's a completely new adventure. I never write my speeches out, and I walk around, sometimes for days on end with thoughts running about in my mind. Then I jot down a few notes, collect any material to which I might have to refer and prepare to argue my case in Parliament – just as if I am in a court of law. And I prepare myself for the cross-examination of the Opposition, if necessary. In fact, I must go further: every day, every meeting I address is a new adventure. Every game of golf I play, every game of chess, every game of bridge is a new adventure ... that is how I look on life".

In Parliament, Vorster operates according to a basic strategy in dealing with adversaries. He either ignores them completely or he chides them gently – or else he hits them with everything he has. There is no grey area between "chiding gently" or "hitting with everything I have" – and he admits this. In discussion, he says: "I must confess, this is my nature, I don't think I could operate differently even if I had wanted to. Look, I regard myself as a politician. People criticise me for not being a 'statesman'. Well, quite frankly, I have never been able to discern when a man stops being a politician and when he starts being a statesman. I think I am just a politician whose job it is to lead his party in the interests of the country; to protect his party from attack, to protect every member of his party from attack. And, against this background, I say that every man who steps into the political arena with me must expect to be either ignored, or chided lightly or hit with everything I have. However, I like to think that even when I do hit somebody with everything I have that I do so with a degree of finesse – I never rant, I never rave, I am never abusive. I do not believe in half measures and if a man steps into the political area with me, whether he be a politician, a churchman, a businessman or an editor, then he must be prepared for everything he gets. And if he wants to squeal when he is hit hard, then he must not step into the arena. I can take it – but I can also dish it out. I don't lose my temper in the House because I know that the man who loses his temper has already lost the fight. Sometimes you get really angry, but then you must not show that you are angry. And sometimes, for that matter, you pretend to lose your temper in order to scare some guy off, in order to get somebody off your back. That is what politics is all about. I could have sued people for libel ever so often. However, I did not because I believe that you expose yourself when you enter politics and that you must be prepared to take the knocks when they come along – even some very hard knocks. I have never squealed and I do not think that I will ever squeal. I just hit back. You must remember that 'n sagte heelmeester maak stinkende wonde[4] ..."

4. Literally: A soft physician makes stinking wounds.

This attitude was confirmed by one of the homeland Chief Ministers who told me after one of their meetings with Vorster that he had been exceptionally pleased with the level of communication – although he was unhappy because of what he referred to as Vorster's intransigence. He said that he had embarked on very severe criticism of Vorster when one of his colleagues suggested he should tone down his invective. Vorster intervened and said: "No, let him say what he has to say. I can take it – as long as he can take my reply".

Vorster makes no bones about his likes and his dislikes, about those people who are acceptable to him and those who are not. His sister Mona once said to me: "John can be very warm – and he usually is. But when he wants to snub somebody or give him the cold shoulder, then he does it infinitely more effectively than any other person I know".

Vorster himself says that he has nothing against people who genuinely differ from him. "But I cannot stand people who have ulterior motives, or people who are disloyal, or people I think are harming South Africa's interests. I will see them, if necessary. I will give them an opportunity to state their case. But the meeting is very formal and that's that. There are some people that I am finished with and one of those people is Albert Hertzog ... so I do not shake hands with him because I am finished with him. In 1967 the Black Sash, for instance, wrote to me and I told my Private Secretary to reply to them that it was a waste of time for them to write to me because I would not pay any attention to their representations. I did this because it was and still is my sincere belief that this organisation is unpatriotic – and I make no apologies for having done it in spite of the consternation my letter caused in the Opposition and in the English-language Press".

Apart from people he identifies as disloyal or unpatriotic, Vorster cannot stand what he refers to as "Important People". "I can't stand an Important Man. From my earliest days in my law practice right until now, I simply cannot take the kind of person who presents himself to you and says either directly or in effect: 'Do you know WHO I am ...'. I cannot stand people who put on airs and who think they must be treated differently because they are IMPORTANT".

His son Willem confirms this. "Father never praised us excessively. We really had to do something brilliant before he would say 'That was very good'. He's a chap who has a mania about preventing a person from getting a swollen head ... he abhors people who show off".

One of Vorster's favourite pastimes is playing chess. He plays a good game – but he can be very aggressive. A colleague who has played with him recalls that Vorster is a good and sometimes unorthodox player. However, the major characteristic of his game is his ability to take advantage of his opponent's slightest mistake. "You make one mistake, give him one opening and, almost certainly, that is the end of the game for you. His one move follows the next so relentlessly that you may as well pack up the moment you realise that you have given him an opening". And Vorster plays politics as he plays chess. Often (in terms of my own observation) his opponents and his critics have made fools of themselves because they have failed to take this into account, because they have failed to understand that when Vorster aims for a particular objective, his first move towards that objective might well be in the diametrically-opposed direction. It takes three, four or even five moves before his direction becomes clear – and then he moves towards his objective with great certainty. Generally, if it is within his power to reach the particular objective, then he reaches it. Because I am cautious, and generally waited before trying to judge any of Vorster's actions, I detected this chess-like approach to political action soon after starting to report politics in 1967. Which meant that I generally waited to see what move number two or move number three or move number four was before committing myself to comment on a particular Vorster line of action.

In playing chess, Vorster takes many a calculated risk – and he does the same as Prime Minister. He conceded: "Taking calculated risks goes with the job. Naturally, with so much at stake, one would not like to take any decision that is not based on the careful and certain examination of all the facts, options and consequences. That is how I would prefer to take my decisions and it is how I take decisions whenever it is possible. But you are often forced to take calculated risks. And when I have to take a calculated risk then I am not afraid to do so. The decision has to be taken and that is where your political aanvoeling (instinct) comes into play. If you have not got political aanvoeling then you can easily make a very serious mistake. Not, of course, that I have not made serious mistakes in my time. Fortunately, however, they have not been very visible ..."

Could he give an example of a mistake? "Of course not. I would be a fool if I started listing my mistakes to anybody but myself ..."

Perhaps in reaction to the care with which he has to take his calculated risks on affairs of state, Vorster takes tremendous chances when he is involved in a pastime like bridge. Comments his son Willem: "He is an outstanding bridge player in the sense that he takes tremendous chances. At times he is even reckless. But I think it is a kind of relaxation because, when it comes to his job, he cannot afford to take chances because the consequences can be unthinkable – and that is why he does it with something that does not matter ..."

When he plays, Vorster plays hard – and he likes winning. He also likes taking bets and he gets great pleasure when he wins a bet because he has outwitted his adversary, generally because of his extremely careful phrasing of the bet. To quote Willem again: "To play golf with him, or even just to walk with him when he is playing golf, is absolutely one of the most enjoyable things I can think of. He's always ready for a bet. He will lie in the roughest of the rough and he will always give you a ten cent bet that he will get out with one stroke. And he wins eighty per cent of these bets. I know that Piet and he played golf one day and I think they were six balls up. Piet was in ecstasy because they could not lose. However, as he told me afterwards: 'Sure enough, he takes a double-or-quits side bet on the last hole ... and we lose everything'. Piet was very unhappy over this".

Piet says: "It is very interesting. He likes choosing his opponents when he plays golf from amongst those who like to win, just as he does. And then he likes people who will – perhaps because he does it himself – constantly remind him of this, who will tell him all the time: 'Look man, I am going to walk all over you at the next hole'. He does it himself. When he plays, no matter whether it is with his children, he will say so often: 'Now, at this hole, I am going to show you ... just watch me ...'".

Willem again: "To tell a good story. This year (1976) we were in the Kruger National Park. It was the day on which the Durban July[5] was due to be run. I cannot remember the name of the horse

5. South Africa's premier horse race.

any more. Let us say it was Left Wing. So he said to me: 'I will give you a thousand to one that Left Wing does not win today'. Well, I thought to myself that I could not miss such an opportunity. And I said to him: 'Good' and I took a rand out of my pocket. He took the money and called Kolbe and John – those are Elsa's little ones – and told them: 'Here is a rand. Go and buy yourselves some sweets . . . Left Wing was scratched this morning!' He really caught me".

This attitude extends to other fields as well. On the very rare occasions that he has the opportunity to go shopping on his own, he likes to go into a small antique shop and buy something small, usually in silver. But he takes a pride in never paying the marked price. It is part of his pleasure to beat the price down, and when he gets home he takes great pride in telling the family that he managed to buy whatever it was for so much less than the shopkeeper had originally wanted.

Inevitably, what he has bought is intended as a present for somebody. To quote Elsa: "He loves giving presents. He gets great joy out of seeing the pleasure a present brings somebody else. But, when it comes to birthdays, he could often not wait until your birthday arrived. If he got the idea for a present a month or two before the time, he would buy it. But then he could never keep it until your birthday. You would get it immediately . . ."

Willem: "He has a philosophy that if you can attach greater importance to anything he has than he can attach to it, then you can have it. I know of many presents that he has received and many things that he has brought home which he has looked at once and then given away – to somebody who would value it more greatly then he himself valued it. To give an example: Pele, the world-famous Brazilian soccer player, sent him a jersey in which he had played and a soccer ball which he had signed. Father gave it to one of the Blacks who worked for us. Immediately after coming home one day, father showed the jersey, which had SFC printed in front and the number ten on the back, to Sam. And, without seeing whose signature was on the jersey, Sam identified it as a Santos Football Club jersey. When he saw the number ten on the back, he immediately said it was Pele's – and true enough, there was Pele's signature on the back. Because father realised that Sam knew immediately what it was and because he realised how much value Sam attached to it, he gave it to Sam for his Black soccer club".

Even when presents are for members of the family, Vorster cannot stand them remaining unopened. Elsa says: "He is absolutely mad about packages. He can become intensely irritated if we go to town, buy something here and there and then tell the shop either to deliver it or keep it for collection the next day. He wants to see things now. He wants us to open them immediately ..." Willem: "I think it reflects his simple humanity. Anybody loves opening packages – but I am not going to show it as much as he shows it. He is terribly fond of opening packages and he is terribly curious to see what is inside. I know how cross he was with Marie and I after our marriage. We went on honeymoon immediately. On our return we went through to Oubos the next day. He was terribly unhappy with us because we had not opened all the wedding presents the night before driving to Oubos. He was very sour because we had not looked to see what we had been given".

Vorster's children obviously adore him. Elsa says: "He made me aware of what the essence of life is, of what it is to LIVE in capital letters. He gave us security and, with his love for us, he aroused the same love in us for him. In a quiet way he made us aware of so many things in life ..."

Willem says: "I never had a father who did my homework for me. I never had a father who built a model aeroplane for me. But I have always had a father who would listen to me if I had a problem and who would give me advice – in his own manner. I always had a father who was available to me at all times. Our relationship was fantastic in the sense that he was an ideal father. Today, I will do anything my father tells me to do. I have a tremendous admiration for my father. But that admiration borders on something about which we cannot talk. I think the basic thing is that I would give him everything I have and do everything he says".

Pieter says: "My relationship with my father is of such a nature that if he tells me to move to another town tomorrow, that I must do something there, take up another job, that I must not continue doing what I am doing now, I would do it immediately – because, over the years, I have found little or no fault in his judgement. He is the sort of man that, if I should disappoint him, this would be the most tragic day of my life. I am as loyal to him as I could possibly be because he is so loyal to me ..."

Elsa says: "His kind of spoiling was always so special. For instance, as a child I can remember that he never left an aircraft without bringing home a glucose sweet for me. Those became 'aeroplane sweets' to me, and it is still that way today. He could give a child a sweet in such a way that it became a very special kind of sweet. And I watch him with my own children. When we go walking – and we are very fond of walking – he has the habit of pulling one or other of them closer with his walking stick. And this generates the very special feeling that grandfather notices me, that grandfather wants me to walk close to him ..."

Elsa again: "If there was one or other problem situation, then we would come together for a family parliament, usually sitting on a bed. And then everybody could put his or her standpoint. For instance, if it was a question of pocket money. Say we did not think the amount was right or that we thought that we should get it on a day other than a Friday, we would talk it out. This kind of thing has lasted right through my life and it was wonderful – especially when I learned that it was not so in all families that the children are able to voice their opinions".

For Vorster his children, and now his grandchildren, have always been a great joy. One of his major regrets about being Prime Minister is the fact that it has kept him away from his children and that it does not give him sufficient time to see his grandchildren. He once said to me: "Grandchildren are God's gift to an old man". And, when he says this, it is with deep sincerity. I can remember having supper with him at Libertas on a Sunday evening. We were speaking of serious matters when he heard the front door opening. Immediately his face softened, his eyes brightened and he said, "There are the children". The subject of our conversation was immediately forgotten as he looked at the door, smiling in eager anticipation. From the moment that little John and Kolbe came running in, all else became irrelevant.

As I mentioned in the first chapter, Vorster is a born Nationalist and, as such, can say very clearly WHAT he believes in, but not WHY he believes. Pressing him on WHY he is a Nationalist, he responded with some vehemence. "Look at this whole conflict between the English and the Afrikaners. Look at it from the English side. They, the English, offered the Afrikaners everything that they had. When we were poor, when we were uneducated, when we were nothing, they were on top of the world – and they offered us access to everything that they had. They ruled the world and they offered us participation in that, but we refused. Their language was a world language and they offered it to us, but we refused. They offered us everything that a mighty empire could offer; we refused it. They offered us titles which were much sought after by the whole world, but we passed a law way back in the twenties which said that South Africans could not accept British titles without permission – and the British have never forgiven us for this. When one places oneself in the shoes of the English who offered us all this, one can understand how puzzled they must have been when we refused. But they simply could not understand and accept that we preferred the small thing that is our own to the big thing that they offered us in all genuineness. To us it was not our own, it was foreign. Perhaps, I can put it to you in this way. When I became Prime Minister, the people of Jamestown went to my father's farm and they cut a piece of olivewood. They hollowed this out and they took a tuft of grass from my father's farm and they placed it in the hollow of the wood. Then they brought it to me. It was seven or eight years ago and it is still as the day they gave it to me – and there are a few things which I treasure as much as that piece of wood and that tuft of grass from my father's farm. Precisely because it came from my father's farm. Without question, there is better wood, there is better grass, there is better soil than that which comes from my father's farm. That is my whole philosophy. There are better cultures than my own. There are better things than my own. But they are not MINE and, however humble, what is MINE is better than the best of the others to me. That is what makes me so determined to guard what is mine and to preserve what is mine ..."

In Martini Steyn Malan, Vorster found the ideal wife, the woman who would complement him almost perfectly. Where he is impractical about domestic matters, she is an almost incredibly capable housewife – a woman who can slaughter an ox, make her own sausages, can her own vegetables and fruit, make her own jam, cater with great expertise, whether it is for her husband alone or for an unexpected crowd of fifty people. She can do everything required of that old-time "wife and mother", and much more. Her fingers literally fly over her typewriter keyboard and, until Vorster became Prime Minister, she coped with a mass of private correspondence herself. But she retained her interest in social welfare. She has her own private files bulging with information about the subject. She is in great demand to open children's homes and homes for the aged. She prepares all her own speeches, digging into her files and reference books and sometimes asking for information from the government department concerned. When the Vorsters moved into Groote Schuur with its Africana treasures, she widened her interests to take these in. Over the years she has tried to bring back to Groote Schuur as many bits and pieces as she can of those which have been moved out over the years. She has tried to identify accurately what is there and to trace every history, to the point where she has enough information now to write a book of great Africana interest on the work she has done in Groote Schuur. And yet she finds time to travel to a large number of functions with her husband (although the tempo of his public engagements has decreased in the last few years), attend a mass of functions herself, maintain contact with her friends, and devote much time to her family.

To the distress of the women's lib community, she believes that her primary function is to provide the environment in which her husband can operate at his best, to take from his shouders as much as she can in order to allow him to concentrate on the essentials when he has to work and to relax completely when he can. However, in spite of all this, she has added dimensions to her life which put her on an intellectual, social and personal level which not many women could match. She explains: "I have been given many more opportunities than most other women in this country to maintain my ties with the things I did in the past. If I think of the opportunities I have ... I'm interested in children's homes and I think I have been in more of these homes than anybody else. I have never looked at marriage and said: 'Help, isn't it a pity that I could not carry on with my work'. I simply went ahead and retained my interest. I become involved in this interest almost every day of my life. Only yesterday I was reading articles on backward children and carefully selecting what I needed for my files. I enjoy myself. I have great opportunities to live my life to the full ... I do not think that I have ever felt frustrated in my whole life. I live every day as it comes – and I live it to the full. That has always been my attitude and it is still my attitude ..."

They are closely attuned to each other. "There is absolutely no difference between my husband's outlook and my own. We have never differed. There is absolutely nothing in his thinking or in his activities which differs from my own. You must understand that we came from the same kind of home, from the same kind of background. Our parents largely shared the same kind of norms, the same political views, the same attitudes to religion, the same outlook on life. Look, what you younger people do not realise is that there was not as much difference in people's background in the old days as there is now. Now things are divergent. In those days you did not have to cope with so many people, with so many divergent ideas. For instance, you could take a young woman from the Cape and one from the Transvaal, put them to discussing things and find that their backgrounds were almost identical. The whole situation was so different then ... younger people cannot understand today what it was like in those days. There was simply no difference of opinion to such a degree that you irritated each other, or tried to convince each other or tried to reform each other. These things simply did not exist. I often think about how divergent things are nowadays. But I suppose that times change and that one must accept and live with those changes. To get back to the question of similar backgrounds and norms. Look at the question of literature. There was little scope for differences of opinion because, when we were students, there was so little Afrikaans literature and what there was was not as divergent as it is now. You could not differ much when it came to sociology because your bookshelves were so small ... there were not then, as there now are, library shelves full of books on sociology."

Of her own major functions, she says: "The most important thing for me is to create a homely atmosphere for John and, naturally, for the children. When he comes home he must know that he can kick his shoes off and relax completely. He must know that he is not going to exchange one set of problems, those of his job, for another, those of his home. He must be able to relax when he comes home, otherwise how can anybody expect him to carry the kind of burden which he does. It would simply be impossible. The running of the house is no business of his. It is my duty to create that wonderful atmosphere that when he enters the door he must feel: 'I can take off my jacket, I can take off my shoes, I can sit down and relax. I am at home'. Whether it is at Groote Schuur or whether it is at Libertas or whether it is at Oubos, it is the same. For instance, when we go to Oubos, I send my personal maid there in advance so that she can clean up and prepare for our arrival so that when John gets there he must be able to walk in and go to his bed and lie down and he must think 'Oh well, and there's my glass of water next to the bed'. And it is the same here. When he comes home to Libertas, he must not say 'Why is this window open, where's this thing and what is that thing doing there?' I look after him and I look after his clothes. I see that he is properly dressed and I see to it that he does not have to worry about anything to do with either his family or his home. I never tell him anything that might worry him, even if it is about the children, if I can keep it over until tomorrow or the day after tomorrow when its impact will be much less. He knows that by the time I do tell him about some emergency, the worst is already over and that the situation is under control. For instance, if a leg is broken, by the time I tell John, it is a question of saying to him: 'Piet or Willem broke a leg but the doctor has already been here and the leg has already been put in plaster at the hospital and everything is OK.' And if I have to go to hospital myself, I do not tell him months or weeks before the time because I know that he will worry. Instead, on the appointed day, I tell him: 'Father, very soon I must go to hospital. I have to undergo an operation. My place is booked at the hospital so don't worry. Everything is OK. I have already arranged everything at home so that it can operate without me and please don't come and see me at the hospital because this will only worry you'. And when Willem was born, I told him: 'My time has come. Please drop me at the nursing home. Then you must go back home and look after Elsa. They will let you know if it is necessary – but please don't come and sit here and worry' . . ."

She does not interfere in his political affairs, or question him about his day. "I know that if he wants to tell me something or discuss something with me that he will do so. Why should I then start asking him questions? He knows that I read nine newspapers every day and that I know what is going on. He knows that he does not have to deal with somebody who needs long explanations. He knows that if he needs my opinions on anything or if he wants to hear my views that he can do so without long explanations – because I share his life. Like today. He came home at lunchtime and he told me something important, something about the affairs of the State. Good and well. He knows that it will go no further and that, if and when he wants to discuss it with me, then I will be able to participate. He is the easiest person to live with because he does not drag you into a thing you do not want to be dragged into".

Like her husband, Tini Vorster is deeply – but not ostentatiously – religious. "We are deeply pious people. We believe in our religion and we worship regularly. We have our private service at home and, if our children are at home, then the whole family gathers round in the room, we pray and we read from The Bible together. When the children are not at home, then John and I do this every evening ... but we do not make a display of our religion".

On the possibility of retirement, Mrs Vorster anticipates no problems, no difficulty in leaving the world of the premiership for retirement at Oubos. "I take each day as it comes and I will take that day when it comes. I will be prepared because we have our house at Oubos, it is fully furnished, we have our personal things there. I have my slippers standing there. I have my gown hanging on a peg there. I have everything there. I can walk in tomorrow and know that I am settled. Remember, as a religious person, I believe God ordains who should do a particular job and when his work is finished, then God sends somebody else to take over. I have never thought that John is the only man who can be Prime Minister of South Africa. I have never thought that I am the only woman who can run Groote Schuur or Libertas. On a good day we found that we were here. We did not fight to get here. We did not tread on anybody's neck to get there. It was just that, on a good day, you found that you were here and, in exactly the same way, on a good day you will move out and there will be somebody else who can take over from you, who can take over from where John stopped ... neither of us are indispensable".

The average weekday at Libertas starts at 6,30 a.m. when Vorster wakes without the benefit of an alarm clock. "I can wake myself at any time. If I must go with you early tomorrow morning and it is necessary for me to wake up at 3 a.m., then I will be awake at 3 a.m. without using an alarm clock. If the kids ever have to go anywhere early in the morning, then it is I who has to wake them up ...". He dozes a bit and listens to the 6,45 Afrikaans news on the radio. Then the morning newspapers are read. "I read all the morning newspapers, here in the Transvaal there are too many of them ...". After a shower and a shave he gets dressed in the clothes Tini has already put out for him. "My wife puts my clothes out for me. If she put out one brown shoe and one black one, then I suppose that I would just put them on without realising. It's no use fighting her. If she wants me to wear a particular tie, then I wear that tie. She has been buying all my clothes for so many years that I have stopped worrying about it".

Breakfast is at about 8 a.m. "My breakfast has been the same, year in and year out – a plate of mealiemeal porridge, a plate of eggs and bacon, or sausage, a slice of home-made bread and black coffee. It does not vary. It has never varied and it will never vary . . .". At the office half an hour or so later, his first task is to look at the day's post. Every letter is answered by his Private Secretary, Johann Weilbach, on the basis of notes Vorster writes on the letters. Weilbach signs all the letters on the Prime Minister's behalf, but Vorster adds a personal touch in the form of a brief note in his own hand to 95 per cent of all the letters that go out from his office. Possibly the day involves a cabinet meeting. But, inevitably it is crowded with people – ministers, visitors, senior officials, his own departmental officials and his own staff.

For lunch, he goes home – without fail. Vorster explains: "I always go home for lunch. Even when I was an attorney, I always went home for lunch – except when I was out of town. I was never and I am still not a man for 'eating out'. I would bring people home for lunch, but I would never go to a restaurant or a hotel for lunch. My lunch is very light, I am basically a very small eater . . . but I believe in having a good, fat breakfast and then I can go without much lunch. After listening to the news, I relax on my back until I leave for the office at about 2,15 p.m. More often than not, I drop off to sleep for a few minutes. Fortunately, I have the facility for switching off completely when I choose and I think that this has been a tremendous help to me over the years . . ."

Vorster generally gets home from his office about 6 p.m. If they do not have guests or if they do not have some form of appointment, supper is invariably taken in front of the television set these days. The meal is generally simple, taken without wine. In fact, Vorster drinks nothing but brandy – and then never more than one or two very weak ones (about a tablespoonful in a glass of water) in the evening when he relaxes before supper. More often than not the rest of the evening is taken up with work. He says, however: "I am getting a bit old now and I try to cut out work at home in the evenings as much as possible – but that still leaves me a great deal to do, both in terms of paper work and in terms of speaking to people".

279

The burdens of the premiership are heavy, but Vorster tries to play golf at least once a week. Twice, if possible. He started playing when he was at university, although the real value of the game never became apparent until he became Prime Minister. "Golf has always been something tremendous for me. It's wonderful relaxation, it's the only exercise I generally get. But, most of all, it is one of the few places where I can escape from being Prime Minister. It's the only place where chaps treat you as an ordinary human being ... and I value that greatly because I want to be regarded as nothing more and nothing less than a human being. I don't really want to be a Prime Minister. You know, I am not one of those chaps who was born wearing striped trousers and fits easily and naturally into high office and all that goes with it. Out on the golf course and in the dressing rooms, we are all the same, irrespective of position or political convictions. I remember Andries Vosloo[6] once asked me to address a meeting in Bedford and a Prog chap came to ask me questions. I gave him merry hell that night and the next morning I found that he was my partner at golf ... and we had a really wonderful game. When I play golf, I never ask for special treatment and, in fact I detest it when, with the best will in the world, people try to give me special treatment. I get changed with the other chaps, I play with them, I shower with them afterwards and have a drink with them. Just being one of the boys is perhaps the most enjoyable part of my golf because then I am not John Vorster the Prime Minister, but John Vorster, golfer".

While golf helps Vorster maintain his sanity during "term", as her refers to his working months, it is during his July and December holidays (each three to four weeks, depending on circumstances) that he really recharges his spiritual batteries and tries to regain the strength he needs to face the massive problems involved in being Prime Minister of South Africa in the pressing Seventies.

The winter holidays invariably follow the same pattern: Hunting in the Karoo or the Orange Free State, ten days or so in the Kruger National Park, followed by another spell of hunting, this time in the Transvaal Lowveld.

Perhaps the most important element of his holiday is the Park. "I

6. MP for Somerset East from 1953 to 1970, Andries Vosloo served as Deputy Minister of Bantu Development from 1966 to 1970 when he became Administrator of the Cape. He retired in 1975.

fell in love with the Park when I visited it for the first time way back in 1945. I was so poor that I did not have a car and so we went with a chap called Muller and his wife. With me were my wife and Elsa who was a tiny baby. We enjoyed it greatly and I have visited the Park every year since then. Sometimes I would go three, four, five or even six times. Time was when I had a friend in Brakpan called Fred Kolbe. Between 1944 and 1953 when I worked at my law practice in Brakpan I used to have tea with Fred just about every morning. He was an estate agent and his offices were near mine. I would arrive at about eight every morning, we would have tea and sit and talk for about half an hour before I would go on to my own office. And it would often happen on a Friday morning that Fred would ask: 'John, are you busy?' If I said that I was not, he would ask: 'Well, are we going?' I would say yes and we would each phone our wives and ask them to pack our suitcases. Within the hour we would be on our way to the Park, just the two of us. Fred and I understood each other so well that it was unnecessary to talk. It often happened that we would not speak a single word during all the time it took us to reach the Park. And often a whole morning or a whole afternoon would pass without us having the need to speak. We would just sit there and soak up the atmosphere and think our own thoughts . . ."

Why is the Park so important to him? "I feel this absolute urge to renew my contact with nature. It is an urge to get as close to unspoilt nature as I can. It is an opportunity to renew yourself, to switch off, to escape from the office of Prime Minister, to become again simply John Vorster . . ."

Hunting is almost equally attractive. "To sleep out in the bush, whether in a tent or under the open skies . . . well, there is simply nothing like it. I like the whole atmosphere of the hunt, the cameraderie, the tracking, the hunting, the element of danger – and the fact that the chaps do not know Prime Ministers around the camp fire and in the hunting field. I have hunted in Rhodesia, in Mozambique, in South West Africa and in South Africa itself. I have shot most animals from elephant down and I will continue hunting for as I long as I am able to".

Whenever possible, Vorster tries to take one of his sons, or his son-in-law, on the hunt with him. Piet recalls: "There was a time when I was with him in Rhodesia when he was invited to help with the culling of elephant. And there I saw something that I thought

281

one only read about in books about big game hunters and big game hunting. Father shot at an elephant which then charged him. I was standing a few yards behind him and I watched as he coolly continued firing until the elephant dropped down in front of him. We measured the distance and it was between ten and fifteen yards ...". Comments Willem: "The hunting field means the same to him as Oubos and the Kruger National Park. It is a place where he can be himself, a place where he can escape the realities of those things with which he is busy all day and the little bit of history that he is helping to write. I think one can also look at a deeper, religious element because, after all, one is nearer to your Creator in nature. I know that this means a lot to him because, even if he is out hunting, every evening The Bible is read, prayers are said".

Summer holidays are always at Oubos[7], a communally owned private holiday resort about 150 kilometres east of Plettenberg Bay. The Vorsters bought into Oubos in 1962 but could not build there until 1966 because the Cape Provincial Administration had frozen coastal resort development. Their first holiday at their Oubos "cottage" was in 1966. The "cottage" was built right on the rocks and the breakers come to within a few metres of the building. From the lounge there are magnificent views of a wild and sometimes breathtakingly beautiful coastline. Once again, the real value of Oubos is the fact that Vorster can escape from his position as Prime Minister. "The fact that I am Prime Minister means nothing to those people. To those guys there, you are just one of them and to the children of the place you could be anybody. When you arrive, everybody comes to say hullo and then they leave you alone. You are free to pop in and talk to anybody if you want to. Conversely, you are free to stay at home and read a book if you want to. You can walk anywhere, talk to anybody and you can be absolutely natural ... you become human again. I had a very good friend Leon Cilliers, who is unfortunately dead now. However, when he was alive, we used to play chess from nine to one every morning. And, most evenings, friends would come over and we would play bridge ... I really like playing bridge and we play a lot of it at Oubos because one has so little opportunity during the rest of the year. For the rest, I walk around, speak to people and I read. I love reading and I am a very fast reader. However, during

---

7. Oubos: Literally Old forest.

'term' I try to read books which contribute to my understanding of what is going on . . . useful books, one might say. But when I am on holiday, I read for relaxation – and then I read cowboy books. I am passionately fond of them and go through them very quickly".

Not that holidays at Oubos are always carefree. "Sometimes, one can say that I have merely set up office there. For instance, the year before last (1975) I had seven conferences and 77 trunk calls. Last year my wife had to give lunch to 70 people one day. I have had Black people from Africa visiting on a number of occasions. Last year I had a Nigerian . . . although I cannot say who he was. You would be most surprised at just how thick and fast the contacts with Africa remain . . .".

Finally, we discussed Vorster's attitude to his children. "Of course, one has tried to be a good father, to talk to them, to play with them, to gain their confidence. Frankly, I am very glad to say that I think both my wife and I have succeeded in gaining their confidence. I punished them when this was necessary, but always showed them that we were still friends. Both my wife and I grew up in very happy, secure homes and I think that this is what we tried to give our own children. Naturally, my political career has interfered considerably with the time I would have liked to spend with my children. But, within the limitations sometimes imposed on me, I deliberately made time to talk to them, to tell them stories, to sit with them when they went to bed. We tried our level best to give them security because that is what a kid wants. And we tried to ensure that they were unaffected by my position, one way or another. You know, I think that if you have to talk to my worst enemies, you will not find anybody who can say that our children made a nuisance of themselves. Nor can anybody say that they misused their position or that the fact that I was a minister or the Prime Minister went to their heads in any way".

Certainly, the children recall getting hidings. Says Willem: "Oh yes, we got hidings, and quite often too. But, when father finished hitting either Piet or me he would always sit down with us and tell us a story. I heard some of my best childhood stories from my father after getting a hiding. It was his way of fixing things up again, showing us that he was not angry with us, that we had done wrong, that we had been punished . . . but that he was not angry".

Now the family is dispersed. Elsa and her family live on a farm in the Philippolis district in the Orange Free State. Willem works in the building industry in Cape Town and Piet, after completing his BA LLB at the University of Stellenbosch, is doing his articles as an attorney, also in Cape Town.

*   *   *

After having closely examined the Vorsters' family over three generations, perhaps the most interesting single element is the degree to which the norms, values and beliefs of Willem Vorster, have been respected and sustained by his son John and passed on, in turn, to John's own children. Not through repression or harsh authoritarianism, but by way of an atmosphere of domestic tranquillity and security, of real respect on the part of one generation for another. As I commented earlier, John Vorster was happy, contented and secure – and happy, contented and secure children rarely question or challenge the values that have provided them with this environment. And both John Vorster and Tini set out to create the same environment for their own children who, in turn, did not either question or challenge their parents' deeper values. Naturally, there have been considerable changes over the three generations. But the deeper values remain intact.

Postscript

In South Africa today, unless you are part of the ultra-conservative lunatic fringe, you cannot turn your back on change. You can either believe in evolutionary change or in revolutionary change. Together with millions of other South Africans, I believe revolution will destroy everything for everybody in this country, that those who might ultimately win an armed confrontation will have got themselves nothing more than the burned and blackened shell of the most prosperous, organised and developed country in Africa. So, while I fear revolution may still be a possibility, I cannot do otherwise than believe in evolution and hope that the quickened pace of evolutionary change will forestall the possibility of revolution. To people such as myself, evolution offers this country its only road to the peaceful change that it so desperately needs.

And, if I believe in evolution, I must take stock realistically of the mechanism that exists to bring about that change. In South Africa, the National Party is so firmly in the saddle, so unquestionably in control of the most important levers of power, that it must be the most vital element in the equation of change. There is no doubt that if the National Party as such wants change, then it will get change. But, unfortunately, the Party as a whole is conservative. If its rank and file had its way, the Party would opt for the status quo every time. In fact, a large slice of the Party has conditioned itself over the years to believe that the slightest concession is the thin end of the wedge that will lead to the end of the Afrikaner's identity, his culture and his traditional way of life.

Certainly there is an element of selfishness in the Afrikaner's make-up. There are few peoples in this world who do not want selfishly to hold on to what they have. With the rest of the Whites in South Africa, the Afrikaner is determined to hold on to his position of privilege. Once again, there are few privileged groups in this world who surrender their privileges easily – including the groups that rule almost every country in Black Africa. Despite this element of selfishness, nobody must underestimate just how strongly the Afrikaner believes in the need to retain his identity (remember Vorster's sharply-delineated words: " ... what is MINE is better than the best of the others to me ...") and how vigorously he will fight if he believes that identity is in danger. So peaceful change in South Africa is largely tied to the National Party and its tempo depends almost exclusively on a) the degree to which the National Party leaders accept the need for change; b) the political skill they are capable of exercising in reaching for that change; and c) the risks they are prepared to take with the party faithful in the process.

The only other important factor in the change equation is pressure. Undoubtedly the National Party Government has made many changes in the past few years in reaction to both external and internal pressure: few governments act differently. Inevitably, any government's greatest problem is trying to reconcile its policies with hard reality — and the more ideologically-orientated the government is, the more difficult the reconciliation. And reality inevitably means pressure for change, some of it overt and obvious, some of it the product of the normal pressures generated by changed and changing circumstances. Pressure comes from many sources. Pressure from the United Nations. Pressure from Western trading partners. Pressure from Africa. Pressure from guerilla insurgents. Pressure from political opponents. Pressure from "verligte"[1] Nationalists who see the need to move more boldly, to adapt to reality more quickly. And then there is pressure generated by internal violence of which South Africa has seen a distressing amount in the Black townships over the past two years.

So, if you accept that South Africa needs evolution and not revolution; if you accept that the gateway to peaceful change is guarded by the basically conservative National Party; and if you accept that the Party can be led into accepting change by its leaders, then you accept the responsibility for change in that vast area controlled by the Government rests squarely on the shoulders of Balthazar Johannes Vorster in particular.

Which provokes three questions. Has he the power? Has he the skill? Does he really want change?

1. Literally: Enlightened.

To answer the last – and most difficult – question first. In my many, many hours of discussion with Vorster, he consistently evaded serious discussion of the future, like a chess player determined not to reveal his moves to anybody. In fact, his whole attitude generates an aura of conservatism which is often belied by the changes which he does make. However, while this aura of conservatism may make it difficult to assess his attitude to change, he does leave vital clues in his speeches. While these clues might not be all-revealing, they do provide the reasonably skilled observer with some help. To give an example: For years I have listened to Vorster telling his audiences, as so many politicians before him, that politics is the art of the possible. Suddenly, during the 1974 election campaign, he told students at Potchefstroom: "People once said that politics was the art of the possible. I tell you here today that politics is the art of reconciling conflicting demands and conflicting aspirations".

I think this philosophy has been the basis of Vorster's actions over the past few years. While Verwoerd basically wanted to adapt reality to his ideology, Vorster has tried to adapt the ideology to the demands of reality. He is handicapped by the fact that politicians (all politicians) inevitably attach more weight to the aspirations of those who put them in power than to the aspirations of those who chose not to – and even less to those who, like South Africa's Coloured, Indian and Black voters, do not even have a vote in the system which currently controls all of South Africa, with the exception of the Transkei. However, despite this handicap, Vorster believes in reconciling conflicting demands and aspirations. Therefore I say he believes in change.

Does he have the power? I think he does. I think he has more power than he would admit to. I think that Vorster's image amongst White South Africans is such that the bulk of the electorate would come close to giving him carte blanche if he stepped out of the framework of Afrikaner Nationalism and appealed direct to the voters. However, because of his commitment to Afrikaner Nationalism, such a step is unlikely. Nevertheless, he does have enormous power within the National Party and a considerable reservoir of support outside the Party should he ever care to make use of it. As I am writing this, South Africa is preparing for a general election, an election in which it seems certain that Vorster will try to broaden the base of his electoral support. This will undoubtedly happen and it will give him more room within which to manoeuvre in the difficult years ahead, to move closer to the realities of the Seventies and the early Eighties. Apart from this, the National Party has agreed to a new constitutional dispensation to be based on separate White, Coloured and Indian parliaments, each responsible for matters of exclusive concern to White, Coloured and Indian people respectively. Each "parliament" will have a Prime Minister and a cabinet. Overall control will be vested in a State President who will be Chairman of a Council of Cabinets which will consist of representatives from each of the racial cabinets (to be selected strictly according to the relationship between White, Coloured and Indian populations). This will give Vorster more direct power than he has now – and a great deal more indirect power. So, to the second question, the answer is: Yes.

Does he have the skill? Undoubtedly. At every stage in his career, his story shows evidence of the skills a politician needs to maintain the balance between what he wants and what he believes he can get away with.

The final variables in the equation of change are degree and tempo. Perhaps the point can best be illustrated by the relationship between two trains, one running on the surface and the other running below the surface. The visible train represents the change that is taking place in South Africa today. For those who are not too blind – or too prejudiced – to see, it is moving faster by the month. In fact, if its progress is seen in isolation, its speed is becoming quite impressive. But the progress of the surface train cannot be judged in isolation. It can be judged only in relation to the progress being made by the underground train, the train of Black and Brown anger, frustration and bitterness. Whether that anger, frustration or bitterness is the result of genuine grievances, agitation or plain pig-headedness (or any combination of these) is beside the point. What is relevant is that the underground train is also running faster each month but it is largely invisible and nobody can say with any degree of accuracy just how fast it is running. Every now and then it gives an indication of its speed when the country is rocked by shock waves like Soweto, 1976 and 1977. But its progress largely remains a matter for conjecture. Only one thing is certain: if the visible train lags too far behind the invisible one, if the underground train reaches its destination

288

before the surface train does, evolutionary change in South Africa must, ineluctably, give way to revolution. If the visible train has a driver, then the driver is Vorster, whose fate it is to be Prime Minister of South Africa at the most crucial point in the country's history.

[Because the underground train is invisible, there is very little agreement in South Africa on whether the current tempo of change is fast enough, whether the degree of change is sufficient.] There are those in his Party who say he is going too quickly; there are some in his Party who believe he is going too slowly. The Opposition and the Opposition newspapers believe almost unanimously that he is going too slowly. Many Nationalist newspapermen, including some of the leading Afrikaans-language editors, believe he is going too slowly. For what it is worth, I believe he is going too slowly. I believe his standing in his Party – and among South Africans in general – is so high that he could do almost anything he wanted to. Sometimes I do not think he realises just how much support he could command from the centre of South African politics (largely that 30 per cent of the electorate who voted for the United Party in the 1974 general election) if he were to woo them with a platform of positive, bold but ordered change.

Of course, there is the opposing argument. If ever Vorster pushed too hard, if ever he moved too far ahead of the rank and file in his party, he would risk being thrown out by the National Party's parliamentary caucus. And, if that ever happened, the National Party would swing to the right because it would have been reactionary forces which unseated him and which would then be in control of the Party. I believe part of Vorster's caution at present is based on fear of this possibility. But I believe an even greater factor is his loyalty to the National Party as an institution and to Afrikaner Nationalism as a concept. I can almost feel his reluctance to move too far ahead of the people he has tried to serve for almost four decades. And he may be correct because a right-wing backlash in the National Party (of sufficient power to unseat Vorster) would be an unmitigated disaster for South Africa as a whole.

Nevertheless, I still believe that he is so obviously in command; that he so obviously stands head and shoulders above those around him in the National Party that he can move much faster than he is moving now. I know history has forced him to walk a narrow road between risking too much and risking too little. And I know that, given the reality of a National Party Government, Vorster is[the only man who can save South Africa (to use words which Vorster once used in an entirely different context) from a fate too ghastly to contemplate.]

But this I also know: the line between pressure which encourages change and which inhibits change is narrow indeed. And there is a very real danger right now that the West – and the United States in particular – is pushing too hard. Under the guise of concern for ALL the peoples of South Africa, they are, in fact, trying to serve their perception of their own interests. Tragically, they appear to be more concerned with what is in their interests than what is in the interests of the people of South Africa as a whole. Or perhaps it is just that they lack the knowledge and the skill to apply pressure positively in South Africa.

To underline the point, let me quote from a recent article by that wise old South African liberal, Alan Paton:[2].

"I decided that when I visited America in May I should try to see Mr Vance (the Secretary for State). I was successful in this and told Mr Vance of my view that the Nationalist – not only through stubbornness, but also through psychological inability – would be totally unable to accept the demand for immediate majority rule in a unitary state.

"What is more, I felt it would deter him from making any meaningful change at all. Pressure from the nations of the North, assisted by Cuba and armed by Russia would finally result in war. In this war, the Afrikaner would be destroyed from without and from within but so would countless others. I have no wish to see Afrikanerdom destroyed because a great deal of the cost would be paid by others. Nor have I any wish to see Afrikaner overlordship continued. Nor have I any wish to live under a government imposed on us by the Communist nations, with the aid of South

2. Paton was Chairman of the Liberal Party of South Africa until government legislation in 1968 made it impossible for multi-racial parties to continue. The Party disbanded rather than become a Whites-only organisation. Paton is a highly-respected author and, occasionally, a shrewd and articulate commentator on the South African political scene. One of his greatest attributes is his willingness to speak out frankly, irrespective of whether this places him under attack – from the Right or the Left. The article referred to appeared in the journal, Reality. It was printed in part in The Star, 2/9/1977

African exiles, some of whom are implacable enemies of the values by which I live.

"Therefore, I urged on Mr Vance that American pressure should be exercised with skill and wisdom. I did not urge America to go easy with the Nationalists. This is no time to go easy, *but I reject utterly a future that can be secured only by devastation.*

"And, what is more, I would not expect the triumph of justice through the weapons of destruction. I do not share the radical view that nothing can be built until everything is destroyed.

"Lastly, I have no personal wish for the destruction of Afrikanerdom. I certainly have nothing for which to thank our rulers. Through their own arrogance they have created for themselves what sometimes appears to be an insoluble problem. They have caused much suffering, much more than the hated British ever did. But the rise of Afrikanerdom has been a great historical drama. I have no wish that it should turn into tragedy ..."

By nature, Vorster is a gradualist – but I believe that this is not the time for gradualism. South Africa needs something bolder and more imaginative. Its Black and Brown people need hope of a better dispensation and its White people need vigorous leadership. Vorster is capable of giving Black and Brown people hope and of giving White people a new lead – that is why I believed it necessary to write this book.

Two Vorster quotes are relevant. When Jaap Marais and others asked him to stand for election as Prime Minister, his brother Koot remembers him saying: "I would' rather be remembered as the man who could have been Prime Minister than as the man who became Prime Minister and made a mess of it". When he was finally elected, he faced the crowds from the steps of Parliament and said: " ... some of us are mentioned in the history that is written, but it is only granted to a few of us to write history – and that is what my predecessor, the late Dr Verwoerd, did in South Africa."

Well, there is no danger that Vorster will be remembered as the Prime Minister who "made a mess of it". Within the constrictive (in my view) framework of Nationalist policy, his achievements have been remarkable. And he has certainly written history. In fact, history may well credit Vorster with having made more real changes than any of his South African predecessors.

But the crucial question is whether Vorster can do even more than this in the vital and difficult years ahead, whether he can exploit the power and the position to cope with the most urgent problems in South Africa's history.

I believe he has the power and the skill to make the changes that are necessary. Only time will tell for certain whether he will agree that these changes are necessary, whether he has the will and the physical capacity to make them.⌐